W9-AZI-458

# FLYING AIRPLANES

*The Pilot's Library General Editor,* Robert B. Parke

FLYING AIRPLANES: THE FIRST HUNDRED HOURS by Peter Garrison

FLY ON INSTRUMENTS by George C. Larson

*In Preparation:*

WEATHER REPORT by Robert B. Parke

PILOT'S AVIONICS HANDBOOK by George C. Larson and Robert Denny

LONG DISTANCE FLYING by Peter Garrison

PILOT'S GUIDE TO PREVENTIVE AIRCRAFT MAINTENANCE
by J. Mac McClellan

*Other Doubleday Aviation Handbooks:*

ANYONE CAN FLY by Jules Bergman

PILOT'S NIGHT FLYING HANDBOOK by Len Buckwalter

THE PILOT'S GUIDE TO FLIGHT EMERGENCY PROCEDURES
by Alan Bramson and Nellie Birch

# *Flying Airplanes*
## THE FIRST HUNDRED HOURS

*By Peter Garrison*

WITH AN INTRODUCTION
BY ROBERT B. PARKE

A PILOT'S LIBRARY BOOK
DOUBLEDAY & COMPANY, INC. GARDEN CITY, NEW YORK
1980

**Library of Congress Cataloging in Publication Data**
Garrison, Peter.
Flying airplanes.
(The Pilot's library series)
Includes index.
1. Airplanes—Piloting. 2. Private flying.
I. Title. II. Series: Pilot's library series.
TL710.G33 629.132'5217

ISBN: 0-385-14594-2
Library of Congress Catalog Card Number 80-7476


PRINTED IN THE UNITED STATES OF AMERICA
FIRST EDITION

## PREFACE

# Why Fly?

November 26, 1962; my first flying lesson. Since then, I am tempted to say, my life has been different. But that would be stretching the facts. A logbook is a piecemeal diary from which one's life can be painstakingly reconstructed like the history of a village from the fragments of pots in a midden. It seems to me from my present vantage point that I have been flying incessantly since so long ago that I barely know the person I was then. The log tells me differently. In what was left of 1962 I flew about 25 hours; in 1963 I crammed in almost 300 hours; but then, between going back to college and being in the navy for a couple of years, I only flew 100 hours or so in the next four years. I averaged about 165 hours a year from 1968 through 1973; in September of that year I first flew my own plane, and have averaged around 270 hours a year since then. As I write this I look back on about 2,700 hours of flying. Compared with the tens of thousands of hours logged by the workhorses of the airlines, mine aren't much.

But even two or three hundred hours a year still means that if my flights average two or three hours I have to have flown every two or three days, mixing the short hops to a nearby field for lunch with longer ones, eight hours over a weekend or fifteen in three or four days, down to someplace hot in Mexico; or sometimes I may have swelled the count rapidly with something really titanic, a flight to Europe or Japan, thirty or forty hours squeezed into three or four days.

So you see that there is something compulsive and obsessive about this activity of flying—for me and for many of my friends and for hundreds of thousands of others. It's not always that useful or that necessary; you have to make it useful or necessary, because you want so much to do it and to keep doing it. You can hardly *need* to go hundreds of miles a week, back and forth, not necessarily for business (though for me all flying is part of the business of collecting what I later process and distribute in the form of articles or books) but just for the sake of doing it, of *going*, of being up there in the sky. Flight is a habit that we find difficult to break. Some of us, at any rate; I'm always surprised, illogically so, when I meet people who used to fly and don't anymore, and don't seem to feel one way or another about it. I wonder, as an alcoholic wonders about someone who looks indifferently at a drink, do they not feel homesick for the sky?

Homesickness is as close an analogy as anything else, I guess; nostalgia for friends, a longing to see a certain face, impatience to get home and into one's own bed again—all those feelings of faint and unfulfilled longing, the desire that produces restlessness, are like the inner itch for the "long, delirious burning blue" of the baneful rhymester.

When I take off in my plane I move into an isolation extreme and radiant. For the first few seconds the streets and houses are streets and houses; I can see the cars still, the people, the dogs and horses. But as the ground sinks away below me it becomes stationary; houses, roads, parks become parts of a texture, no longer individual entities. The earth, which constantly dates itself when viewed at eye level with its cars of a certain vintage, its advertisements for films and products, its pedestrians dressed in certain fashions, its newspapers, its timetables of lunch hour, rush hour, wee hour—this same earth, seen from an airplane, is without precise date. It is obviously the modern world; I see highways, cities, airports; but their location in time has lost all precision, while their location in space (as if the emphasis had merely shifted places) seems more clear and precise. The sky, while I was on the ground a distant backdrop, now seems more and more like an enveloping medium, an ether, engulfing the globe. At ten thousand feet, flying in smooth air, I am peaceful, remote, timeless, unhurried. My activities are reduced to contemplation and to the small, negligent, reluctant movements, like those of a person half asleep in the sun by a pool, with which I keep the plane on course.

It is quite possible to bring my problems with me to this height, but it is also possible to leave them behind. The earth combines the qualities of a real thing, seen close at hand, and a map whose abstraction separates it from every vestige of reality. A highway seen from the air reveals, as it does on a map but not when we are driving along it, its human purpose: it connects cities far apart, which we can see from above. We see the meaning of the road and sense its personality: the boldness with which it slices through a hill, its tentative meanders as, in a more pensive mood, it seeks a way across a rolling river plain, its sudden defeat and deflection by a rocky escarpment, and the accelerating, anticlimactic triumph with which, now at its ease and self-assured, it penetrates suburbs and plunges among the skyscrapers. Rivers likewise tell a story of time and struggle, obstacles and easements; I see the oxbow bend and the two old houses back to back on opposite sides of a lobe of forested land, and know at once that children from the two houses had two ways to join up, one along the riverbank, which was longer but easier, and the other by the path through the woods where, in pairs, safe from detection, they skittered away from the path into forts and fastnesses and with trembling hands compared genitals. I see the sadness of the isolated farms, the gaiety of water, the decaying buildings that have never known wealth, the disconsolate animals, the unplanted furrows and the arabesques traced by a fanciful tractor hand, the island of trees to which everything seeking coolness came, the wavering, radiating tracks of the cattle. In land that has never been subjugated I see the filigree of stream branchings, precisely like the branches of a two-dimensional tree or the lacework of dendritic rocks, all manifestations of the same elusive abstraction, a mathematical law which, like the creator himself, leaves plentiful signs but itself is never seen, and the meaning of whose being is therefore always in doubt. I see from a hundred miles away the first mountains rising from the plain, the diminishing cultivation, the ridged, rebellious ground, the barrier before which wagon trains halted in amazement and Indian hunters turned as one turns on reaching the fence surrounding one's property. I parallel a massif, black outcrops of rock supporting catenoids of snow like a vast tent city of complex and marvelous design; its cold fatality, inflexible, monstrous, powerful, and impassive as the sea, frightens me. What creatures disturb those virginal geometries? And beyond them the ocean stretches like a sheet of frilly foil, melting confusedly into mist, throwing up a path of light at the end of which, remote as a neighboring galaxy, the Japanese conduct their business.

From a mythical sea full of monsters one turns to comfortable and familiar ports: the big airline terminals with their endless tarmac, the curling trains of baggage carts with flattened, rectangular locomotives, the liners nosing up to the buildings like cattle at a trough, the liveries of the carriers and the flashing white and red lights, the smell of jet fuel; or on the other hand the pretty country fields, the acres of grass and clover, the dilapidated structures in which recur the routines of modest businesses, and the unforeseeable characters, youth or old man, mother or girl, unknown actors, comedians without stages, who come to fuel our planes and show us where to park.

It is impossible, while airborne, to have any intercourse with the ground. You look at it as a work of art; an irregular lake, surrounded by trees, and a refinery with its pipes, towers, and tanks seem to have been set side by side on a tessellated plain as a deliberate allegory of the rural life and the industrial. On the other hand, you develop a certain intimacy with the sky itself and its innumerable personalities. Its architecture is monumental. You fly among clouds in which simple solid forms, planes, cylinders, truncated prisms, all freshly cast in wet concrete, conjoin at odd points and angles into a crystalloid mass, like that of certain modern buildings; through them, down slanting chutes, the humid earth can be glimpsed; and up above, solid as a mountain of snow, sunlight falls upon a hemisphere of cloud, and, on a palette of gray, there lies a scrap of palest blue. The French novelist Marcel Proust speaks of the sky chasing cloud and overtaking it, as though they were playmates, consubstantial, coplanar. For a pilot that is a difficult image to accept, because he knows that one of the essential and poignant facts about the air is that always, somewhere above the clouds, even on the blackest day, the sun is blazing in an empty sky. After an instrument climb, when you burst out of the clouds on top, the sudden rematerialization of the world, its abrupt endowment with dimension, position, speed, and height, resemble those sudden and risible reorganizations of matter that occur when film of an explosion is run backward. You feel, in miniature, the relief and sense of well-being that you would feel on being told by a doctor that your tests for some dreadful disease had been negative.

Nightfall brings its own particular conditions. As evening comes the landscape sinks, like a slowly foundering ship, into an aquatic gray, a smoky indistinctness increasingly undifferentiated, until we mistake the reflection of an instrument light upon the windshield for the last rosy scrap of sunset; and then the darkness is complete, and the world seems to contract until it extends no farther than the cabin windows.

Night is an introspective time. Lights dot the blackness below and above in equal profusion; there is almost nothing to watch, and so one turns one's eyes inward. Sometimes, however, I have glimpsed at night powerful visions: meteor showers, the aurora borealis, a wall of lightning storms, or, most stunning of all, the earth floating in space, as astronauts must see it: a black horizon in the foreground, and, behind that, light-years of emptiness.

I cannot imagine life without these moments, these contacts, this sight or an immense scale which bears the same relation to the sights of daily earthbound life—the view from the window beside which I write, with its rail yard, acanthus, moth, mountain, and haze—as the end of a novel or biography, with its mysterious hint of a grander meaning or symmetry, does to trivial details of plot and character within the book.

The impression of being at the threshold of infinity, on the remote margins of time, has been very important to me. Its importance no doubt has not been due to any property of the sky itself, but rather to the fact of my having invested so much time and effort, and experienced so many things, in the act and ramifications of flying. When one has hurried homeward through skies whose racing clouds have seemed to share one's impatience; peered anxiously through darkness at the battlefield of thunderstorms through which one must fly; when the drooping rain and the piercing sun have seemed on hundreds of occasions, year after year, to echo one's own feelings, as the backdrop that an old painter placed behind his subject reflected metaphorically some essential quality of the figures in the foreground; then the sky is as important a place as the familiar scenes of childhoood or one's own home. Yet, oddly enough, as the experiences of flying become more and more intimately part of my life, the act of flying becomes more and more boring and routine, so that I have to take care, when I fly, not to feel restless or impatient, but instead to sit emptyheaded and alert until the rotation of a knob and the shifting of lights that accompanies the automatic switching of my fuel tanks, though it occurs only once every five minutes, seems virtually continuous.

But obviously not everyone who flies feels the same things that I feel, though I think that most pilots who have been doing it for a while probably share my paradoxical sense of simultaneous fascination and boredom. Those who have not flown for so long, on the other hand, have a livelier relationship with aviation, like people at the beginning of a love affair, for whom every word and glance is laden with significance.

Private planes are noisy and in them it is often hard to talk; so one spends one's time in reflection, looking out, reading. The silent cockpits of airliners encourage, on the other hand, a tedious affability, small talk, a social routine that excludes the sense of mystery, the spontaneous generation of dreams. One can grow tired of even the most unbelievable views, particularly in the most believable company. Still it is the dream of many general aviation pilots to ensconce themselves once and for all in the front office of an airliner.

When I ask pilots why they like to fly, their answers don't go very far. If it isn't your business to write about a subject, I suppose there isn't much reason to spend a lot of time thinking about it. People usually say that it's fun. One friend says that it gives him lots of time to think. No one says that it gives him access to a heavenly other world. One woman likes flying who you might think would not: her husband was killed in the crash of a private plane. A year later, she resumed flying herself. "I like flying because I hate driving," she jokes—but then goes on to say that she finds great satisfaction, "a high," in doing something well that she had not been sure that she would be able to do at all. "Flying is difficult. If you do something wrong—instant judgment."

Perhaps many women would find that satisfaction, having been raised to think that there were things that, as women, they were not equipped to do. For them, the first solo is a colossal thrill, setting the final stamp upon a daring enterprise.

There are also plenty of practical reasons for flying. It is pleasant to bring within easy reach a much larger radius of action than the car permits—just as the car pleasantly brought within the compass of a single day places and events which previously had been, of necessity, isolated in the compartments of separate outings, separate days. If you like to ski you can go farther to do it with less strain. If you like the desert, go to the desert, spend the afternoon and evening, and come back home. Go to Canada or Mexico or the Caribbean. Visit someone a hundred miles away for a couple of hours. Airplanes give you that power; simply as tools they are delightful. But they also have their own character, and one feels a keen enjoyment in getting to know them, conquering their rebelliousness, making the most of them. Some airplanes are bores, some have thrilling personalities; some are elegant, some clumsy. You become fond of some of them as you do of certain automobiles or boats.

For me it is a long way to go, to put myself in the place of people who detest airplanes, although I know many such people. Their perceptions are completely different from mine. For them the fact of being high above the ground in a fragile device, with the fear that that naturally produces, remains always in the foreground.

The act of flying appeals to ancient instincts. The oldest heroic poems betray an admiration for what is swift, what leaps high into the air, what goes far afield—the virtues of warriors, hunters, and of the animals that were the most dangerous and the most difficult to hunt. To go where it is impossible to go, to climb where there is no foothold, to see things beyond the edge of mortal seeing—only gods, magicians, and heroes could do those things. An airplane in flight is beautiful not because it gets somewhere its pilot wants to go, or even because it gives him a godlike perspective on the earth; it is beautiful because it is itself godlike, and the atavistic part of our psyche which is no different from the psyche of the most ancient man sees instantly that divinity, and gazes at it in wonderment. Most kids would like to fly; it's automatic. I think anyone would like to who has not thought about it too much. That's what Hamlet meant: everybody longs to fly, and then "the native hue of resolution is sicklied o'er with the pale cast of thought. . . ." If one feels any fear of it at all, flying requires that one hold one's breath and take the plunge boldly. Fear dies out and leaves a reward behind. I have known many people who fly, and some who have, for one reason or another, given it up. But I can't think of anyone who was sorry that he had been a pilot.

CONTENTS

## INTRODUCTION

A glance at the history of aviation will reveal that one of the principal beneficiaries of World War I was the airplane. Before 1914, it was an oddity struggling for identity. After the Great War, it was swift, sleek, and altogether appealing and romantic—a vehicle of mighty knights. It was also a machine of vast promise. Revered seers spoke of huge armadas of transports carrying the people and goods of the world. Military men of vision predicted mighty fleets of bombers would lay waste any aggressor's country. And small personal airplanes were thought to be just around the corner.

The airplane of the 1920s was, it seemed, always newsworthy. There were records of every description being set. Luminaries of every stripe were pictured going for a ride. Aces of the recent conflict were reported to be founding airlines or joining aircraft companies. Then, of course, there were always accidents, forced landings, hairy escapes from death, and fatal crashes. And withal there was the image of the pilot to report on and to nourish. No wonder that in spite of the risk, a good many people wanted to learn to fly.

Learning to fly was a particularly daring undertaking in those days. There were, at first anyway, no training airplanes and no recognized instructors. There was no curriculum and no license. But perhaps the most fearsome of the hurdles to be overcome was the initiation that an instructor was expected to administer, early on, to assay a supplicant's determination, courage, sincerity, manliness (be he man or woman), and willingness to put his trust in the instructor. This consisted of subjecting the student to the most terrifying and sick-making series of aerobatics of which the instructor was capable.

If the student never returned it was accepted that he would not have made a good pilot anyway. If he came back for more it was with the tacit understanding that he could be subjected to unmerciful verbal abuse, and dealt with profanely within the often narrow limits of the instructor's vocabulary. If the student failed to perform a maneuver up to the expectations of the instructor, he could expect to be regaled with the rhetorical refrain, "What are you trying to do, kill us both?"

The principle behind this unsettling treatment was simple enough. The instructor was trying to establish a stress situation in which a difficult task would be made more difficult by his hounding the student, often unreasonably, until only the most dedicated would continue and only the most determined would survive. It was thought to be for the student's own good.

Something of this thinking persists to this day in spite of modern audio-visual presentations, smart-looking ground-based simulators that allow a student to become familiar with the cockpit while sitting in a cozy room, and instructors who must submit to periodic re-evaluation by the FAA. All too often circumstances conspire to show that some flight schools still feel that a strong measure of unanticipated difficulty is not all bad for the learning process. Ask any pilot and he will corroborate this finding with a few tales of incredible oversight or plain neglect that occurred during his training. That he persisted, you can see; and since he won his wings you may wonder if the strength of the system is not illustrated by his being a pilot. What proponents of this harsh approach tend to overlook is the large number of people who find the shortcomings of the system intolerable and perhaps even dangerous, and drop out. Who can say whether or not these well-intentioned souls would not have made good pilots.

When the industry and the FAA do turn a mildly critical and examining eye on their possible shortcomings and inquire of newly commissioned private pilots as well as dropouts, what were their grievances as well as their praiseworthy experiences, the results are pretty much what you might expect. On the less satisfactory side there is often surprise and disappointment expressed at the casual and sometimes formless aspects of flight training. Given the cost and seriousness of the subject, a good many respondents feel a lack of direction and objectives in the airwork. And the bright new customized ground schools are sometimes criticized for their closed circuit aim of trying to groom a student for the FAA written test rather than preparing him for thoughtfully exploring the fundamentals of flight.

Whatever the shortcomings of flight training today, however, one must hasten to add that conditions are infinitely better than they have ever been. Having said that, it must also be observed that there are still some yawning voids and awful slightings of critically important concepts in most flight training programs today. Moreover, most packaged flight training courses—for all their benefits of programmed learning and careful organization—leave little room for reflection, rumination, and instructive hangar flying. That's one reason for this book.

Another has to do with the fact that the training airplane is an awful place to learn to fly. It is cramped, bumpy, drafty, often smelly, and far too noisy to conduct thoughtful conversation. Yet this is the environment where the student must spend most of his time with his flight instructor. All too often the result is that the student learns what he is supposed to do from shouted and necessarily abbreviated commands combined with hand signals. Much as the instructor might like to have a more relaxing and stimulating atmosphere in which to explain the intricacies of the airwork, he is for the most part trapped in a system that allows him little choice. There is a fairly high priority on getting the student in the air and on spending a minimum amount of time on the ground. In the air, the instructor must concentrate on teaching flying skills and developing aeronautical judgment often at the expense of explaining in sufficient detail why a maneuver should be performed and what is going on aerodynamically when an airplane moves through the air. In the absence of the opportunity—and, it must be admitted, sometimes the ability—to explain the intricate and ever changing balance of forces that are at work on an airplane during the airwork maneuvers, an instructor must all too often resort to the "follow me through" method of teaching in which a maneuver is demonstrated and the student attempts to mimic the flight instructor's movements, albeit without having any notion of what he is trying to accomplish.

A careful rereading of the above will reveal that this is not a blanket condemnation of the ability and skill of flight instructors. On the contrary, it should be said early and often that most flight instructors are diligent, dedicated, hard-working airpersons of great skill and ability.

It may just be that developing the skills and the judgment to fly an airplane well is one of the most challenging and satisfying accomplishments available to ordinary mortals. By the same token, nobody says that coming by those skills is going to be easy and no responsible person believes that the techniques for passing on those skills to newcomers have been perfected. If there is any certainty about this business, however, it is that the better the understanding of the principles and the greater the familiarity with the details, the higher the chances of success. That's where this book comes in: merely reading as much of it as you can understand will give you some idea of the concepts with which you'll be dealing when learning to fly, and will introduce you to the abbreviations and terms that will shower around you when you go to any airport.

The subjects treated in this book are the ones that years of experience have shown present the greatest difficulty to beginners. The presentations cover areas that flight instructors often have the most trouble making clear, and the attitudes and points of view in *Flying Airplanes* are those that we believe will prove to be the most practical and worthwhile.

If you've never flown before, it is certain many portions of the technical and mechanical explanations will elude you. Don't worry. That is to be expected and it is not important. If there are large portions of the book you don't understand after you've received your private pilot license, then is the time to be concerned. In the meantime, read what you can understand and what intrigues you and leave the rest. After you've built up half a dozen hours of flight instruction you'll find that most of the sections that seemed impenetrable are suddenly clear. If you take our advice, then, you'll read as much as you can before you fly, read it once again after you solo, and go over it thoroughly a third time after you've earned your license.

Besides reading this book to familiarize yourself with the range of ideas you'll be dealing with in learning to fly, you'll find that indirectly there are answers to questions that you might hesitate to articulate. The principal one might be: Are the time and energy necessary to get a pilot's license more than I can afford to spend? Another might be: Is the subject matter too tough for me? And another: Is the theory so abstruse and the mathematical requirement so advanced that I will not be able to keep up? What about the need for superior coordination and quick reflexes?

We could give you an abbreviated answer to those questions right now, but then you might miss some of the extraordinary pleasure and satisfaction of reading *Flying Airplanes: The First Hundred Hours*.

ROBERT B. PARKE

# FLYING AIRPLANES

# 1

# *Instructors, Schools, and the Private License*

Learning to fly is not much more difficult than learning to drive a car or ride a bike, so far as the handling of the airplane is concerned. Perhaps it seems more difficult than these because we are usually older when we begin to fly airplanes and more resistant to new learning. But the skills involved, the coordination, the simultaneous management of several motions, are not new to us; they are only presented in new combinations.

What is different now, however, and makes learning to fly an airplane and thereafter using one more difficult for everyone, is the modern flying environment. It used to be normal for a student to solo in eight or ten hours; now it is not uncommon to go twenty hours or more before solo, and the reason, most instructors agree, is less in the type of aircraft or in the nature of the syllabus than in the crowded, distracting, and unfamiliar airport environment of urban areas: the swarm of airplanes interrupting the student's rhythms and the at first incomprehensible radio talk that bombards him. Some of the ill effect of the crowding and regimentation is in the distractions it produces and the compromises of his natural instincts which it forces upon a student; some of it is pure intimidation—the fear of making some idiotic mistake in full view and hearing of a dozen seasoned and impatient pilots.

People who learn to fly at small, not-so-busy rural airports without control towers are in a way better off. They are better off too, perhaps, if their instructors entirely relieve them of having to operate the radio. Even at an uncontrolled field, radio is important; a unicom frequency, as it is called, usually 122.8, is used by pilots and a ground station (if there is one) to make communications whose purpose may range from announcing one's arrival in the traffic pattern to asking the ground station to place a phone call, or finding out whether the restaurant is open. Even if there is no one else in the pattern, it's a good idea to announce one's position from time to time for the benefit of any arriving aircraft planning to enter the pattern. But there is no reason to saddle the student with this task in the beginning.

The first thing to learn in flying is how to fly the airplane; this task under way, all the other aspects of aviation may gradually be brought into the cockpit. Learning to take off and land will be easier if the student can concentrate on it and nothing else; so if you have a choice, a small uncontrolled field may be a better place to begin your search for flight instruction than a big controlled one.

Not all flight instructors will agree even with this modest proposal, I should admit. Some, particularly those who do most of their flying at busy urban airports, will feel that the early exposure to congestion is important for the student. It gives him a taste of the way things are really going to be. The only time radio will be a problem anyway will be in the pattern; and much of the flying course will be spent outside the pattern. And indeed I have been at once touched and irritated on encountering pilots arriving in the big city for the first time who go on and on about all the traffic and the hustle and bustle and the confusion and crowding. The traffic patterns of big airports are certainly the places where a novice endangers the greatest number of his fellow pilots in the shortest time. He has to know what he is doing. So, if I feel that a quiet airport is the best place to practice takeoffs and landings, I should add that never to have visited a busy airport during one's training would be a very stupid omission.

However, convenience is an overriding consideration. People usually find it difficult to schedule their flying lessons into a busy routine. Since it is best, above all, to fly fairly frequently while learning, the best airport is the one you can get to most often and most easily, and the best school is the one that has sufficient airplanes and instructors to schedule you as frequently as you like and when you like.

In picking a school you are likely, in a city, to suffer from an embarrassment of riches. The small airports will have one or two and the larger ones, perhaps a dozen (except for the largest airports in the largest cities, which sometimes cater almost entirely to big business aircraft and to airliners, and have no flight schools at all).

The phone book is a good place to start. My Yellow Pages go from "Flexible Shafting" to "Floats—Metal, Glass, etc.," without stopping for "Flight Instruction." Under the improbable heading of "Aircraft Schools," however, no fewer than thirty-three are listed. Omitting those that cater to airline flight engineers-to-be and aspiring aircraft mechanics, I still find quite a choice. They are located at the various airports in the area; the ones within thirty minutes of me happen to be Burbank, Whiteman, San Fernando, Van Nuys, Santa Monica, Torrance, Compton, Long Beach, Hawthorne, and El Monte. Quite a choice. Where to begin? Well, if I worked, I might figure that I am likely to do most of my flying at six in the evening, after work; or at six in the morning during the winter months, when it will already be dark in the evening. I would like to avoid traffic, so I figure that I would be going *to* the evening lesson during the rush hour and returning *from* the morning lesson during the rush hour. I want to be going against the traffic, and since the traffic goes in opposite directions morning and evening, this reasoning will exclude one entire group of airports and include another. Alternatively, I might consider that during the summer months Los Angeles is often subject to an overcast condition during most of the day, and that it is more persistent in one area of town than in another; on that basis I might decide that one group of airports was preferable because they were likely to have better weather. This is the kind of weather information that a pilot might be more aware of than most people; so I might consult a pilot friend on the matter. I might also consult a pilot friend about the conditions at different airports, the traffic densities, the takeoff and landing delays. And I might ask him or her about the types of airplanes in which I could take my training.

Several different models are used for trainers. The opinions of veteran pilots or even of instructors of their relative merits are not necessarily reliable, since a new student might possess an entirely different but perfectly valid set of perceptions. The most commonly used trainer for many years has been the Cessna 150, recently renamed, with a slightly more powerful engine and several other changes, the 152. Like all single-engine Cessnas this is a high-wing airplane. It has a small cabin with relatively poor visibility, and a 100- or 110-horsepower engine. The competing Piper trainer is called the Tomahawk, and it is a much newer, slicker-looking airplane with a T-tail, a low wing, and a roofed bubble canopy that provides visibility far superior to the Cessna's. Despite its cleaner and more modern appearance, however, the Tomahawk does not perform any differently from the Cessna. Grumman American used to make the Trainer, which is a low wing, like the Piper, with good visibility, and slightly better performance than the other two. Piper Cherokees, which are four-seaters and have 150-hp engines, are still used as trainers (they were Piper's entry in this market for many years before the Tomahawk was introduced). A few big, four-seat Beech Sports are used for training, and a two-seat Beech trainer, the Skipper, remarkably similar in appearance to the Tomahawk but a little less graceful looking, has recently appeared.

A small flight school or a private instructor might use some less conventional trainer; a Piper Cub, for instance, or an Aeronca Champ, or one of the modern derivatives of the Aeronca—the Bellanca Champ or Citabria. These are all taildraggers; that is, their landing gear consists of two main wheels in front and a small third wheel at the tail end of the fuselage, as opposed to the now prevalent "tricycle" arrangement of three wheels of about the same size, two beneath the wings and one beneath the nose. Taildraggers sit on the ground differently from tricycle gear airplanes, nose-high; they also handle differently in landing. Their devotees speak of them as "real airplanes," as though nearly everything built since 1950 were some kind of substitute. More skill is needed to land a taildragger, and so it is reasonable to suppose that a taildragger student may be sharper than his "nosedragging" counterpart. But it is nothing to make a great issue of, and the vast majority of pilots today have trained in tricycle gear airplanes and only fly tricycle gear airplanes. If they begin to fly taildraggers, they need a few hours of instruction to "check out" in the special techniques.

You might find that, rather than considerations of location or local weather, the type of trainer you would get to fly at this school or that might make up your mind. It would be quite understandable if you fancied yourself more in the sleek little Tomahawk than in the stodgy-looking Cessna.

Instructors like to debate the relative merits of different trainers, and you might find one saying, for example, that the Cessna 150 or 152 is an excellent trainer for the same reasons that make it an imperfect airplane: it is underpowered, draggy, has a quirky stall and poor visibility. But these very flaws would make the student particularly aware of power, skillful in stalls, or attentive to traffic. I feel certain that in any case the instructor matters more than the airplane, and that the differences among the airplanes can easily be made up by the differences among the instructors.

You might learn to fly in an airplane with a bubble canopy, and if your instructor kept harping about traffic you might absorb as much of a respect for it as if you had learned to fly in the 152. As far as stalls are concerned, most pilots who get a private license are never going to stall again, or they will do so only very rarely, for biennial flight reviews or checkouts for renting airplanes; and for those purposes, if you can stall one airplane, you can stall them all.

Some flight schools advertise Veterans Administration approval and an FAA-approved curriculum. For the private license the VA approval is inconsequential, because veterans' benefits do not extend to private license instruction, only to advanced ratings. As for FAA approval, it is, so far as I can tell, meaningless, like FAA opinions on the whole. It does not mean, though I suppose the holders of FAA approvals would like you to believe that it did, that some sublime lord high instructor has closely examined the school and decided that it conforms to the official definition of an ideal learning environment. It simply means that, on paper at least, certain criteria have been met. But it so happens that these criteria are of no definite importance.

Apart from cost, which I will get to in a moment, what is going to concern you when you are learning to fly is the skill and personality of your instructor and the overall environment of the school. Now, a school might consist of anything from a free-lance instructor hunkering down with you under a tree to explain the theory of a maneuver before going up with you in his Cub, to a thoroughly organized chrome and glass institution with dozens of instructors and battalions of secretaries and clerks behind long counters scheduling you, collecting your money, selling you books and paraphernalia, and calling in your instructor on a beeper. The instructor can be a salaried employee of a school operating a whole fleet of airplanes; or he might be a free-lance pilot who habitually is associated with a particular fixed base operator (FBO), is covered by that FBO's insurance policy, spends the hours between students lounging in that FBO's lobby, and rents planes there for lessons; or he might be a pilot who enjoys instructing, has some other profession, takes one or two students at a time as a recreation, and uses a plane of his own or rents one. There is no absolute requirement, no pattern for a flight school, even though the term "school" seems to suggest something formally defined. The private license requirements simply call for so and so many hours of dual instruction with a licensed flight instructor, and so and so much solo; ground school (which can simply be conversation before and after lessons with that same instructor, or might consist of scheduled evening classes of thirty or more students) is not formally required, and I, like most people who learned to fly more than ten or fifteen years ago, did not take it at all.

It is, then, a matter of business convenience that flight instruction is provided, often, by large formal institutions called schools, or even "FAA Approved" flight schools. Really the only necessary organizing thread in a course of flight instruction is that provided by the student himself.

Prospective students like to have prices quoted to them, and then to anticipate that when a certain expenditure has been made, they will have their license. Would that flying were so simple. The wiser approach is to forget about the final price and look at the hourly rate. Fancy schools will probably charge higher rates; city schools will charge higher rates than country schools, even though the country environment is possibly the better one. The rate will be compounded of the hourly cost of the airplane and the hourly cost of the instructor; otherwise put, there will be a dual and a solo rate. Sometimes you might have an opportunity to rent an airplane "dry"—meaning that you pay for the fuel yourself but get the airplane for a lower hourly rate. Renting dry will not usually make a great deal of difference in the final cost, but it might make it possible for you to defer some of the cost of lessons by shifting it onto a gasoline credit card. (Most schools accept some credit cards anyway.)

If someone offers a normal trainer, like a Cessna 150, for an abnormally low rate, say $10 an hour, you might suspect that he will be cutting corners on maintenance. The lowest and highest rates in a given area for the same model of trainer will rarely be more than $2.00 apart—though East Coast rates may be $4.00 an hour higher than West Coast rates, perhaps because, with better weather, the West Coast planes get better utilization. The lowest prices anywhere are probably in southern California, with a new 152 going, in the late 1970s, for $17 an hour.

The total cost of the license will usually be about $1,200 to $1,500, though it could go quite a bit higher if you did everything in the most expensive way possible and were a slow study besides. The national average of time spent training for the private license is about 60 hours. The FAA minimum requirement is 40 hours, and in the past that may have been a reasonable figure; nowadays, a good student flying in a very simple environment might still make that figure, or even be ready for the test before having the necessary time logged. But don't be too impressed by the fact that an FAA Approved flight school can sign you off for the check ride at 35 hours, while others have to go to 40; the chances of your completing the curriculum in 35 hours are infinitesimal.

(The private license taken in a sailplane might run $1,000, only a small savings with the significant disadvantage that it does not entitle you to operate a powered aircraft. The transition to power from gliders is not particularly easy, and if your ultimate goal is to fly powered aircraft, your best bet is probably to get the single-engine land private first, and then take up soaring, if you like, later. Soaring is very highly thought of by nonpilots, and I think that more people have asked me whether I flew sailplanes, on hearing that I was a pilot, than any other question, though lately curiosity about hang gliding has been gaining; but it is a sport without utility, and one which, in spite of the absence of engines, is nearly as costly to pursue as power flying.)

Rather than worry about the cost of getting the private license, you should, if you wish to worry, worry about the long-term costs of flying or of owning an airplane. If you are going to fly enough to remain reasonably capable, or are eventually going to buy a plane, then the cost of the private license is a minor initial investment. If the private license seems like a serious financial obstacle, on the other hand, you should question whether it is wise to invest so much in something that you may not be able to afford to use later on. Do not imagine that once you are a pilot opportunities to fly cheaply will rush to offer themselves to you. They won't.

You might weigh the comparative costs of different schools, if you have a choice, simply in terms of the total number of benefits that they provide. Assume that the amount and quality of instruction will in every case be the same; it may not be, but there is no way to correlate the quality of instruction with the place where it is obtained. Then compare the different types of arrangements—FBO, flying club, dealer training center—in terms of their other benefits. The FBO will probably offer rental airplanes and free-lance instructors and a place to sit for ground discussions, but little more. The flying club will have discount airplane rates, but initiation fees and dues which when prorated against the amount of flying you do may add up (depending how much you fly) to as much as or more than the commercial hourly rate. The dealer-connected training center will usually offer a deluxe package of instructional materials, possibly some kind of programmed learning course, with computers, logs, all the paraphernalia included. Beech Aero Clubs provide this as well as a ready-made club atmosphere with bar, lounge, company, and planned activities; and the price is correspondingly high. The Beech Aero Club scheme was dreamed up by a marketing head who had to figure out a way to push Beech's unattractive line of low-powered single-engine trainers and personal aircraft. Some people have denounced it as a ripoff, and others have been very pleased with the clubs; no doubt the different locations, combined with the different people who go to them, allow of various degrees of satisfaction.

The dealer-connected schools have an ulterior purpose; they want to establish your brand loyalty early. It would be an exaggeration to denounce them as a sinister plot on the part of the manufacturers of airplanes; the loyalty of the individual instructor to the underlying scheme is not likely to be very strong, and the ready-made instructional materials are bound to be of a certain value. Their overhead will be higher than that of a simple FBO, but part of it may be written off against the factory's promotional budget. Again, the way to measure one price against another is to subtract the part spent on instruction, assuming the same 60 hours at all schools; and then see what you get for the balance.

One feels inclined at the outset of one's novitiate to purchase a lot of equipment that supposedly is needed by pilots. Typical items include large chronometers with concentric dials crowded with numbers; digital watches giving Zulu time; fancy sunglasses; aluminum computers that can figure out drift angle and Mach corrections; electronic calculators specially intended for pilots; chart cases; plastic place mats made of aeronautical charts; decorative relief maps of states; tumblers decorated with antique airplanes; aeronautical cuff links and ties; copies of the inescapable poem *High Flight* printed on imitation parchment with burnt edges, glued to a piece of wood similarly damaged; "pilots' belt buckles"; magazine subscriptions; and, as they say in the ads, much, much more. None of this stuff is worth a damn. Beginners are persuaded to buy the items in the belief that flying is going to be a complex, specialized, demanding activity that will require them, or that all pilots have them. There may also be an element of vanity involved, and the primitive notion that when you possess all the paraphernalia of a pilot, you are a pilot.

I am a pilot, and I don't own a watch or sunglasses. I have a warped plastic computer that I use infrequently, and then only to find density altitude or true airspeed or, very occasionally, to figure an ETA. These basic tasks can be executed with the simplest cardboard disc computers—the kind companies give away as favors. I have a twenty-dollar Novus scientific calculator in the plane, but only in case I need it for some calculation that pops up in my train of en route meditations; it is inferior to the plastic disc for all flight calculations except adding up a series of leg lengths, and that can be done on the margin of a chart. I used to have a chart case, but I could never find a place to put it in the cockpit and ended up distributing the VFR charts here, the IFR book there, the flashlight in another place.

I do not have one of the plastic protractor/rulers that you are supposed to use for navigation; they always warp, and anyway you can rarely spread a chart out flat in the cockpit. Instead, I have something called a Jimmie Mattern Navigation Computer, which is a combination of a circular calculator with a pair of dividers, and serves very well for en route navigation. Jimmie Mattern, who was a pioneer long-distance flyer in the twenties and thirties, gave it to me; he lives in Palm Desert, California, and that is the only address given on the device. It's very handy.

When you start flying long distances, certain items are good to have: basic tools, a small survival kit, a sleeping bag, some rope; a small cassette player with headphones (the kind that covers your ears) can provide welcome entertainment on a boring flight; a pad and pencil; a good book (in case you have to wait for weather). But for flight instruction you don't need even these.

On the other hand, one item you ought to have for all flying, which is very cheap and very valuable, is a pair of earplugs, or a supply of them. Two types commonly available at airports are the rubber Com-Fit, consisting of three diaphragms on a stem, and E.A.R. plugs, which are simply little cylinders of yellow plastic foam that you can dispose of when they get dirty (they ordinarily pick up dirt from your fingers more than from your ears). Airplanes are very noisy, and long exposures to them will damage your hearing. Earplugs seem to offer considerable protection, and they will not interfere with your ability to understand speech or the radio. I find the E.A.R. plugs the most effective and comfortable, and they are also very cheap, though FBO's sell them with a bigger markup than mail order houses do. Plain cotton, on the other hand, is completely ineffective.

Supposedly the last word in earplugs is the custom-made rubber type, which fits your ears and no one else's, and is molded right in your ear, producing, at least when I had it done, a remarkably delightful sensual experience, something like having someone's tongue in your ear. But let us pass on. As far as the ability of these things to keep noise out is concerned, I was not impressed with mine. It seemed to me that the fine hairs in the ear held the skin slightly away from the plastic plug, and left a passage for air and therefore sound. Someone provided me with a vial of vaseline with which to coat the plugs before sticking them into my ears. This helped the noise attenuation, but it gave me greasy ears, and one day the vial tipped over in my glove box, melted, and gave me greasy charts as well. Really, it is very difficult to do better than the E.A.R. plugs.

So much for equipment. We are a nation of compulsive buyers, and the temptation to equip ourselves for every activity is almost irresistible. So if we want to go out into the wilderness we buy hundreds of dollars worth of down bags, weightless backpacks, lunar boots, transubstantiated foods, and titanium cookware only to meet on the trail a whistling man with a dog, a ranger who has lived there all his life who is on a three-day, eighty-mile circuit of cabins with an army surplus bag on his back, a sack of rice, some cans of soup, and a package of Oreos. He is wearing sneakers. It is the same with aviation. A beginner spends a hundred dollars on a lot of gadgets and only later, slowly, does it dawn on him that his instructor, who has four thousand hours and flew Crusaders on carriers, has nothing but a Timex with a broken band in his pocket and a ballpoint pen in his shirt.

So far as books are concerned, instructors have their favorites. Look through several to see whether one seems more congenial to you than another. If you are the sort to learn well from books, you might pick up several, even ones not specifically intended for private pilot courses, such as William Kershner's *Flight Instructor's Manual,* which will give you the subject from the instructor's standpoint in great, in fact excessive, detail. My purpose in this book is to describe some of the fundamental ideas underlying aviation and to try to give a newcomer a glimpse of an experienced pilot's perspective. Other books may have different purposes, and for the private license you might want one that describes each step in the curriculum so that you can review at home, and that gives systematic explanations of the regulations, normal procedures, navigational techniques, aeronautical theory, and so forth, to prepare you for the written test. For most beginners, the books are too exhaustively detailed. Eventually, you have to know all the material, or at least have to have known it at one time and to know where to look things up; but to facilitate learning, you need less detail and more of the broad view. So, when you are looking for a good instruction manual, pick one that is fairly short and of recent vintage. Forget the piece of kindling called the "Pilot Instruction Manual—Federal Aviation Agency," which is out of date. Not that flying, essentially, has changed much; but the chapters on parachutes, spins, tailwheel taxiing, float flying, and so on have very little to do with the modern private license; and the writing is uninspired. Even though this book has the apparent blessing of the FAA (which hasn't been called Agency for years, by the way; it's the Federal Aviation Administration), it's a waste of money. Kershner's *Student Pilot's Flight Manual* is good, if rather discouragingly thorough; if you had to teach yourself to fly alone, yoke in one hand and instruction book in the other, this would be the one to take. Wolfgang Langewiesche's classic *Stick and Rudder* is the only masterpiece on the subject of learning to fly that I have seen. It is a thorough and correct introduction to the theory of flight for the practical aviator, and any pilot who takes his flying seriously ought to have read it carefully. It too is dated, but being a really fine book, it does not suffer much from age. *Stick and Rudder* seems to be free of errors and misconceptions; if it says one thing and your instructor says another, suspect your instructor, and keep quiet. When I learned to fly, I didn't use any book at all, and it is quite possible to fly skillfully with a complete misunderstanding of some of the principles of flight. Most pilots do it all the time. Unless your jaw needs exercise, don't get into arguments with people about how things work. Read, listen, compare, and practice. You are certain to be exposed to misinformation or contradictions about the theory of flight; don't get worked up over it. It is the unavoidable consequence of nonscientists inhabiting a field that is, on the scientific level, quite complex.

Which brings us, via the school, the equipment, and the books, to the most important element in your learning—the instructor.

What you are going to be learning when you study for your private license is, on the entire scale of aeronautical practice, baby stuff. The private license is variously derided as a license to go out and kill yourself and a license to go out and start learning how to fly. It is certainly true that a pilot with a private license and 60 hours total time is only barely prepared for the eventualities the air can offer him; henceforth, he will learn from experience. Significantly, after the private, one does not as a rule immediately start working on the commercial or the instrument rating (though one can). Usually one first starts "building time."

Anyway, however challenging the curriculum may appear, it is pretty simple stuff, and so you don't need to cast about for the proverbial grizzled veteran to engage as your instructor. A callow youth will do just fine; in fact, he may do better, for various reasons. Just as a person who teaches second graders how to read does not need a thorough acquaintance with world literature, a flight instructor does not need to be a retired fighter pilot. The reading teacher mainly needs enthusiasm for the job, love of children, patience, and some knowledge, gained by practice or study, of teaching. The flight instructor needs, *mutatis mutandis*, the same qualities.

Not many instructors have chosen to be instructors for their whole lives. Some instruct for diversion; some are filling a hiatus between other jobs; some are building time in hopes of landing with the airlines or in some other kind of commercial flying; only a few do it for a living, always have, and intend to go on. It isn't very pleasant work, after all; put yourself in the instructor's place and imagine the hours spent in a cramped and noisy cockpit, feeling that one thing should be done and suffering through another, and waiting for students, some of them quick but others painfully retrograde, to grasp what seem like simple and self-evident principles. Some people are much better at it than others, and there are some who are not good at it at all. Flight instructing is like any other profession; there are a few people who do it brilliantly, a majority who do it well enough, and a number who do it badly but do it anyway.

Getting a poor instructor is unfortunate, but it is not unlikely, any more than getting a poor teacher for the second grade. Unless the incompatibility is so great as to make learning impossible, a bad instructor will, at most, cost you a few more dollars than merely an average one. As I have already said, a few extra dollars are not so important as they seem, because flying is such a costly activity that the price of the private license is only a drop in the bucket. Between a *very* poor instructor and a *very* good one there will be a bigger difference in time and money spent and, more important, in the amount of enjoyment you get from your lessons.

But the influence of the teacher on the student is even more far reaching. An instructor who builds a student's self-confidence, self-reliance, and self-control may affect his flying ability and judgment in subtle ways. I can imagine those influences having, over years of flying, incalculable effects.

But how can the student, who is innocent of all the fundamentals and the nuances of aviation, tell a good instructor from a bad one?

The classic bad instructor, according to a friend of mine who saw himself going bad and quit instructing, is the one who is "burned out." He has instructed so much that he has exhausted his enthusiasm; students no longer intrigue or challenge him, their quirks pass him by, their problems or blocks leave him indifferent. He is worn out. His attention seems to be elsewhere or to be nonexistent; when you are executing a maneuver, he is looking out the window, visibly distracted. He is impatient, and grows angry at repeated failure to do a maneuver properly or to grasp the principle behind some exercise. An instructor who is irritated easily, who gets impatient, or, worst of all, who shouts at you, is not worth going on with. Tell him that you are not paying to be abused and get another instructor. The loss is his, not yours.

Less obnoxious but no more helpful is an instructor who does not make things clear to you. Aviation is not very obscure; it is mostly practical, and its tricks and secrets are not difficult to learn. If you repeatedly fail to get the point of something, or of everything, after several explanations, there are two possible reasons: either you are extremely obtuse or your instructor is not communicating well. Never hesitate to say that you don't understand something, and make your instructor go through it again. If it doesn't get clearer, talk to someone else; there are so many different ways of explaining things that one person's method may succeed where another's has failed. If you find that your instructor has trouble getting through to you, consider trying someone else. My burned out friend says that the most interesting thing about flight instructing was adapting the curriculum to the student. You realized right away, he said, that the approach that worked with one student would not necessarily work with another, and you had to choose, or invent, your methods anew with each student.

There is the possibility, of which instructors are aware, that you have very little aptitude for flying, and that if you are having problems, this is the reason. Or you may have the aptitude, but not the attitude. Occasionally an instructor will drop a student, send him away, because he finds himself hopelessly incompatible with him or, what is even more difficult to say, feels that he would be a bad pilot. Instructors have their stereotypes of bad pilot material: for instance, a hurried, successful, confident professional who thinks he knows everything, is used to calling the shots, and adapts with difficulty to the humble role of student. Or a Marine karate instructor with a violent temper. Or a congenital stumblebum who trips over things and whose hands shake under pressure.

If an instructor tells you he thinks you ought to reconsider your decision to learn to fly, you should consider both the possibility that you and he had a personality conflict, and the possibility that he is right. But even if he is right, you can still go on if you must. Plenty of pilots were made of "bad pilot material."

Do not expect, on the other hand, that your instructors will heap praise on you if you are doing well. There is one school of pedagogic thought that holds that praise is a great goad to student effort, and another that dismisses it as an opiate. For myself, I don't believe any instructor ever told me, apropos of anything more general than a single execution of a particular maneuver, that I was doing well. Much less that I was a "good pilot"; I have never heard that commendation except from people who were not in a position to know and simply assumed, because I was an aviation writer and had flown long distances, that I must be whatever is meant by a "good pilot." I have seen pilots who I myself thought were much better than I as well as much worse, and I conclude from the fact that after all these years I am still alive, and have damaged only one airplane, that I am at any rate an average pilot. I attribute the lack of praise from my instructors, who have been many, to some unwritten law; but perhaps I was always so embarrassingly bad that they could not bring themselves to lie to me, even for kindness' sake. At any rate, don't expect praise; if you get it, consider yourself lucky, but don't get carried away with it. Praise may tell more about the instructor than about the student.

Many instructors are women, and people are liable to wonder whether they would be better advised to engage a male instructor or a female. I doubt there is much to be said in general, but in particular cases the sex of the instructor might make a difference. I have usually preferred female instructors, I think, and among males I have preferred those who had what could be called, without slight to them, a feminine manner—by which I mean one that is mild, easy-going, sympathetic, and patient; in other words, grandmotherly. I have difficulty with instructors who are tense, impatient, brusque, elliptical, or who seem to place their own competence in unflattering juxtaposition to mine. I have, however, also had female instructors who had, conversely, what I would broadly characterize as masculine characteristics, and with whom I did not enjoy learning.

The element of enjoyment seems to me important, but even here I am not sure that I am not misplacing my priorities. I had a very enjoyable time learning helicopter flying from a woman instructor, and then proceeded to fail the flight test—quite mysteriously, since I could easily perform the failed maneuver the day before the test and the day after it. The only reason I could find for that failure was reluctance to terminate the course. I do not mean that I was enamored of my instructor; that would, I think, do nothing to help one learn. Only that I was having a good time and didn't want it to end. I protracted my instrument training to an incredible length for a similar reason, I think, and blew the flight test on that one too (with a female examiner, by the way). All this shows, if nothing else, that it is not a final catastrophe to fail a flight test. So far as the sex of instructors is concerned, however, it clarifies little, and I doubt there is much to clarify. I would think that female instructors, at least those who are pretty, must get very tired of airborne mashers; but aside from that, the important differences are among personality types, not sexes.

Often your first lesson will be an introductory one, half an hour long, intended to awaken your interest, persuade you of the accessibility of the matter, and determine that on leaving the ground you do not immediately panic or begin to feel sick. This initial introduction over, your instruction begins in earnest.

The curriculum is laid out by the Federal Aviation Administration in Part 61 of the Federal Aviation Regulations and published as a "Flight Test Guide/Private Pilot Airplane." This is a complete list of the maneuvers that may be required of the candidate on his flight test. Not all will be or the test would take all day; but one has to be more or less prepared for all of them. Some are fictions; for instance, the guide says that the applicant may be required to demonstrate night takeoffs and landings. I very much doubt, however, that more than one applicant in a million does so, because flight examiners, like most other people, work during the day and go home at night. Perhaps above the arctic circle, during the winter, there are exceptions. In reality, the examiner will subject the candidate to a random selection of tasks, each examiner and each season and locale having its fashions and favorites.

When you take the flight test, you will already have passed the written test. The written, as it is commonly called, is notoriously one of those exams that seem entirely to miss the essence of the subject they cover. Information of which any pilot ought to be aware, such as the behavior of weather systems or the importance of various causes of accidents, is passed over, while questions about the papers that must legally be aboard the airplane and certain details of flight planning, course calculation, and nomenclature dominate the test. I don't remember what papers have to be aboard myself; I know how to work out a wind triangle but I have never—not once—done so in real life; and I have to think hard to distinguish between bearing, course, heading, and magnetic variations, simply because none of these problems ever arises in real life. The written test is a formality, and studying to take it is one thing, training to be a pilot another.

The flight test will begin, however, with an oral test that will recapitulate some of the kinds of materials which fuel the written, and pass from that into more practical considerations of planning and executing a flight. The examiner will be interested in seeing whether you understand certain general principles. You will have to solve a weight and balance problem; plan a cross-country flight, taking into account wind and weather, and computing distances and times and headings; file an imaginary flight plan; and discuss various emergency procedures. You will go out to the airplane and preflight it under the eye of the examiner. You will then take off on the simulated cross-country flight, which during its first leg will be terminated; and you will perform a series of maneuvers. You will finally come back and land, sit through the endless ritual of the typing of the temporary license, and you will be—though like one who has lost his virginity, you will feel and look no different—a private pilot.

You are likely to find the weight and balance problem particularly harrowing, since a single mathematical error can be very hard to locate, and can turn your results to junk. If you make a mistake, however, all is not necessarily lost. What the examiner is likely to be looking for here, as everywhere in the test, is a good understanding of the concepts involved, not supernatural powers of multiplication and division.

The flight test requirements from which your examiner will compile your ordeal fall into several categories. The first is basic flying skills; you have to be able to fly an airplane straight and level, and to maintain a heading with some appearance of purpose and accuracy, make turns without losing or gaining a great deal of altitude, and roll out at the desired heading. You have to be able to "slow fly" the airplane—that is, to make gentle turns at a very low airspeed, just a few knots above the stalling speed—and you have to demonstrate a number of stalls and recoveries. Implicit in this selection of tasks is an evaluation of your ability not only to perform the task itself, but to set it up. If the examiner tells you to slow to 60 knots, he expects you to reach that speed in a reasonable period of time, stabilize it, and maintain it accurately without gaining or losing much altitude. This can be the most difficult part; slowing down to 60 knots without changing altitude is actually a more difficult task, involving more variables and taxing one's coordination far more, than turning right and left a few times at 60 knots. In order to prepare yourself for this aspect of the test, you should memorize the power settings at which maneuvers are performed. This makes setting up the maneuver much easier than if you had to discover the power settings anew each time.

These basic maneuvers demonstrate your ability to handle the airplane at various airspeeds, and to make it do what you want it to do—go up and down, go fast and slow, go straight, and turn. Another category of maneuver is designed to test your ability to handle the airplane while distracted. These are more complex tasks, using objects on the ground as reference points for circles, S-turns, rectangular courses, figure eights, and so on. The applicant (as the person taking the test is styled) usually imagines that there is some ideal line through the air, visible to the examiner but not to him, to which he must hew, and that the measure of his success or failure will be the sum of his deviations from that line. Actually, the test is more subtle. The examiner is interested in seeing how naturally the applicant handles the airplane while his attention is forcibly engaged by something other than the instrument panel. Does he increase back pressure as he steepens the bank in order not to lose altitude in a turn? Does he notice wind drift quickly and compensate for it? Or is the airplane always miles ahead of him? These maneuvers, which in most cases depend on the presence of wind for their difficulty, are actually easiest to perform if the wind is quite strong. In a light wind it is often difficult to tell whether drift is due to the breeze or to the pilot, and one has to depend on a factual knowledge of the direction in which the wind is blowing to determine when and how much to compensate. In a strong wind it is not necessary to know which way the wind is blowing; you can easily see the airplane being blown along, and the correct compensations become instinctive. If there is no wind at all, the test will take place anyway, but the ground reference maneuvers won't have much spice. In that case, the examiner might postulate a wind and ask you for an explanation, as you go around the course, of the corrections you would be making for it. This would be the most difficult task of all, and not a very meaningful one either, since it would test the student's articulateness and powers of visualization, and not his ability to fly an airplane.

A portion of the test takes place under the hood. This hood (which became a household word, at least temporarily, when the student pilot who was struck by a Boeing 727 at San Diego in September 1978 was reported on national television to have been wearing one, producing in the minds of many the vision of hundreds of amateur pilots flying around hooded like Klansmen) is a gadget that blocks the student's view to the side, like a horse's blinders, and above, like a visor, and obliges him to manage the airplane solely by reference to the instrument panel. Thus it simulates, very crudely, the conditions inside a cloud—omitting, however, the terror that the non-instrument-qualified pilot feels because the cloud, unlike the visor, cannot be taken off at will. It was always my impression that for a hood to work, the student had to want it to work. You would put it on and the instructor or examiner would say, "Can you see outside the aircraft?" And you would say no (of course), although really you could without too much trouble. At any rate, you put on the hood and then, in theory by instruments alone, without peeking, you repeat some of the basic maneuvers—straight flight, turns, climbs, descents—while keeping the airplane under control; and the examiner asks you to find out where you are by radio aids, and to use a radio facility to establish a course and follow it. These are the tasks you would have to perform if you inadvertently got into weather. You might also have to do a recovery from an unusual attitude by reference to gyros only.

At various points in the test you might have to cope with, or say how you would cope with, simulated emergencies. You will, for instance, have the engine chopped on you unexpectedly at some point, and you will have to find a suitable place for a forced landing, and then make the approach, without power, to a position from which a safe landing is more or less assured. When I was confronted with the chopped engine on my private test, I shifted into high gear. We were several thousand feet up, but I felt, for some reason, that I had to choose a landing place as soon as possible and not waste a lot of time maneuvering; so I picked a reasonable-looking field in which we might have totaled the plane but certainly survived ourselves, and said, "I would put it down there." "How 'bout this airport over here?" the examiner said, nodding at the medium-sized airport off his side of the airplane. I admitted that the airport might be preferable, and circled down to a position on final approach far too high to make a good landing. "Don't you think we're a little high?" the examiner inquired. "Oh," I replied, "when you drop the gear and flaps this thing comes down like a brick." For some reason, perhaps because he was not acquainted with the Comanche 250 himself, the fellow accepted this thoroughly disingenuous assertion, and went on with the check ride.

The most important part of the check ride, it seems to me, is the landing phase. For one thing, landings and takeoffs include, to some degree, most of the other maneuvers required on the ride; and they are certainly the phase of flight in which mistakes can be the most costly. Whether or not you can hold heading and altitude is not vitally important as long as you can take off and land.

There are four types of landings and takeoffs that may be required: normal, crosswind, short field, and soft field. Since there are differences of opinion even among experts about how these are to be performed, what is mainly at issue again is your understanding of the principle of each maneuver, and your air of being in command of the situation. Only to a certain extent, however; in a short field landing, for instance, a good air is no substitute for a short landing. These are not very difficult maneuvers; except for the judgment of the approach path, which has some instinctual quality or "feel," the landing and takeoff requirements are less difficult than the maneuvers by reference to the ground. But more weight is probably given to landings and takeoffs by many examiners, who realize that these are the maneuvers that one must be able to perform, even if one can perform no other, in order to fly safely, or for that matter to fly at all.

In my experience, and judging from the caliber of pilots that I have seen and heard tales about, a perfect performance is not necessary to pass the private flight test. It seems, in fact, that you can blow half the test and still pass handily, though this may perhaps be less true today, when some slight attempt has been made to tighten up the requirements for pilot competence, than when I took my test. I remember clearly that I was in the dark about many maneuvers, notably ground reference maneuvers and crosswind landings, up to and beyond the time of my taking the check ride. I must have done some things very badly. Some I barely did at all; for instance, I forgot to put on my seat belt until I was on the downwind leg of the final landing on returning to the airport after, I assumed, failing the test. I had not failed; why not, I cannot say.

Time and chance have vindicated the indulgence of my examiner; it turned out that I could fly after all. But the check ride and the license that I got from it were far from proving that. They were in fact hardly more than a formality—only, as I said, a license to go learn to fly.

Why examiners are so indulgent, I don't know. Perhaps they make generous allowances for nervousness brought on by the check ride situation; if so, however, they are doing the student a disservice, since an in-flight emergency will make him at least as nervous as an FAA examiner can. Perhaps they are simply grading on the curve, adjusting their standards to the average quality of the students that come before them, so that over the years, by imperceptible stages, the quality of students declines because there is more pressure to finish the private course quickly than to finish it perfectly. Perhaps it is simply that we are a nation of kindly, lazy people who do not have a fanatical devotion to doing everything in the best possible way. In any case, standards for pilots are quite low. For instance, to mention a palpable example, 70 is a passing grade on the written test. Assuming that the written test is representative of the real flying environment (it isn't, but evidently somebody thinks it is), are we to suppose that an acceptable pilot can be wrong, while flying around up there, 30 percent of the time? That 30 percent of the time new instrument pilots are going off on the wrong heading to the wrong station at the wrong altitude, misinterpreting their charts and misreading weather reports? You would think, flying being a matter of life and death, that 90 might be considered a passing grade, but not 70.

I don't know whether this laxity matters. It would be difficult to connect accident statistics with the quality of instruction in a convincing way, since many seasoned pilots have accidents, and weather, which is the cause of so many of them, is nearly impossible to give practical instruction in. I wonder whether there is not also a feeling behind the indulgence of the FAA that the aviation industry would suffer hardship if pilot licensing requirements were more stringent; fewer people would become pilots, and so fewer would buy airplanes, radios, and so on. The FAA and the industry are no doubt not in conscious collusion, but they have sympathies and contacts that make them operate as a team, despite their ostensibly opposing roles, in somewhat the way the branches of government check one another but execute, in the broad view, a unified policy. It is a commonplace that the government bodies that regulate industries and the industries themselves draw from a common pool of personnel; and that government does not fail to consider the impact of its policies on profits and employment. So it would not be particularly surprising if the desires of the aircraft and equipment manufacturers for a large market were a deterrent to reform of the instruction and licensing system.

You find out when you have your private license in your pocket that you still have a lot to learn. I made several long round trips during the time between getting my private license and getting my instrument rating, on which I started working immediately upon finishing the private: Los Angeles to Salt Lake City, Los Angeles to Boston, Los Angeles to Mexico City. I had a few close calls but did not get hurt. Except for one or two occasions, I was lucky in my choice of weather; but I did a few stupid things that I now look back upon with disbelief. It is easy to be less lucky. One friend of mine got his license, didn't fly for a couple of years, then got hold of a plane, loaded his wife and another friend into it, and set off across the country. He ended up more or less landing the airplane in a snowstorm on a mountainside in Texas, where it remained. His wife was injured, but not severely. That was lucky too, although there is a point in the survival of misfortunes at which I wonder if it makes sense to say that one was lucky, when the misfortune itself was so unlucky.

In fact, to put the private license into perspective, you could think of your flying career as consisting of three stages: the training stage, before you get the license; the stage of chance and luck, for the first few hundred hours after you get it; and then the stage of experience and, presumably, competence. The chance and luck stage is shorter for some people, but a few seem never to graduate from it.

The single factor that above all else must determine the course of one's experience after the private is the amount of time one manages to spend flying. Nothing is worse than to check out anew every month or two to take your family on a weekend trip. If you are going to fly, you ought to fly a lot. Not that you would entirely forget how to land, any more than you would entirely forget how to ride a bicycle; but flying is a complex activity in which many things must be kept in mind, and it is only practice, the continual renewal of your familiarity, that ensures that the right things will be in your mind at the right times.

# 2

# *Money*

It may be, as the ads say, that anyone can fly; but not anyone can afford to fly. Flying is an expensive activity. Not uniquely so, perhaps, but it's right up there among the champs.

How much would it cost, people ask, to get a pilot's license? They imagine that once you have the license you can fly, and so automatically you will fly. Not so. Getting the license is expensive enough; but doing something with it is much more so.

Of course, it depends what you mean by flying. There are cheap ways to get airborne. In the twenties people used to put together flying contraptions out of materials found lying around the barn; and then they would jump off the roof of the barn to try them out. The broken leg was probably more expensive than the contraption. You can still do the same; and, inflation having taken its toll, the medical bills may be a much greater multiple of the cost of the flying machine than before. But you also may not get hurt; so hang gliding is the cheapest way to fly. It is a sport, however, not a means of transportation. You can buy or build a hang glider fairly cheaply—though as the technology of hang gliding has developed, it has become increasingly costly, like all sports. I know a Rogallo in a garage that you could probably pick up for $100. One of its owners died, one moved away and forgot about it, and the third broke his arm so badly in it that it could not be properly reassembled (the arm, not the hang glider). So you could probably get that one for a song. There are lots of others; people buy toys like that, eventually lose interest in them, and stick them in their garages; so you can locate one, get on top of a hill, and fly.

That is the only kind of flying for which no license whatever is required. The latest hang gliders are pretty fancy machines, and you can stay aloft in them, in good conditions, for hours; the only thing that formally distinguishes them from sailplanes, for which a license is required, is that they are foot-launched, whereas sailplanes are towed into the air by a winch, an automobile, or, most commonly, by a powered airplane. Some hang gliders even have motors.

Hang gliding is a sport, and to stay with it you have to develop a powerful liking for it. Its only purpose is to enjoy the sensation of flight. Soaring is the same sort of thing, on a much grander scale. But soaring is probably the best way to find out what pure flying is like, and whether or not you really enjoy it. Not that most pilots get into aviation through soaring; most go down to a local flight school and get a ten-buck half-hour ride.

Soaring is more expensive, as you might expect, than hang gliding. Compare a formal hang gliding course with a formal soaring course. The hang gliding course will usually involve an introductory lesson (ground school plus a flight or two) for $35 or so; subsequent lessons at $25 a day until you have learned basic maneuvers, turns, safe landings where you want to land, and so on, until with $140 or so invested you are on your own. A used hang glider in good condition bought from a non-disenchanted person will run $600 to $800; a new one of the Rogallo type $1,000. Rigid wing kits start around $900 and require 150 hours or so of building time.

Soaring, on the other hand, begins within the framework of the FAA private license. When you take up soaring, you are working on a license that can eventually be converted to one for powered aircraft. To solo a sailplane usually takes 6 to 8 hours of flying time, perhaps 35 tows (at $10 to 2,000 feet), and costs $500 to $600. Another $300 to $400 will take you the additional 7 hours to the private license, which entitles you to carry a passenger in a sailplane. If you get interested in soaring as a hobby, you might pick up a used ship for $6,000, maybe a little less. You'd also probably want a trailer for it. So you can see that soaring is roughly five to seven times as costly, stage for stage, as hang gliding.

You might imagine that the experience gained flying sailplanes would stand you in particularly good stead when you start to fly powered airplanes. But it doesn't; a sailplane pilot might have a slight advantage in knowing how to maneuver an airplane; but so far as landing and taking off are concerned, he may actually have developed habits that he will have to unlearn for powered flying. Some of the solo time logged in the sailplane can be carried over against the license requirements for the single-engine land rating; but not enough to make a saving, since sailplane flying is actually more expensive per hour, unless you hit upon lots of lift, than power flying.

The kind of flying this book is about is the kind for which you get a license called "Private Pilot, Airplane Single Engine Land." It means flying airplanes with an engine, with several seats, with wheels, in which you go from place to place, sometimes with family or friends, for business or for pleasure. It can be a sport—airplanes can be raced, stunted, built at home, restored as antiques—but it goes far beyond being a sport. It becomes almost a way of life—to the point that the mention of an "occasional pilot" makes other pilots raise their eyebrows skeptically—and it turns out to involve the kind of investment that only a "way of life" can justify. Or a business—and using an airplane for business, in one way or another, is the classic way of turning the expense into a tax benefit, and thus making it bearable.

The cost of getting the private license will be at least $1,500. Once you have the license, you will want to do something with it, and since most people don't buy airplanes right away, you will be renting them for a while.

The trainer in which you did your pre-license flying will have been a two-seater, and will have rented for $12 to over $20 an hour, depending on age, equipment, and type. If, now, you want to take a weekend trip with your family, you will want a four-seater. A typical one would be a Cessna 172—one of the all-time best-selling airplanes. It will probably rent for at least $5.00 an hour more than the 152, and there will be certain provisos attached to its rental, usually that you fly it two or three hours on each day that you have it. If you rent it for a weekend at $25 an hour, it will cost you at least $150, no matter how little you use it. Three hours in a 172 is about 350 miles; so you could, for instance, fly that distance Saturday morning, arrive at noon, and leave for home at four on Sunday and be back in time for dinner and before dark.

*This 1972 Piper Cherokee 140 B, a 2-place, 130-mph model, makes a good trainer or pleasure aircraft.*

Fuel costs would be included in the rental cost of the airplane. Overnight parking would not, but it is surprisingly cheap: usually $2.00 or $3.00 a night, $5.00 a night at the busy urban terminals. Most airports used by private planes don't have landing fees, but a few do. Usually they're pretty reasonable—a dollar or two. Again, the big metropolitan terminals charge the highest prices, and they are easy to avoid.

One of the great inconveniences of flying is that when you get to the destination airport, you're often stranded. In some places you can get public transportation near the airport, and when there are airline flights to an airport there is sometimes limousine service into town. Hotels and motels will often send a car around to the airport to pick you up. You can rent cars in many places. In the boondocks, where you would think the problem would be the worst, you usually have the easiest time: someone at the airport gives you a lift or lends you his car. At a few places you still find an "airport car," keys in the ignition, for the use of itinerant pilots. You put some gas into it to show your appreciation. Aviation stands, strangely, with one foot in the future and one in the past.

Sectional charts were $1.85 each the last time I looked, up from 50 cents when I bought my first ones. You don't need much else to fly. Maybe a pair of pants.

Since your transportation bill is going to run $160 to $175 for a two-day, 700-mile round trip, you might as well go somewhere that you can't

*The proverbial Piper Cub is still being hand-made in limited quantities. This 2-place taildragger is for sale at slightly over $30,000.*

go by airline for $70 and that's too far away, or over too difficult a route, to reach by car in the same time.

The rates for frequently rented airplanes give a pretty good indication of the real hourly cost of owning the planes, which is normally about 70 to 75 percent of the rental rate. Old airplanes rent for less because their depreciation is lower. There is, however, one big difference between an airplane you own and one that you rent: utilization. A popular rental in a good area might fly over 1,000 hours a year; the cost of insurance, depreciation, and hangar space or tiedown, on an hourly basis, would be quite low. But a privately owned airplane may fly much less than that—in fact, it almost always will, unless the owner leases it to a fixed base operator for use as a rental.

For a garden variety four-seater, depreciation might run $1,600 to $2,000 a year; insurance, $1,200; and storage from $150 a year (for tiedown out of doors) to over $1,000 a year (for hangar space at a fairly busy general aviation airport). Fuel, at this writing, is selling for $1.25–$1.50 a gallon, and oil for the same price as automotive oil, that is, about $1.00–$1.50 a quart. A four-seater with a 160- or 180-hp engine will use about $10 worth of fuel and oil per hour (equal, by the way, to 8 cents a mile, more or less).

Maintaining an airplane is also expensive. Scheduled maintenance for this airplane may cost $2,000 a year at first, and every 1,500 to 2,000

*One of the new generation of turbocharged 200-hp singles from Piper, the Dakota, is priced at about $75,000 with suitable equipment.*

hours of operation, the engine will have to be torn down and overhauled, and that will cost around $4,000 to $6,000, depending on its condition. Unscheduled repairs can be costly, not only because of the labor and parts but because of lost flying time. Replacement parts for airplanes are ludicrously expensive, and in many cases (alternators, starters, oil filters, etc.) the aircraft part looks suspiciously like an automotive one—the resemblance sometimes goes as far as identical part numbers—and costs two or three times as much. Recently I replaced several parts on my engine, a Continental of 210 horsepower. Four sets of rubber shock absorbers cost $280 wholesale. A fuel pump, again wholesale, was over $500. A year ago I had a piston ring break while I was on my way from Los Angeles to Boston. The cylinder was scored and had to be replaced, and the installed cost of the new one was $750, including the trade-in of my old cylinder, which would be reworked and resold. I could perhaps have worked out a better deal by getting a cylinder from a friend in Los Angeles and having it shipped to me, but there were pressures to do otherwise. For one thing, it would have meant staying a couple of extra days where I was, which I didn't want to do. For another, a repair shop

*This twin-engine 6-place aircraft, the Cessna Skymaster, has its engines on the fuselage, providing center-line thrust.*

doesn't like to have customers bring in their own parts; it's like taking your own food to a restaurant. The mechanic makes money on parts; if he can't do that, he'll make it elsewhere, and if I had managed to bring the parts cost down, the installation bill would almost certainly have gone up.

The so-called leaseback arrangement, in which you buy an airplane and then lease it to an FBO who uses it as a rental, makes the airplane a business property; there are attendant tax benefits, and the income from a leaseback covers most of the fixed costs of operating the airplane. The airplane deteriorates more rapidly, however, in the hands of a variety of renter-pilots who have no reason to take extremely good care of it; and it is not always available at a moment's notice.

Our garden variety four-seater would list, equipped, for about $40,000. The usual financing arrangement would be 20 percent down with seven years to pay, and a simple interest rate of about 13 to 15 percent. Monthly payments under this arrangement would be about $550. (All these figures, by the way, are subject to rapid inflation—more rapid, apparently, than the rate for most consumer goods. However, their proportions to one another will remain fairly constant unless, for instance, there is a sudden doubling of the price of fuel—which is quite possible. To correct these figures to the time at which you are reading them, you would have to determine the average equipped price, out the door, of a Cessna 172 or Cherokee Warrior, and augment all the costs here by the ratio of that price to the $40,000 mentioned above.)

*The Lance II, the turbocharged top of Piper's Cherokee line. It will carry 6 people at 200 mph at altitudes up to 25,000 feet.*

*Two Beechcraft models. Top, the twin-engined Baron can carry 6 people at well over 200 mph. Bottom, the Beech Bonanza, with essentially the same fuselage, features single-engine operating economy but costs almost $100,000.*

The list price of a new airplane includes 25 percent for the dealer. In other words, his cost is 75 percent of list. He can bargain within that spread; and somebody who likes to hustle airplanes, or who is trying to get himself established, might sell for no more than $1,000 over wholesale. He makes money in other ways; for instance, for bringing in the loan to a bank he will get a kickback of $500 or so—a "broker's fee." If he makes only $1,500 or $2,000 on a sale, he is still doing fine so long as he sells several airplanes a month—and that is why he has to be a good hustler.

The dealer's share of the list price of avionics is higher: usually 40 percent of list. This is quite significant when you consider that a $30,000 airplane can easily have $10,000 worth of equipment aboard—so that a lot of a dealer's potential profit can be in options. (In Cessna's case, they put in their own radios, under the ARC brand name, at the factory and sell them at bargain rates designed to prevent the purchaser from buying a bare-bones airplane and equipping it himself, or through his dealer. This bothers some people, because ARC avionics have a particularly bad reputation.) A basic VFR avionics package, consisting of Nav, Com, and transponder, can be had for $2,000; good quality basic IFR equipment, with dual Navs, dual Coms, ADF, transponder, marker beacons, glide-slope receiver, audio selector panel, and so on, costs upward of $7,500.

These are all prices for new airplanes and new equipment. Used airplanes, like used cars, can be a better bargain than new, for the same reasons: they have already undergone the first blow of depreciation that occurs when a product ceases to be unowned, while their utility and performance are sometimes superior to those of new ones. (An excellent example of this is to be found in the light twin market, where none of the airplanes now in production—Piper Seminole, Beech Duchess, or Grumman Cougar—is the equal of the now discontinued Piper Twin Comanche.) The maintenance costs of airplanes necessarily rise with age, and in particular the buyer of a used airplane has to look at the age and condition of the engine(s). Since they must be periodically overhauled at a cost of several thousand dollars, engines that are nearly at the end of their TBO, or time between overhauls, promise a large expense in the near future. Engine time is recorded in logs and on an hour meter in the tachometer, and most engines will go from 1,200 to 2,000 hours between overhauls.

*An early model Beech King Air still commands a good resale price.*

The engine is the single biggest maintenance expense in an airplane, and the more expensive the engine, and the more of them there are on the airplane (two is the usual maximum), the higher the operating costs will be. Sometimes one buys a new engine outright rather than overhaul an old one; incredible as it may seem, the engine of an economical four-seater costs $7,000, while that of a fast 4–6 seat retractable with a turbocharger might easily sell for over $20,000.

Price is generally proportional to performance; and the least expensive plane you can get—a battered two-seat tandem taildragger like a Cub or a Champ—will cost, in flyable condition, upward of $5,000 and will offer performance barely superior to that of a balloon. Reasonably good used four-seaters start close to $10,000. Many people wonder if they could not get into flying more cheaply by building an airplane from scratch, or from a kit, or buying such airplanes, which are called homebuilts.

Homebuilts are, in fact, cheaper to operate than factory airplanes because you can do your own maintenance, and they are usually inexpensively equipped in the first place. Some of them have very good performance, but very few are four-seaters. Buying them is risky, unless you are sufficiently knowledgeable to make a very thorough inspection or to hire a professional mechanic who can. Since each is different from every other, common sense is the only guide to judging them.

Several kits are available for one- and two-seat airplanes that can be built in a fairly short time. The late Ken Rand's two-seat KR-2 achieved the remarkable speed of 250 mph with Rand alone present; but it was strangely influenced by the presence of other airplanes, and was regularly clocked at only 150 mph by other airplanes flying alongside.

Burt Rutan's two-seat canard VariEze (pronounced "very easy"), built entirely of fiberglass and plastic foam, cruises at upward of 180 mph with a 100-hp Continental engine, and can be built for between $5,000 and $10,000 in around 1,200 man-hours.

Another Rutan design, the Quickie, is a single-seater similar to the VariEze in structural concepts, which uses a tiny 18-hp industrial engine and manages to cruise at over 100 mph on about 1 gallon of fuel an hour. It is the ultimate in economy and efficiency, exceeding as it does 100 miles per gallon, and can be built in about 400 man-hours from a kit that costs less than $4,000, including engine. But while the VariEze is arguably an airplane intended for transportation, the Quickie is principally for recreation.

There are many other homebuilt designs and kits, or partial kits, on the market. At the other end of the kit spectrum from the ones I have mentioned is a competition acrobatic biplane called the Christen Eagle, a kit for which, engine included, costs $27,000 and requires 2,000 to 3,000 man-hours to assemble. Most homebuilts are not available as kits; instead, one buys plans and some hard-to-fabricate parts from the designer or from independent vendors, and works more or less from scratch in one's home shop.

In my case, I designed and built my airplane, called Melmoth, entirely from scratch, using no existing parts (which was a mistake): it required over four years of full-time work to get into the air, and another year to get the bugs worked out. The cost was about $15,000. Obviously, I could have gotten airborne sooner and less expensively by buying a commercial product, but not in such style; and I think that most people who build homebuilts do so either because they like the style or because they like to tinker. I think it would be unbearable to regard the whole process of building the airplane—which is nearly always very long indeed—as a regrettable delay and an obstacle to one's actually having and using an airplane. So strong, in fact, is the love of building for its own sake that many home-builders, after they finish a project, sell it and begin another. They like flying well enough, I suppose, but they would rather be home building a plane.

I have concentrated on the low end of the aviation price spectrum, on the assumption that most people approaching the field for the first time would be interested in the least expensive way to get into it, not the most expensive. But it is amusing to see how much, rather than how little, one can spend on an airplane.

Three-hundred-horsepower four- to six-seaters with retractable gear are going for about $90,000 new these days. A light twin, whose performance is inferior to the big single's, costs upward of $100,000, and a twin like the Cessna 310, which carries up to six people at 220 mph, costs over $150,000. For a Beech Baron 58P, which is like a Cessna 310 but pressurized, figure upward of $350,000.

Those are private planes that regular ordinary people might fly for personal pleasure or for business. This is a rich country. They go higher. Anything with two turboprop engines starts at $600,000. Some people own these for fun, but mostly they are business planes—which often means that businessmen own them for fun. They can run up to a million or so. That is also where the very cheap, bargain basement jets, Cessna Citations and Learjets, start. Figure $650 an hour to rent a Lear, pilots included. We can put you in a nice jet for a million, million and a half. If you want something a little bigger (there isn't anything faster) we have a slightly used beauty here, hardly even dusty, a Gulfstream II, only three million!

I understand that King Khaled of Saudi Arabia purchased a 747 from Boeing for his private use, which with special equipment about which I can't even begin to speculate, but including, I would think, at the very least, a titanium Jacuzzi using light water, is said to have cost, in round figures, $127 million.

The picture is not so discouraging as it seems, however, if you are

*Near the end of the line of business aircraft is the 4-engine 10-place Lockheed Jetstar.*

willing to make some compromises. Joint ownership is one, if you can get together with one or two other people on a schedule of utilization. Airplanes tend to spend most of their time on the ground anyway, and so it is possible to divide their use among several people without too much inconvenience, so long as everyone doesn't insist on going away on the same weekend.

Another is the do-it-yourself approach to an airplane. Not building it yourself, which goes beyond the amount of time, effort, or skill that many people have to spend, but getting a second-hand airplane and fixing it up. A Cessna 172 ten years old, somewhat the worse for wear, will give the same performance as a new one, and cost $10,000 rather than $40,000. Two or three families might get together and buy one for cash, avoiding the high interest rates. Repainting, upholstery repair, corrosion removal, and minor mechanical cleanup can be done by enterprising owners, and many mechanics are willing to let an owner do the light work on an annual inspection if they feel that he can do it competently.

Though the cost of an old airplane is quite a bit lower than that of a new one, there will still be high fuel prices, insurance, and engine and avionics repairs to contend with. There is no way to make an engine overhaul cheaper, other than to make a bad job of it, because most of the cost is in parts, not labor, and most parts replacements are simply inevitable. As is the case with automobiles, however, it is not necessary to go first class in everything other than the engine; an old Volkswagen will get you to the same places as a new Mercedes. To some extent, you can reduce your costs simply by abandoning the desire that your airplane be highly prestigious and squeaky-clean; to a further extent still, by putting a good deal of personal effort into ownership. A used airplane is probably a good investment; it will hold its value if you take care of it, and it may soon be the only way for a person of average income, who cannot deduct his airplane from his taxes, to own one.

# 3

# *How an Airplane Flies*

Until a lifetime ago, people still debated whether a flying machine were even a possibility; now a small child can fold up a piece of paper in such a way that it flies, or glue together bits of wood and paper in such a way that they fly *well*. The principles of flight are so simple that, once understood, they make it appear that almost anything could fly, provided a large enough engine were hooked to it. Indeed, airplanes have limped back from war missing so many parts that they were barely recognizable; and yet they still flew.

The essence of the flying machine is its wing. Wings come in all sizes and shapes, but the wings of the class of airplane that we are concerned with—small private planes—are all quite similar. They are more or less rectangles roughly six times as long as wide, and with a thickness about a seventh or an eighth of their width. These proportions are not magical;

they simply represent a convenient compromise between aerodynamic efficiency and structural convenience.

What makes this piece of lumber fly is the shape of its cross section, which is called an airfoil. Airfoils come in a variety of shapes, but they have certain features in common: a rounded leading edge, a pointed trailing edge, and smoothly curved upper and lower surfaces. Usually, they are thickest at a point between a quarter and halfway back from the leading edge. They always go through the air with the leading edge first, as its name suggests.

Taking a typical airfoil, such as is used on many modern light airplanes, we can make a couple of observations about it. Begin with two imaginary lines; one runs through the middle of the shape, halfway between the top and bottom surfaces; this (the dotted line) is called the *mean line.* Another is a straight line drawn from the leading edge to the trailing edge; this (the dashed line) is the *chord line.* If an airfoil is symmetrical, as are the tail surfaces of most airplanes, the two lines coincide; most wing airfoils, however, have a humped shape, with the mean line curving up in a shallow arc above the chord line. This overall curvature of the airfoil, called *camber*, aids in producing maximum lift with minimum drag, but it is not essential. Some airplanes, notably acrobatic ones that need to fly upside down as well as right side up, use symmetrical airfoils.

Now, as this shape moves along through the air, it generates an upward force, called *lift*, a backward force called *drag*, and a tucking or plunging force called *pitching moment*. Both lift and drag are related to the *angle of attack*, which is the angle between the chord line and the direction of flight. (It is often defined as the angle between the chord line and the relative wind—the relative wind being simply another way of expressing the motion of the wing through the air. Whether you think of the air moving past the wing, like a wind, or of the wing moving through still air, the effects are the same.)

Generally, the lift of a wing gets greater and greater as its angle of attack increases, up to a certain point—15 degrees or so—where the lift suddenly diminishes sharply, while the drag suddenly increases. This unpropitious combination of events is called a *stall*—nothing to do with the engine—and the angle of attack at which it occurs is called the stalling angle of attack. Pitching moment, on the other hand, is largely unaffected by angle of attack.

There's an important point here to get clear in your mind at the very outset. Angle of attack is *always* considered relative to the direction of flight (or relative wind); it has nothing to do with the wing's position in relation to the horizon. This may be confusing, because airplanes usually fly parallel to the horizon, and one habitually thinks of angles of attack in relation to the horizontal. But a plane can stall going straight up, or straight down, or any way you like, so long as the angle of the chord line to the direction of flight exceeds the stalling angle of attack.

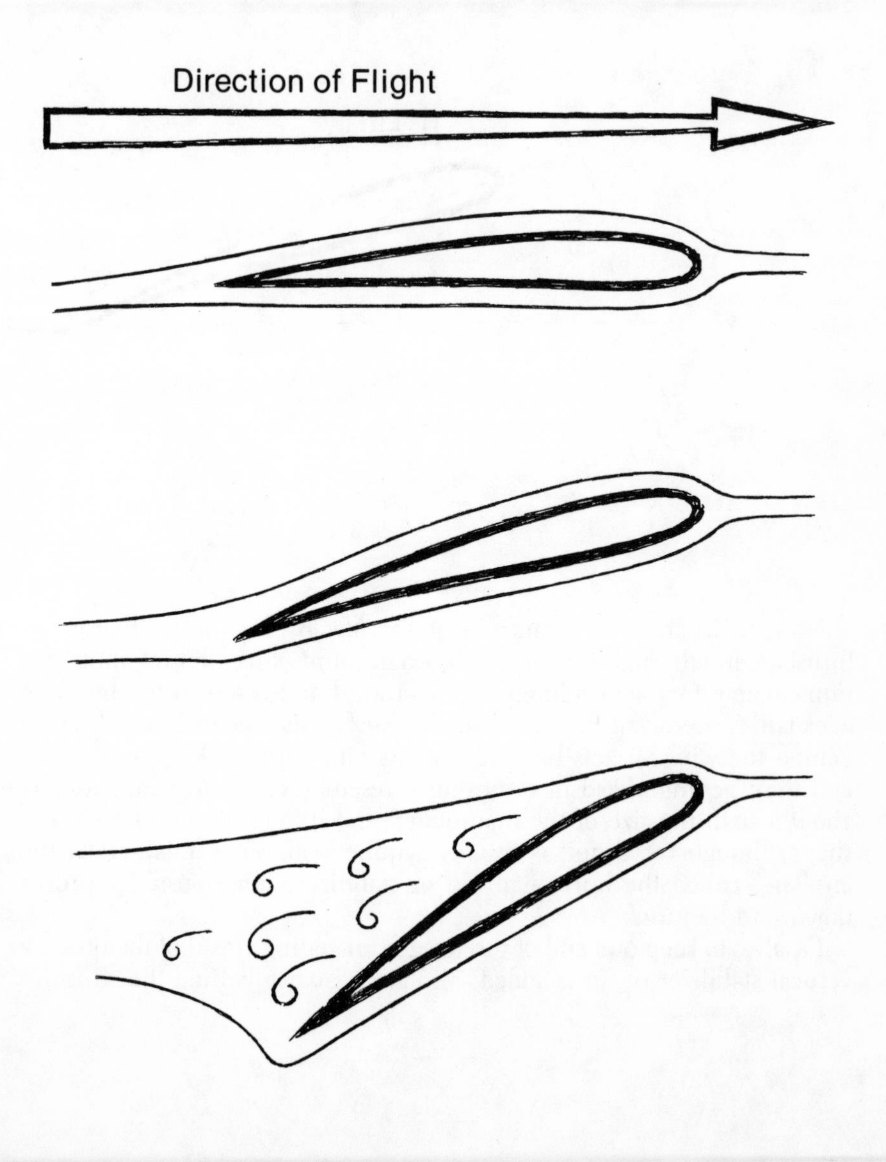

So: moving through the air, leading edge first, a wing produces lift; the greater the angle of the wing to the oncoming air, the greater the lift, up to a certain point called the stall, where lift sharply diminishes, drag increases, and continued flight is difficult.

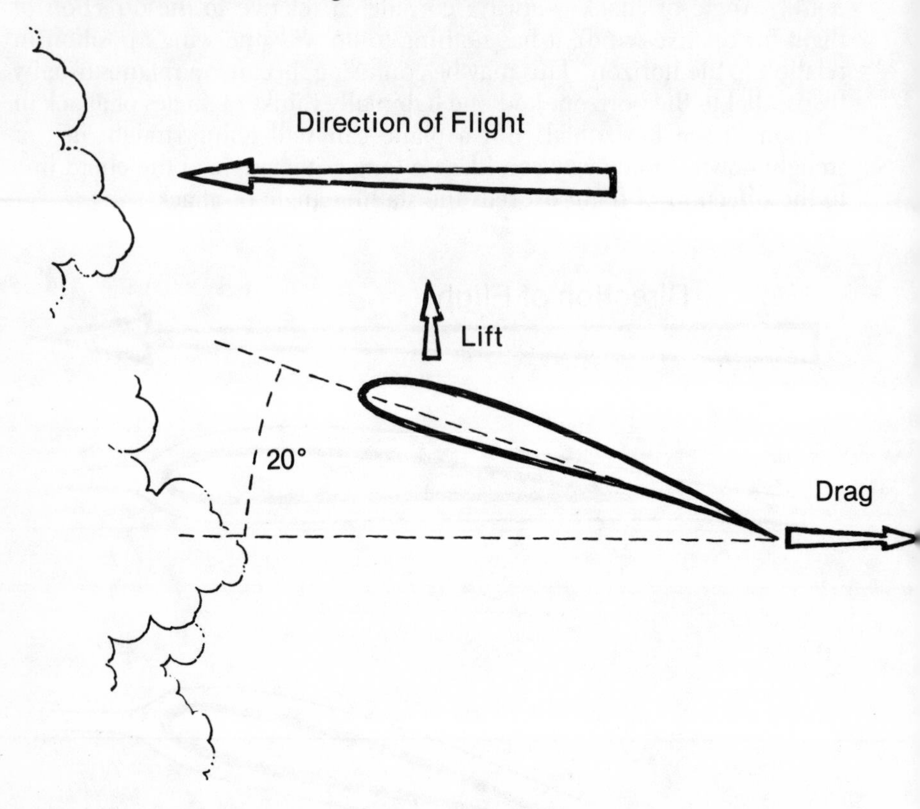


Now, by itself a normal airfoil is not *stable.* By this I mean that if you thrust a wing through the air it will, on account of its pitching moment, immediately tuck its leading edge downward and begin to tumble nose over tail. To prevent this, a stabilizing surface is attached at a distance behind the wing. It acts like the feathers on an arrow, keeping the rear end from getting ahead of the front; it resembles a small wing, usually about a sixth the size of the main wing, and it too is made in an airfoil shape, though the airfoil is usually symmetrical, since this part of the airplane, called the horizontal tail or stabilizer, must push upward or downward by turns.

Finally, to keep one end of the wing from getting ahead of the other, a vertical stabilizer or fin is added, also at a distance behind the wing.

We now have the makings of an airplane.

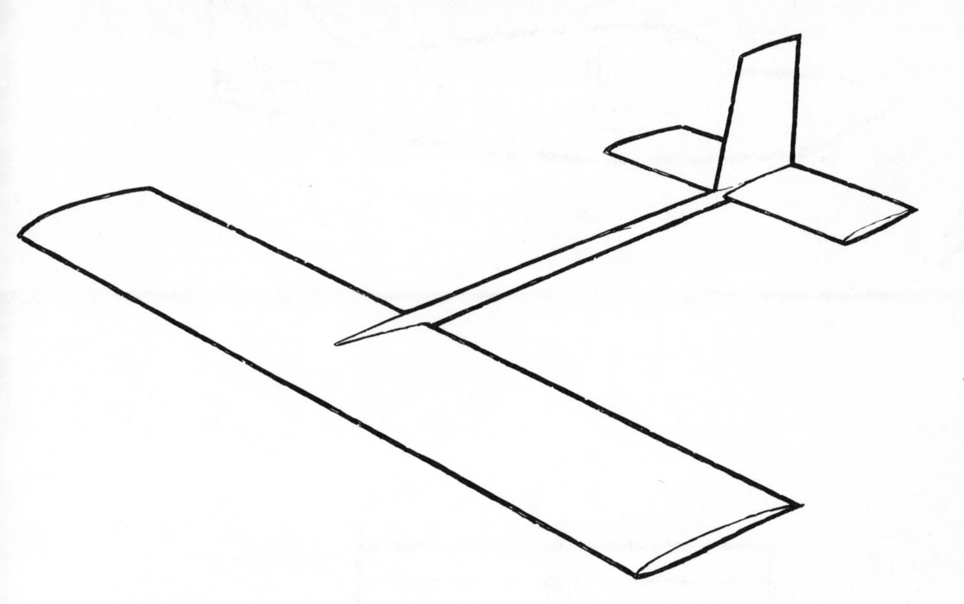

A few things are still missing: a place to put people, an engine, landing gear, and a way to control the whole works, so that it goes where the pilot wants it to.

The structural connection between the wing and the tail surfaces (which, by the way, are also collectively termed the *empennage*, pronounced EM-puh-nazh) is enlarged to contain a passenger cabin. The engine is attached to the front end, along with its propeller; together, they balance the weight of the tail, so that the complete airplane will more or less balance about a quarter of the way back from the leading edge of the wing to the trailing edge. This balance point, to which we will return later, is called the *center of lift*, and it is said to be located near the quarter-chord point.

The landing gear, which usually consists of two main wheels and one nosewheel, is secured to the wings or fuselage in such a way that the main wheels are somewhat aft of the center of gravity, the nosewheel well ahead of it.

We are left with the matter of the control surfaces.

So far, I have mentioned two types of movement of the airplane around its center of gravity: the pitching movement, which is counteracted by the horizontal stabilizer, and the yawing movement, which is counteracted by the vertical stabilizer.

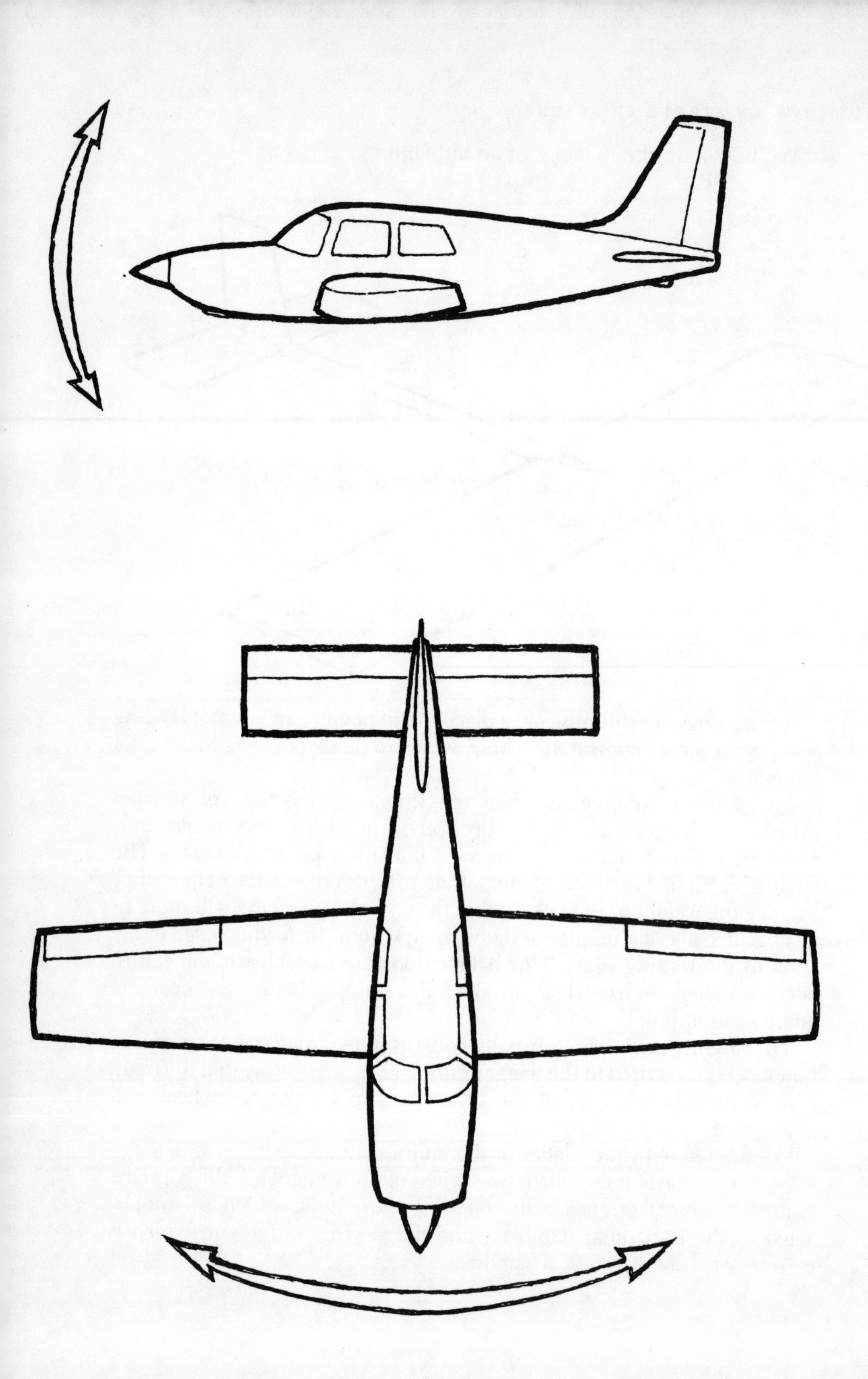

Obviously, there is a third motion: rolling.

If you think about it, you will see that these three types of movement, in various combinations, account for every possible evolution of an airplane in the sky, no matter how exotic. Lest the prospect of perverse combinations seem alarming, I should mention that in normal flying, the pitch angle never exceeds 15 degrees; the yaw angles are negligibly small; and roll angles of more than 40 degrees are uncommon. The entire repertory of motions of an airplane in normal use, therefore, is not larger than that of a bicycle traveling on mildly hilly roads.

I say a bicycle and not a car because, like a bicycle, an airplane banks in order to make turns. Thus, in an airplane you never feel the sideways force during turns that you do in a car; you can drink your tea without fear of spilling it.

The controls work in the three axes named: the pitch axis, the yaw axis, the roll axis. The elevator controls pitch, the rudder yaw, the ailerons roll. Generally speaking, the control surfaces consist of a hinged portion of a larger surface; by deflecting it one way, you produce a force the other way, just as when you put your hand out a car window, you can make it rise or drop by deflecting its trailing edge down or up.

Thus, to increase the wing's angle of attack, for instance, as you would want to do on landing, you deflect the elevator upward:

By pushing the tail down, you raise the leading edge of the wing, since the whole airplane always pivots around its own center of gravity (represented conventionally by the checkered circle).

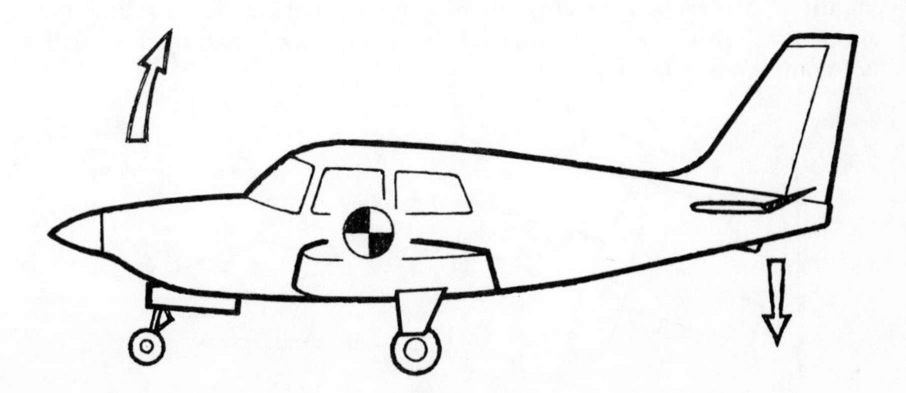

I'll come back to the practical use of the controls later, but I'd like to call your attention to a difference between the roll axis and the other two that makes it behave a little differently. Here is what the three axes look like:

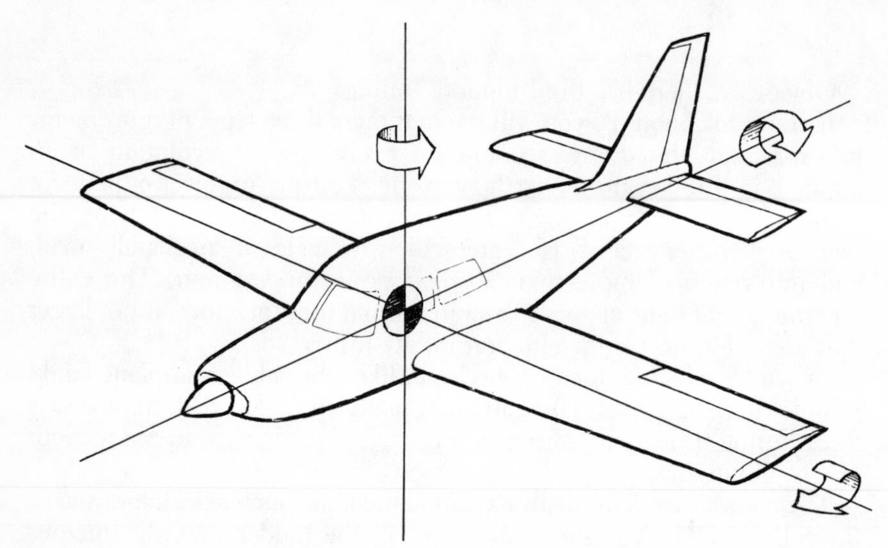

Each axis is like an imaginary shaft, passing through the center of gravity (called the CG), about which the airplane can pivot. Notice that the yaw and pitch axes are both at right angles to the direction of flight, while the roll axis is aligned with the direction of flight. The result is that while a deviation from neutral in pitch and yaw makes the airplane look different to the oncoming air, and produces a restoring force, in roll this does not occur.

If you deflect the elevator upward, for example, the nose of the plane will come up; but at a certain point the nose-down restoring force of the stabilizer will exactly neutralize the nose-up force of the elevator, and the airplane will *trim out* at that angle of attack; in other words, the nose will not come up any farther.

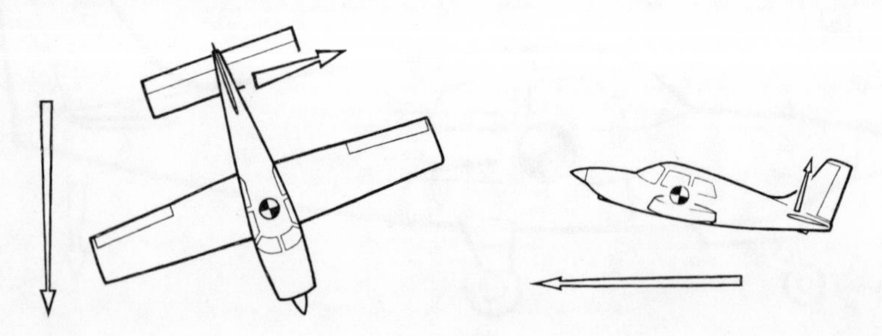

But in roll, all that happens is that when you deflect the ailerons, the airplane starts to roll and keeps on rolling. To establish an angle of bank, you roll into the bank with the ailerons, and then stop the roll with opposite aileron, and finally keep the ailerons approximately neutral during the turn.

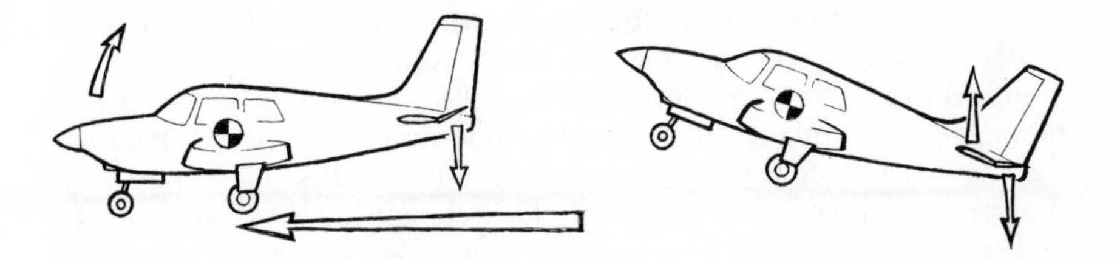

There are two ailerons, one on each wing, and they are linked together in such a way that when one goes up, the other goes down. The downgoing aileron pushes its wing *upward*, and the upgoing aileron pushes its wing *downward*. Thus, when I talk about "opposite aileron," as I just did, I mean right-turn ailerons as opposed to left-turn ailerons—*not* the one on the right wing as opposed to the one on the left wing. They work simultaneously, always; they are one control.

The wing and empennage are called *flying surfaces*, and the ailerons, elevator, and rudder are called *control surfaces*. The arrangement that I have described is the conventional, familiar one; but it is not the only one that can fly. Airplanes have been built with no empennage at all; they are made stable by special airfoil sections and by control surfaces located at the trailing edge of the wing. A familiar example of such a design is the Concorde, the Anglo-French supersonic transport, which has a wing of what is called a slender delta planform; that is, it has the shape of a long, narrow triangle and no tail surfaces whatever. An alternative arrangement moves the wing to the rear of the airplane, places another lifting surface at the front, and then by distributing the weight of the airplane properly between the two surfaces—that is, by putting the center of gravity between them and proportioning their areas accordingly—produces a stable airplane. This is called a tandem wing arrangement or, if the front wing is much smaller than the rear one, a canard. In the last five years a single designer, Burt Rutan, has developed a series of canard designs of increasing ambitiousness, and all of them seem to demonstrate, in one way or another, the superiority of the canard arrangement to the conventional one. Whether this achievement will be a mere flash in the pan or will alter the course of airplane design remains to be seen; mere convention is very powerful, if only by its familiarity.

The heart, the genius, the essence of the airplane is the wing. People forget this; when imagining the improbable ultimate catastrophe, they say, "If the wings fall off," as though the fuselage were holding up the wings. If the wings were to break off, they would not fall; they would depart upward and the fuselage would fall. All the other parts are the servants of the wing; and the wing is the servant of the pilot. When you fly an airplane, you are flying a wing.

Among private airplanes, the wings are, as I said before, all quite similar. Curiously enough, they are almost all of about the same size—around 150 to 180 square feet. The reason for this is that the faster and more powerful airplanes make do with proportionately smaller wings than their lighter but slower and less powerful counterparts. By going faster, they get more lift out of a given area. The relationship between wing area and weight is expressed by a number called W/S, or wing loading (W stands for weight, S for surface—confusing, but conventional). An old-fashioned light trainer like a Piper Cub has a wing loading of about 10 lb/sq. ft.; a six-seat light twin will typically have a wing loading about thrice that. By going faster than the Cub, the twin makes its wing develop three times as much lift per square foot. It does not have to go three times as fast; lift increases with the square of speed, and so the twin need only go about 1.7 times as fast as the Cub, other things being equal.

This brings us to the relationship between angle of attack, lift, and speed. It is the most important single relationship in flying, and although many pilots don't understand it, they would be better pilots if they did. It's not excessively complicated, but it has a few pitfalls which I'll try to avoid.

We have seen that, at a given flying speed, the magnitude of the lift can be increased by increasing the angle of attack. Lift is measured, like weight, in pounds or kilograms or what have you. In normal flight, lift is equal to weight. I repeat: in *normal* flight, lift is equal to weight. By "normal" I mean any condition not involving an acceleration—that is, a turn, a pullout into a climb, or a pushover into a descent; during level cruise, steady climb, and steady descent, *lift is equal to weight*. If lift were not equal to weight, something would happen to change matters. For instance, if lift were less than weight, the airplane would begin to accelerate downward. The direction of flight would change, but the angle of the chord line at first would not. Now the angle of attack is somewhat increased, because the direction of flight is more downward. The stabilizer is no longer properly aligned with the direction of flight and produces an upward push, which causes the nose to come down, restoring the angle of attack to its previous value. But now the airplane is pointing downhill and will begin to pick up speed like a rolling car. More speed produces more lift, until the lift becomes equal to the weight. After a few oscillations, our airplane will have settled into a descent, at a slightly higher speed than before, and the lift will have become exactly equal to the weight.

Notice the circular nature of this arrangement. Insufficient lift produces a descent which increases speed which increases lift. But the descent continues: it is supplying the energy to overcome the drag produced by increasing the speed. During a steady descent, lift is equal to weight, but engine thrust is less than drag. Contrary to what you might intuitively imagine, a descent does not imply a lack of lift; it implies a lack of power.

Similarly, a steady climb represents not excess lift but excess power. Only during the transition into a steady climb or descent is there a temporary imbalance between lift and weight.

Generally, in unaccelerated level flight lift is equal to weight, and thrust is equal to drag. An imbalance, produced for instance by a change in throttle setting or by a change in angle of attack, results in an acceleration to a different state where balance is again achieved.

Hiding at the center of this relationship is the concept of trim. For the pilot, trim is a little knurled wheel or crank, between the seats or on the ceiling of the cabin. With this control he adjusts the angle of attack so that the airplane climbs, descends, or flies level, as he wishes. The stick or yoke, of course, also controls angle of attack; but without trim, you would have to exert a constant force on the controls to hold any airspeed or attitude other than one particular one. Trim allows you to eliminate control forces and fly hands off.

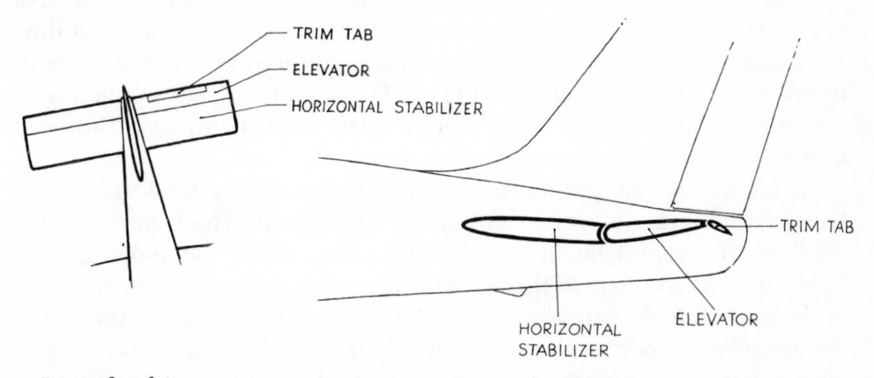


It works this way:

Normally, if you let go the controls, the elevator will trail directly behind the stabilizer. But by adjusting the position of a small movable portion of the trailing edge of the elevator, you can make it sit trailing-edge-high or trailing-edge-low. In the illustration, a downward position of the trim tab has produced an upward float of the elevator; this in turn increases the angle of attack of the wing until the force of the up elevator is neutralized by the stabilizer (see p. 42 for a refresher on this point).

Plainly, by adjusting the position of the trim tab the pilot can cause the airplane to seek any of the whole range of possible angles of attack. He can still control angle of attack with the yoke or stick, but if he releases the controls, the attitude and speed on which the airplane will eventually settle will depend on the position of the trim tab.

The full complement of cockpit controls, therefore, consists of pedals which control the rudder (step on the right pedal to turn right); a yoke or stick which controls pitch and roll (pull the yoke or stick back to raise the nose, push forward to lower the nose; tilt the stick right or left, or rotate the yoke like a steering wheel, for roll); and a wheel or crank for setting pitch trim. There may also be trim controls for the roll and yaw axes, but they are of minor importance, and most small airplanes do not have them at all.

There is a misconception so often heard from laymen that I may as well talk about it here, among the basics, as elsewhere. It is the notion that an airplane needs its engine to remain aloft and that the heavier or larger an airplane is, the worse it glides. Typically, even people who realize that with its engine stopped an airplane will still glide, will suppose that at any rate a jetliner would not make a very good glider. The opposite is true.

The engine is necessary because to remain aloft an airplane must have forward speed, which produces drag, and so the airplane needs a source of energy to overcome drag and maintain forward speed, just as a car, rolling in neutral on a level road, will slow down gradually because of friction, unless it receives an input of energy. This input can be supplied by a descent; and a gradually descending airplane will maintain its airspeed against drag just as will a car rolling downhill.

As for the gliding properties of airliners, the glide ratio—that is, the flatness of the glide, or, in automotive terms, the shallowness of the gradient that would be sufficient to keep the rolling car moving—is a function of what is called the aerodynamic cleanness of the design; it has nothing at all to do with the weight. Jet airliners happen to be very clean designs—that is part of the reason for their high speed; and so they will glide better than will light airplanes, whose windmilling props produce a great deal of drag.

This is not to say that an airliner would settle to the ground like a dry leaf. It would glide flat but it would glide fast. It would reach the ground sooner than would a light airplane starting its glide from the same height, but it would cover a greater horizontal distance before reaching the ground, and arrive at a greater horizontal and vertical speed. It is because of its high horizontal speed that an airliner without power, landing in a bean field, is less safe than a light plane in the same fix; but it would not fall like a brick. Far from it, an airliner would, in fact, glide nearly as well as some sailplanes.

# 4

# *What All Airplanes Have in Common*

Although the manufacturers of airplanes, like the manufacturers of cars, would like to have you believe that the differences in outward appearance are of tremendous importance, this is rarely the case. The configuration favored by the largest manufacturer, Cessna, for its single-engine planes, fuselage slung underneath the wing, has the trivial advantages of providing shade and protection from rain to people standing by the plane, and of allowing easier boarding and a better view straight down. The low-wing configuration used by most other manufacturers—which in view of the primary importance of the wing ought really to be called a high fuselage configuration—lends itself to a simpler installation of retractable landing gear, gives some nervous passengers a feeling of support, and makes it easier to fuel the airplane as well as to check visually if there is adequate fuel in the tanks, which are normally located in the wings. In textbooks and in the wind tunnel, the high-wing arrangement appears to have some aerodynamic advantages; but in actual practice these become insignificant and only the mundane practical benefits of each configuration remain.

There is little to choose between tapered wings and rectangular ones, swept-back fins and upright ones, T-tails (where the stabilizer is set atop the fin) and normal ones, despite the implications of advertising copy. Each feature has some theoretical advantage, but it is invariably obscured by a thousand less obvious effects.

The remarkable thing about general aviation airplanes, in fact, is their uniformity. Like cars, they resemble one another to the point that you can go from one to another with little transitional uncertainty. Their qualities are much alike, partly because federal requirements make it so and partly because the science of their design is so thoroughly conventional.

There are certain conspicuous standouts: the Bellanca Viking's silky ailerons; the sexy styling of the now discontinued Cessna Cardinal; the remarkable speed of the Grumman Tiger and the Mooney 201. Pilots develop favorites and defend their choices with ardor; but if one steps back a bit, the members of a given class—and classes are broken down mainly by engine size—are birds of a feather. What differences there are, are not among makes and models but among types and classes. One four-seat 150-hp fixed-gear single-engine plane is about like another; but it is worlds apart from a 600-hp light twin.

The distinction in feel and performance between planes of markedly different wing loadings and engine sizes are the ones that lure pilots farther and farther up the rating ladder. A student often starts out in a small two-seater of 65 to 150 horsepower—most likely a Cessna, Grumman, or Piper trainer. When he taxies, he can feel the breeze rocking the airplane, which seems as light as a small sailing craft, and when he opens the throttle for takeoff the acceleration is gentle. The airplane takes off and lands at highway speeds, and cruises no faster than 120 mph—which for an airplane is very slow indeed. The cabin is small, the engine is small, and the wing is large. This class of airplane is said to have a low wing loading—a large wing area in proportion to its weight—and a relatively high power loading. These qualities make it slow and gentle, like the kind of horse on which you would teach children to ride. The landing approach, flown at perhaps 70 mph, gives plenty of time for assessing one's position and speed and for making corrections. The landing itself, at around 50 mph, is lazy, though it may not seem so to the beginner, who sees everything as very hasty and furious; and the ground roll is short, so that the point on the runway at which the touchdown occurs is not overly critical.

As one gains experience, one almost always wants to move into faster types of airplanes. The manufacturers have been at pains to provide easy stepladders of types up which the ideal customer climbs, as he seeks greater speed and sophistication at, of course, rapidly increasing cost. Cessna's four-seat model 172, for instance, has flying qualities that are almost indistinguishable from those of the 152 trainer, and its cockpit equipment is about the same and similarly arranged. Thence one moves, presumably, to the slightly more demanding 182 or 182 RG (retractable gear), with the additional complications of cowl flaps, constant speed propeller, retractable gear, and higher speed. The next step might be to the still faster, still bigger, perhaps turbocharged Centurion. Then, getting ever richer or deeper in debt, one might "trade up" to a twin and then a twin turboprop until the ultimate move is made to buying a jet. The graduations in Cessna's single-engine line are so small and subtle as to be almost imperceptible; but if you were to go from a trainer straight into a Centurion, for instance, you would be aware of a considerable difference—bigger, perhaps, than the difference between the Centurion and Cessna's docile jet, the Citation.

The Centurion, which is a six-seat airplane with retractable landing gear and an engine of 285 horsepower, is a far heavier airplane than the 152; but its wing area is only slightly greater. To the pilot, the higher wing loading makes itself felt in a number of ways. The airplane is less responsive to turbulence: it has a "stiffer ride," and it does not jump into the air as a trainer does but seems to slide smoothly into a climb. After liftoff comes a short spell of heaviness, a transition to climbing speed, while the landing gear and flaps are retracted and the airplane gradually gains 30 or 40 mph. The pressure on the yoke makes the pilot feel that he is helping to hold up the airplane as it accelerates toward the trimmed climb speed of perhaps 100–120 mph.

The control forces, especially in pitch, are higher in the faster, heavier airplane. In the landing pattern, which is flown at 90 mph rather than 70, there is less time for corrections, and the touchdown point is more critical, since the landing roll will occupy a greater portion of the runway's length. All in all, a more precise touch is required throughout the flight.

The light twins fly much the way airplanes in the Cessna Centurion/Beech Bonanza class do, with the added complication of two engines. With wing loadings three times that of the trainer, and two engines totaling as much as 800 horsepower, the medium and "cabin class" twins dwell in a new realm of speed and performance. In taxi, they are as solid as a car. The takeoff begins with a definite acceleration, and the airplane is racing down the concrete at nearly 100 mph when the pilot lifts the nose. Turbocharged, pressurized, often operating completely on instruments under constant surveillance of ground controllers, they are extremely demanding when they are demanding, and at other times they are nearly self-sufficient. Usually they are equipped to execute most of the flight automatically. The pilot may reduce his role to that of a programmer, executing the takeoff and the landing manually, but directing the airplane through the rest of the flight by pushing buttons and setting radio frequencies. Mechanically complex, they are comparatively trouble-prone and consequently costly to operate. In return, they repay the investment of pilot effort and owner cash with high speed and nearly all-weather capability.

For the pilot working his way up the rating ladder, jets are the top rung. A business jet, such as the now nearly legendary Learjet, is a paradoxical machine. On the one hand it provides the pilot with visceral excitement in proportion to its dazzling performance. On the other hand, being a near-silent, smooth, air-tight life-support system for its occupants, separating them from the lethally tenuous atmosphere at 40,000 feet and almost requiring, because of the poor handling qualities of planes at that height, to be flown by the autopilot, a jet drives its pilots into an isolation very remote from the sensations of flight. There is almost no sound, no vibration, no bounce, no rush of air, no sense of motion. You have difficulty convincing yourself that anything is really happening. Because of the speed and weight of jets, even acrobatic maneuvers performed in them take place with a stupefying slowness. If you turn a small trainer up on edge, it will drop its nose and start diving in a couple of seconds. In a jet, five seconds, ten seconds will pass as the nose slowly arcs downward. It seems forever before you think you ought to level out. Jets combine the fact of speed with the sensation of slowness. They feel heavy in flight, partly because controls are difficult to displace at high speeds and partly because of their high wing loadings, a jet having ten times the wing loading of a Piper Cub. In spite of that heaviness, jets climb in a thrilling way that no other airplane can match. A lightly loaded Learjet can climb at 10,000 feet a minute; a pilot will shake his head and smile, knowing, but not trying to describe, the sensation of that ascent.

The trainer and the jet are remote from one another, but the distance is in style, not in substance. They are flown the same way, using the same skills. The left hand is on the yoke, the right hand is on the throttle. (In light single-seaters and tandem two-seaters, especially the older ones, the throttle is on the left; but the transition is easily made, almost unconscious in fact. The arrangement may date from a time when high control forces suggested putting the stick in the stronger hand.) The rudder pedals and the brakes are under the feet, and the rudder pedals work the opposite way to what you might expect: pushing the right pedal away from you makes the airplane turn or yaw to the right. Although this is a different arrangement from that used on a sled or a horse, it has the advantage of allowing you, if you want to make a particularly sharp turn while taxiing, to step on the rudder pedal and on the brake at the same time on the same side. This causes the plane almost to swivel around that main wheel.

The throttle works like the accelerator of a car, except that it is in the hand rather than under the foot, and unlike the accelerator of a car it does not have a spring returning it to idle. It remains wherever it is put. Pushing it forward increases the power, pulling it back all the way lets the engine idle. The throttle of a turbine-engined airplane, that is, a jet or turboprop, is called the *power lever*—a more general term that abandons the anachronistic reference to the butterfly throttle of a reciprocating engine.

Certain basic instruments are needed for flight. Even they are not indispensable; early pioneers in aviation flew with no instruments at all, but they also had a lot of accidents. Once you have decided to have some instruments, the first and fundamental one needed is the airspeed indicator. Because of the phenomenon of the stall, there is a certain minimum speed at or below which it is hazardous or impossible to fly. For other reasons every airplane has a certain maximum permissible speed based on the strength of its structure. There is thus a band of speeds that is safe, and an airspeed indicator provides a reliable and convenient way of remaining within that band—better than guessing from the flapping of the fabric as the pioneers used to do.

Beyond the airspeed indicator, every other instrument is to some degree a luxury. But this is a luxurious age. An altimeter is necessary for flying in airways, which are defined by certain altitudes; a compass is a considerable aid to navigation; and so on: each instrument provides the pilot with some piece of information that he needs or may sometime need. The huge instrument arrays of complex airplanes baffle only people who do not understand the questions they are designed to answer. Once you understand flight, you understand those instruments. At any given moment, the pilot is only interested in a few of them, and all pilots are interested in the same few: airspeed, heading, altitude, vertical speed, position. They define everything that is of continuous concern. The rest tell about the state of the systems and engines: pressures, temperatures, quantities, rates of flow and rotation, voltage and amperage, and so on. They are items of little interest, because they rarely change and are automatically regulated. The pilot glances at them from time to time to verify that all is well. If something feels wrong, he looks at these instruments for a clue to the problem, but for the most part he ignores them. The only instruments that really count are airspeed, heading, altitude, vertical speed, and position. They count in a Cub and in a 747 or a space shuttle. They are the prime parameters for navigating through three-dimensional space. Look at any instrument panel, large or small, simple or bewildering, and those few essential instruments will cluster right in front of the pilot, underscoring the fact that in any type of airplane, however simple and slow or fast and complex, the process and sense of flying are the same.

The airspeed indicator does not measure speed directly; it measures ram pressure, as you might judge how fast you were driving by putting your hand out the window and feeling the pressure of the air against it. The analogy with the car requires making an important distinction, however. In a car, what actually concerns you at all times is groundspeed, not airspeed. Measuring groundspeed by reference to air pressure requires the assumption that there is no wind. The situation in an airplane is quite different. The airplane is supported on air; so long as it measures its speed with respect to the surrounding air, it has no way of knowing whether, or in what direction, the surrounding air mass itself is moving, except from a circuitous calculation in which measured airspeed is compared with observed progress over the ground. The airspeed indicator has nothing to do with groundspeed—the actual rate at which you are traveling from one place to another. To compute groundspeed you have to time yourself between two points a known distance apart. In practice, this rarely needs to be done, and never with pinpoint precision.

But the airspeed indicator not only does not tell you your groundspeed; it does not even tell you your real airspeed. Because the airspeed indicator deduces speed from the impact of moving air, it is affected by the diminution of air density with altitude. It is therefore necessary to distinguish between *indicated airspeed* (IAS), which is what your airspeed indicator reads, and *true airspeed* (TAS), which is the actual velocity of the airplane through the air. Indicated airspeed diminishes with altitude for a given true airspeed. For instance, an airplane traveling at 150 mph at 10,000 feet will show only 130 mph on its airspeed indicator. The IAS is an indicator of flight condition; the TAS is used for navigational purposes and for bragging. TAS is derived from IAS by a simple calculation performed on a circular slide rule. In the course of a flight, each type of airspeed might interest the pilot at a different stage. During the takeoff and climb, he is controlling his IAS; the rotation and liftoff speed, and the speed for best rate of climb, will be indicated airspeeds. When he levels out to cruise, if he is not sufficiently familiar with the airplane to know its performance by heart, he may take out his little circular slide rule, or "pilot's computer," and convert the IAS into a TAS by a simple operation.

Now he knows how fast he is moving through the air, but he does not know for certain how fast the air is moving over the ground—that is, how the wind is affecting him. To discover this, he would time his flight between two points on the ground whose distance apart he can measure on a chart. From this he calculates his *groundspeed* (GS).

Notice, now, that the airspeed indicator had nothing to do with finding groundspeed. However, by subtracting the TAS from the groundspeed, or vice versa, he can find out the *wind component*. This is the contribution being made by the wind; but he still cannot tell which way the wind is blowing, or how hard, because a wind component of minus 10 mph, for instance, could represent a direct headwind of that speed, or a quartering headwind of twice that value. Their effect on the airplane would be of the same magnitude, with this difference: a quartering wind or a crosswind will make the airplane drift away from its track, while a direct headwind or tailwind won't. Still, it is hard to tell, without an elaborate analysis that no pilot would ever waste time performing, the exact magnitude and direction of the winds aloft.

The altimeter measures the static pressure of the air surrounding the airplane and displays it as an altitude above sea level rather than in pounds per square inch, inches of mercury, kilograms per square meter, or millibars, which would be normal measures of atmospheric pressure. The instrument is adjustable by the pilot to compensate for local variations in barometric pressure. A small window on the face of the instrument displays four digits on a drum-counter mechanism; they can be set from about 28.00 to 31.00, which are about the most extreme sea level barometric pressures likely to be encountered. Before takeoff the pilot sets the altimeter to the known field elevation; if a local barometric setting is available from a tower or Flight Service Station he may compare it to the setting showing in the window on his altimeter. They should be the same. If they are not, he may make some mental note, such as "set the baro .06 above the true setting," and eventually have the instrument checked. En route, and at his destination, he will get local readings from ground stations by radio and change his setting as necessary.

Conventional altimeters such as are found in light airplanes have two conspicuous hands resembling those of a clock, and a third less noticeable hand or pointer. The "minute hand" indicates hundreds of feet, the "hour hand" thousands, and the third hand tens of thousands. The third hand is important because 10,000 feet and 20,000 feet look the same as sea level, so far as the position of the other two hands are concerned. Errors in interpreting altimeters have led to some remarkable incidents. At times, however, altimeters have no doubt been blamed for mistakes that were really the intentions of the pilot. An airliner flew into water short of its destination under a low ceiling which, over the water, turned to fog. Presumably the pilot was trying to duck under the overcast and come into the airport just below the clouds. He was ignoring the altieter, not misreading it. But the crew offered as a defense the claim that all three of them—pilot, first officer, and second officer—misread their four altimeters. Hardly plausible, but an example of the bum raps that are pinned on this unfortunate instrument.

Heading, or the direction the airplane is pointing, is read from a plain magnetic compass. When the heading changes, the compass, which is floating in liquid, takes a while to stabilize, and so it is difficult to change to a new heading by the magnetic compass alone. Most airplanes use a gyrocompass or DG (directional gyro) for precise maneuvering. The DG cannot sense North, so the pilot sets it to coincide with the magnetic compass; it then displays turns with little or no error, and no lag or overrun. Since the DG is a gyro instrument, however, it slowly precesses and may need to be reset every fifteen minutes or so.

The vertical speed indicator is the least indispensable of the basic instruments, because a pilot could get a rough idea of his vertical speed simply by watching the altimeter. The VSI, like the magnetic compass, is subject to the same kind of leads and lags, though for entirely different reasons. It does, however, provide the pilot with useful indications of altitude trends.

Finally there is the matter of position. The term is ambiguous; it can mean, in the case of a person, standing up or sitting down. It can mean in New York or in San Francisco. In airplane parlance, notions like standing and sitting are called *attitude*, and *position* refers to geographical location. There is no single instrument to measure geographical position; the pilot, in his role of navigator, makes use of various sources of information to keep track of it. In clear weather and familiar surroundings, he simply looks around him, as you do when driving a car. When he is flying blind in a cloud, he navigates by radio signals.

Attitude, consisting of the position of the airplane about three axes—pitch, roll, and yaw—is displayed on two instruments. One is called the needle and ball; it was the original gyro attitude indicator—the kind Lindbergh used. It consists of a vertical needle that can tilt to either side and a black ball in a curved glass tube below it. The ball is used to indicate the need for an application of rudder. If the ball is centered, fine; if it lies to the right of center, right rudder will bring it back. You *step on the ball* to make it come back to center. Perhaps it helps to think of it as something squishy or slippery under your foot. When the ball is in the center, the way the needle is tilted is the way the nose is turning. In other words the tilt of the needle corresponds to a bank, and you could think of the needle as representing the vertical fin of the plane. But if the ball is not centered, the reading of the needle goes awry; and so the needle is better thought of as indicating rate of heading change than angle of bank. In Lindbergh's time, the proper procedure for using the instrument was first to step on the ball, and once you had it centered to level the wings by reference to the needle. This led Lindbergh himself often to speak in his books about stopping an inadvertent turn by stepping on opposite rudder—a procedure that is entirely incorrect by today's thinking, in which turn is primarily controlled by the ailerons, not the rudder. The contradiction arises, in fact, partly from the fact that planes like the *Spirit of St. Louis* had rather evil handling qualities, but mostly from the peculiarities of the needle and ball as an attitude indicator.

Because the needle and ball was a confusing instrument to use, it has been supplanted by the artificial horizon, though most airplanes still carry a needle and ball, or some version of one, as a backup instrument. The artificial horizon is so simple that a person who has never flown before can easily learn to fly by one, just as if it were a game in an amusement arcade. Again using a gyroscope, it provides a line that always remains horizontal with respect to the real world, however the airplane banks. Thus, even when you are flying in clouds and can see only gray all around you, you can see the position of the horizon by referring to this instrument. The horizon line also moves up and down in response to pitch movements of the airplane, so that the pilot can see whether he is nose-up or nose-down. The airplane itself is represented by a small "toy airplane," seen tail-on, which is fixed on the instrument face.

A less common alternative arrangement has the horizon fixed in the instrument and the toy airplane banking and pitching in relation to it. If one ignores the illusory verticals and horizontals produced by the instrument panel and cockpit, however, and looks only within the circle of the instrument, the impression is the same, and veteran pilots find no advantage in either type. Some studies have shown that novices adapt more quickly to the moving-airplane type of display, but it has not supplanted the more traditional moving-horizon type.

Early aviators were surprised to discover, and slow to admit, that they could not remain upright in clouds without some kind of attitude indicator. One might think—and laymen generally do think, encouraged by the mention of "seat of the pants flying"—that, just as one can remain upright and walk about with one's eyes closed, one could keep an airplane upright by the same inner sense of position. *It doesn't work.* The reason it doesn't work is that the force which we interpret as gravity when we are standing up, and which enables us to judge our verticality, becomes confused in a turning airplane with a centrifugal component. In an airplane, as on a bicycle, one feels no sideways force when the airplane banks; the force is always straight downward. So an airplane spiraling down toward the ground in a cloud feels, to its occupants, who may not have long to live, exactly as though it were cruising along straight and level. To further complicate matters for the seat-of-the-pants pilot, the inner ear's organs of balance *can* detect rolling acceleration; so we feel the onset of a moderately rapid roll, but when the airplane is stabilized in a bank we soon conclude that it is right side up. If we then roll back to level, the ear feels as though we are rolling into a bank in the opposite direction. Remarkably violent impressions can be produced by certain motions of the plane or of the head; one can be convinced that one is gyrating wildly when one is in fact sitting perfectly still, upright, and level. It is because the sense of balance is useless in an airplane that attitude gyros are necessary; and it is because the ear's illusions are so powerful that the art of instrument flying is difficult to learn. Powerful discipline is required to obey the commands of an instrument panel when your head, your whole body, cries out for you to do otherwise.

These, then, are the basic instruments needed for all-weather flying. Not all airplanes have all of them, but all all-weather airplanes have all of them in one form or another. They are easy to recognize and interpret, and once you have learned to use them in one airplane you can use them in any other.

# 5

# *Engines*

The engines of small private planes are made by two manufacturers, Lycoming and Continental. They are all of the air-cooled flat opposed type; that is, they are flat engines, like those of VW bugs or Corvairs, with the cylinders arranged in opposing rows along the sides of a crankcase. Each cylinder is separate from the others, with individual heads, unlike those of automobile engines, which have a single head casting for a block of cylinders. Some have carburetors, others have fuel injection of a simple kind (continuous flow into the intake manifold at each cylinder), with engines of less than 200 horsepower generally having carburetors. Incidentally, the engines of 200 horsepower or less generally have four cylinders, and more powerful engines have six or, in one case, eight.

These engines are mechanically similar to automobile engines, apart from the difference in their basic configuration. There is, however, one important difference. In an automobile engine, the spark plugs (of which there is one to a cylinder) are fired by voltage coming from the electrical system, of which the battery and generator are essential parts. If the generator fails, the battery will eventually discharge, there will be no more spark, and the engine will stop. As a matter of principle, the number of systems whose failure could cause engine stoppage is in an airplane kept to a minimum; and so in lieu of the automotive ignition system airplanes use the magneto system, which was used on cars when they had no electrical systems. A magneto is a self-contained generator that stores up a pulse of electricity as it turns and discharges each time a pair of contacts touches. It is geared directly to the engine and provides a spark so long as the engine is turning. Airplanes have two of them, and two spark plugs to each cylinder, mainly for safety. The spark, as well as the running of the engine, is completely independent of the airplane electrical system and is unaffected by the battery, generator, or master switch. The airplane's engine will continue to run regardless of failures, or deliberate interruptions, of the airplane electrical system.

The engine controls available to the pilot are somewhat different from those found in a car. There is, to begin with, no choke, which is the system, automatic or manual, on a car by which a rich mixture is supplied to the engine for starting. In an airplane that enrichment, if it is required, is produced by priming or by running a fuel pump before or during the start. The throttle is manual, since in an airplane you usually set the power and leave it, rather than modulating it continuously as you do when driving. If the airplane has a fixed pitch propeller, as all trainers do, it is analogous to a car with only one gear, and so lacks an rpm control; rpm is determined by throttle setting and forward speed. With an adjustable propeller (they used to be called, quite descriptively, "variable pitch," but with the addition of a governor they have come to be called "constant speed" propellers), the pilot has a prop control, which is always found alongside the throttle.

The airplane also has a mixture control, but unlike the choke it is used to make the mixture leaner, not richer. The fuel-air mixture in a car may also be leaned, but only by adjusting a screw on the carburetor; since cars do not regularly operate through a wide range of altitudes, mixture compensation is not important for them. Airplanes, on the other hand, must operate efficiently at all altitudes, and so they are provided with a mixture control.

Finally, there is a control on carburetor-equipped engines called carburetor heat, which is used in certain weather conditions to prevent the formation of ice in the carburetor.

All these controls are provided with some sort of friction locks to prevent them from vibrating out of position in flight, and they are generally of one of three kinds: the simple push-pull cable, the vernier, or the quadrant type. Verniers are the most delicate and precise type of control, and so they are nice to have for mixture and prop; but I don't like a vernier throttle because it is difficult to operate rapidly, and on a throttle its precision serves no purpose. Carb heat controls are usually infinitely adjustable plungers, but one is well advised to have them either fully on or fully off, and so they may as well just be a two-position lever.

Quadrant controls used to be used only in multiengine and military planes, but they have begun to be popular in smaller planes, probably because of the aura they carry of something bigger and more important. They are useful in a twin because it is easy to operate two of them at once. Seaplanes often have overhead throttle quadrants, which are annoying because they lack (as panel-mounted quadrants sometimes do) a surface on which to rest your arm, or even the heel of your hand or a fingertip, to serve as a reference in making small adjustments.

The sense of operation of these controls is generally consistent: pushing the control forward produces more of whatever it controls—more power, more rpm, more fuel per pound of air. Carb heat, on the other hand, works the other way: more heat comes when you pull the control backward. Mixture gets leaner as you pull the control back, but doing so may bring more power, whereas pushing the mixture forward may, under certain improbable conditions, cause the engine to run roughly or even quit. I mention this because there is a tendency, when one detects a loss of power or rough operation in flight, to react by pushing everything forward, and this is not always the best solution.

Trainers have meager engine instrumentation: rpm, oil temperature, possibly cylinder head temperature, and some kind of ammeter. The more complex the airplane, the more elaborately it is instrumented, and the greater the pilot's ability to adjust with precision all the parameters of the engine. As a student pilot, you will be concerned with only three variables: engine power output, engine rpm, and engine temperature (as indicated, usually, by oil temperature).

Heat is the great enemy of engines, and air-cooled engines run, to begin with, quite hot. The temperature at which the engine runs will be a function of its throttle setting, mixture setting, and the forward speed of the airplane, the last because it affects the amount of cooling air available. Convention dictates that while airplane engines are capable of running continuously at maximum power (or rated power), we only use maximum power for takeoff and initial climb, and we never cruise at more than 75 percent of rated power; often at less than that. (Lately a few manufacturers have begun giving performance figures for cruise at 80 percent power in order to make the same airplanes look better for the next model year. Nothing has changed, except in the willingness of the manufacturer to stick his neck out a little farther.) The power level at which an engine is run is probably not so important a determinant of its longevity and health as the manner in which it is operated—the same as is true, I guess, of human bodies. With ample instrumentation and a good understanding of conditions inside an engine, you can keep an engine healthy in spite of working it quite hard; on the other hand, you can think you are going easy on an engine and really be hastening its demise.

For example, after takeoff people will often back off a little on the throttle because they feel that this makes things easier for the engine during the climb. The contrary is true. Most airplane engines are provided with a system that enriches the mixture at full throttle and makes the engine run cooler. When you back off full throttle, you actually make the engine heat up; it is better to leave the throttle fully forward during the climb and let increasing altitude gradually diminish the power output. By the same token, people think that by leaving the mixture rich during the climb they will keep the engine cool and thus be kind to it. But above three or four thousand feet, at full throttle and sea level mixture, the excess of fuel is so great that it begins to foul spark plugs and cools the engine excessively, possibly pulling cylinder head temperatures down below the minimum recommended level. So it *is* desirable, in fact, to lean during the climb. The problem in trainers, paradoxically, is that they are not equipped with the necessary instrumentation to permit you to do so; and so one ends up being trained to do some things in exactly the wrong ways. Most likely your instructor will tell you, as students have been told for years, not to lean below 5,000 feet—a pernicious rule that you will later have to force yourself to unlearn.

With a fixed pitch propeller, you will find the propeller tending to overspeed the engine when you level out after a climb, and you have to throttle back to keep the engine within limits. As you climb, getting into regions of lower and lower oxygen supply, the engine power diminishes and the prop slows down; so you keep advancing the throttle until it is fully open. Thereafter, your fuel consumption and speed will be determined by mixture and altitude. Depending on the characteristics of the propeller, the altitude at which full throttle produces no more than the maximum (or "red line") rpm may be from 6,000 to 11,000 feet. A prop that keeps engine rpms low at high speed is called a *cruise prop*, and one that keeps them high at low speed a *climb prop*, because each is most effective in the one regime or the other. Manufacturers select a prop to give the best compromise, in their opinion, between climb performance and cruise performance. A constant speed prop, on the other hand, is adjustable, and will give a range of engine speeds at any throttle setting, making available maximum power regardless of forward speed. Trainers, generally, are rather underpowered and are provided with climb props. They do not spend a great deal of time cruising, and so a high cruising speed is not important to them. The single performance parameter most important to a trainer is undoubtedly its rate of climb, and this will be a function of the airplane's weight, wingspan, and engine power. This relationship will hold true for all airplanes; a large wingspan, light weight, and large engine will tend to make them climb well; short span, low power, or heavy weight will make them climb badly.

You will learn, as you become familiar with your trainer, the takeoff, climb, and cruise protocols which the flight school has adopted. These are not necessarily correct—there is a great deal of misunderstanding of engine management, even among instructors—but while in school you will have to adhere to them. Several points are worth keeping in mind, however. One is the observation that I mentioned earlier about throttle setting during climb. It is not a kindness to an engine equipped with automatic mixture enrichment to reduce power during the climb. Another is the point about too rich a mixture leading to other problems, mainly plug fouling. During the climb, it is good to lean the mixture for best power above about 3,000 feet. Best power mixture is simply the setting at which the rpm is highest; you will detect the rise, followed by a drop, in rpm as you lean the mixture. In cruise, however, the mixture ought not to be at best power, which is too rich, wasteful of fuel, and conducive to plug trouble, but at the leanest setting consistent with smooth running. You keep leaning, in other words, after rpm has started to drop, until you notice a distinct change, a roughening, in the tempo of the engine. You then enrich the mixture *very slightly* (I always see people overdo this re-enrichment) until the engine is just on the very edge of roughness.

Because a fixed pitch prop makes rpm a satisfactory gauge of power output, one engine instrument that it would be useful for students to get acquainted with is omitted from trainers: the manifold pressure gauge. I learned to fly in an airplane with a constant speed prop, and so used a manifold pressure gauge from the start; but even so, for a long time I didn't know what manifold pressure meant, though I knew some rules about how to use it.

The manifold pressure gauge is usually calibrated from some minimum, usually 10, to a maximum of 35 or more units. It behaves strangely. When the engine is at a fast idle, it may read lower than at a slower idle, but in general the more you advance the throttle, the higher the mp. However, with the engine shut off entirely the mp is the highest of all—right around 30 when the airplane is at sea level.

The units it measures are called "in. Hg," which stands for "inches of mercury," Hg being the chemical shorthand for that metal. Air pressure is what the instrument is measuring; but it is measuring *absolute* pressure—that is, pressure above a vacuum. So just sitting there at sea level with the engine off, the instrument reads the ambient pressure, which prevails inside the intake manifold. That pressure is about 30 inches of mercury (it varies depending on weather conditions, and is, incidentally, the pressure you set in the little window of your altimeter under the name of "local baro setting"). When you start the engine and idle it slowly, the instrument reads about 15 inches, because the cylinders are sucking in air through the intake manifold, and the throttle is nearly closed; the engine is sucking against a blocked passage, and so the manifold is at a low pressure.

Now, as you advance the throttle, the pressure at first gets even lower; this is because a small amount of excess fuel makes the engine pump quite a bit faster, without greatly increasing the flow rate of air past the slightly opened throttle. As you keep opening the throttle, the trend changes: the rpm, that is, the pumping action, increases slowly, but the manifold pressure rises as the throttle opens, and at full throttle it is just an inch or two below the ambient pressure. It will always be a little below the ambient pressure at full throttle, unless the engine is turbocharged, because there is always some resistance to air pouring through the manifold past the throttle, even when the throttle is wide open; and this resistance registers as a loss of manifold pressure.

Atmospheric pressure diminishes about 1 in. Hg per thousand feet of altitude above sea level; so from a "standard pressure" at sea level of 29.92 in. Hg, it diminishes to about 25 inches at 5,000 feet, 20 inches at 10,000 feet, 15 inches at 15,000 feet, and so on. (The relationship is obviously not linear, nor does it continue until there is no pressure at 30,000 feet; but it holds true in the range of altitudes, up to about 15,000 feet, in which lightplane pilots are most likely to be interested.) So in Denver, with the engine stopped, the mp gauge will be reading 25 in. Hg; and at La Paz, Bolivia, only 17 in. And in those places the greatest mp available at full throttle will be slightly below those values. The maximum power available at full throttle will be accordingly diminished, and the performance of the airplane reduced. This effect of altitude upon power output is one of the most important facts about aircraft engines, and it must be considered carefully.

To start with, it is not altitude in the sense of absolute barometric pressure that ultimately determines power output; it is what is called *density altitude*. Now, density altitude is a measure of air density, not altitude, though it is given in feet. It refers to a standard profile of the atmosphere, an average atmosphere, so to speak, in which, corresponding to each height above sea level, there is a certain pressure and air density. The atmosphere is constantly changing, but by knowing the pressure and temperature we can deduce the density of the air at a given moment and place, and this density will appear on the chart of the "standard atmosphere" beside a certain altitude. So we name that altitude to describe the density. Note that a given density altitude does not correspond to a particular actual altitude. Higher temperature makes the density altitude rise, lower temperature makes it drop, so that, for example, a temperature of −20°C at 11,500 feet pressure altitude, or of +20°C at 7,700 feet pressure altitude, both correspond to a density altitude of 10,000 feet. Finally, pressure altitude is not true altitude either, but the altitude shown on the altimeter when the baro setting is 29.92 in. Hg.

Now the density altitude tells us how much oxygen is present per cubic foot of air; and this information reappears, in the form of a maximum power output available, in the airplane or engine handbook. The important thing for the pilot to absorb is that the power available to him is influenced by *both altitude and temperature*, and that at some density altitudes which he may quite routinely encounter in his flying he will not be able to operate safely with loads which normally are well within the capability of the airplane. In other words, a 100-hp engine will be that only at or below sea level density; above it—and most of the time one is above it—the engine will be weaker, and sometimes it will be so much weaker as to pose a positive danger of which the pilot has to be aware.

Turbocharged engines are an exception. Equipped with exhaust-driven compressors that deliver air at near sea level density to the engine at altitudes up to 15,000 feet or more, they virtually cancel the ill effects of diminished density at any altitude at which an airport is to be found. However, relatively few airplanes are turbocharged (though it is becoming an increasingly popular feature), and the beginning pilot is most unlikely to find himself in a turbocharged airplane for quite a while; the airplane he is flying will be what is called normally aspirated.

Manifold pressure and rpm to some extent mutually affect one another. With a fixed pitch prop, increasing manifold pressure (in other words, opening the throttle) increases rpm. On the other hand, with a constant speed prop, reducing rpm increases mp (because the engine, in its guise as air pump, is working more slowly). Together, mp and rpm spell power; either can be used to increase or reduce power output.

As a rule of thumb, one is always told to keep mp and rpm "square," or to have the rpm "higher than" the mp. This rule is based on the fact that, purely by coincidence, the numbers on the tachometer and those on the mp gauge are the same, 2500 rpm being abbreviated on the gauge, for instance, as "25"; and normal power settings often involve the same numbers on both instruments, for instance 2400 rpm and 24 in. Hg, which a pilot would call "twenty-four/twenty-four." Now, it is true that, like an automobile engine when you step on the gas at low speed, an airplane engine will suffer from detonation, known and heard in cars as knock or ping, if the mp gets too high when the rpm is too low. However, the "square" rule, like the never-lean-below-5,000-feet rule, goes too far; it is like proposing that you avoid highway accidents by never leaving your house. In fact, most engines can operate comfortably at settings like 24/2100; the particular limits for each model of engine can be found in the engine handbook, which is part of the material that usually can be found in some pouch somewhere on the airplane. It's useful to know the limits, because you might find that your airplane is much quieter at 2100 rpm than at 2400; but if you felt that you couldn't run more than 21 in. Hg at 2100 rpm, you would never want to cruise at that rpm because there would be so little power available. If, however, you can safely cruise at 24/2100, then you have a useful setting that will increase your enjoyment of flying; so it's worth knowing about. Similarly, on a hot day you might take off and find that, if you pull your engine back to 25/2500 for the climb, the cylinder head temperature goes up rather than down. This is because of the full throttle mixture enrichment valve I mentioned before. You would like to stay at full throttle, but you don't want to exceed the engine limitations, and you might suppose that that means reducing rpm. So you might, as I always do, leave the throttle fully open after takeoff and reduce rpm only, knowing that 28/2500 is an acceptable power setting. As you climb the 28 will quickly drop down to 25 anyway, and the engine will have stayed cool.

Airplane engines are tough, simple engines, designed not for extreme efficiency but rather for the last refinement of reliability. That they all look very much alike should not be taken to mean that they are the final and perfect product of an evolutionary process. It is so expensive and so risky to develop and test a new engine and then to get into the business of manufacturing it that nobody wants to do so for the relatively small light airplane market. Lycoming and Continental are a couple of survivors, and the engines they build were state-of-the-art in the forties. If they are still state-of-the-art today, it is because this is an art that hasn't gone very far.

There are, of course, other types of engines available—turbines, jets, rotaries, liquid-cooled V-8s, two-strokes. But turbines and jets are too expensive and too inefficient for light airplanes, and the rest simply haven't had the testing and development that would be necessary for their adoption by airplane manufacturers. Some small two-strokes were tried in a small homebuilt called the BD-5 a few years ago, with disastrous results. Curtiss-Wright, an aeronautical firm of long experience, has worked on a rotary (or "Wankel") engine for airplanes but has not put one into production. Several small firms are developing modified automotive V-8s with the intention of selling them to the operators of agricultural spraying aircraft, who wear out engines at a great rate and need something less costly to purchase and maintain than conventional airplane engines. But for general aviation airplanes of the kind that new pilots will be flying, there's only one type of engine—a Lycoming or a Continental.

# 6

# *Maneuvering and Stalling*

The hours you spend in the airplane preparing for your private license will cover a variety of subjects, but the principal ones will be pattern work and air work. Pattern work is essentially landing and the procedures for safe and orderly arrivals and departures. It will most probably include radio communication.

Air work is, on the other hand, pure flying. The private license requires that you be able to perform certain maneuvers proficiently; you spend hours practicing them. The maneuvers are mostly simple ones: turns, climbs, descents, stalls, slow flight. Various ground reference maneuvers are also taught, with the intention of training you to handle the plane more or less automatically while looking outside the cockpit. If you were working on a commercial license, you would attack another class of maneuver, including the lazy eight and the chandelle; a chandelle is a climbing 180-degree turn begun at cruising speed and ended at stalling speed; and a lazy eight is not an eight at all, but a continuous series of swooping 180-degree turns, alternating left and right, while simultaneously climbing and descending.

The purpose of the so-called ground reference maneuvers is to develop your ability to fly the airplane when distracted from the instruments and controls, though the ostensible purpose is merely to train you to compensate for wind. Pylon turns require no particular effort if the wind is nil; when there is a wind blowing, however, you have to compensate for it at every point of the maneuver if you want to follow the prescribed ground track.

The method of correcting for wind is intellectually very puzzling to a beginning student. The goal of the maneuver of circling around a point in a wind is to stay the same distance from the point at all times; in other words, to describe a circular ground track. If the wind were nil, this would be easy; you would put the point off your wingtip, start turning, and adjust your angle of bank so as to stay a constant distance from the point. Mind you, even this simple-sounding maneuver is not that easy. When I was a child I used to wonder how people in cars knew how much to turn the steering wheel in order to go around a corner. My puzzlement was misplaced; I should have wondered how pilots know how much to bank to stay a constant distance from a point.

Part of it is experience; you know, after you have done a few hundred turns, how tightly you will have to turn to stay at a fixed radius from a point (or, to put it another way, to keep the point stationary with respect to your wingtip, which, so long as there is no wind, will also keep it at a constant distance if your angle of bank stays the same). But when you begin learning these maneuvers you will have made very few turns close to the ground, and none with your attention on some fixed object; so experience is not there to help.

The rational procedure to follow in a no-wind condition is to seek the correct angle of bank by a process of gradually diminishing errors, a series of "cuts" at it. Your instructor will begin by demonstrating the maneuver, having probably explained it beforehand (without effect) on the ground. Note the angle of bank that he uses; it may vary somewhat, but at least note the approximate angle. Note also the distance between you and the pylon; just try to get a rough idea of these two values. When you try the maneuver, fly on a tangent to the intended circle, and begin your turn when the point is off the wingtip at more or less the proper distance. If you are closer than you intended, you will need to bank a little more steeply; if farther away, less steeply.

At the moment that you begin the maneuver, look at the instruments

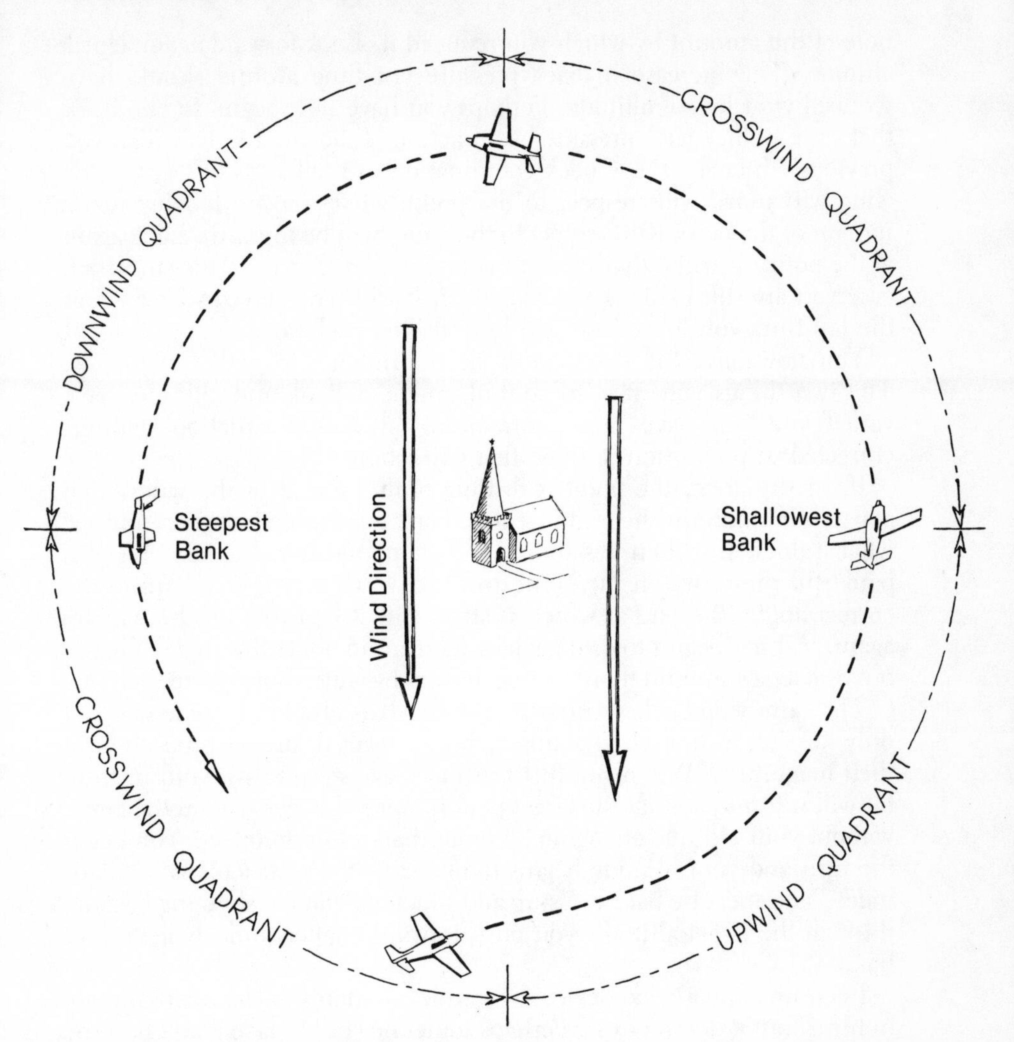


and out the windshield, and roll the airplane into a bank at about the same angle the instructor was using. When you have the bank stabilized, the ball is centered, and you are not gaining or losing altitude too drastically, look out at the point. Watch it long enough to see whether it is drifting ahead of or behind the wing. If you cannot detect a definite drift right away, look forward again, check your altitude and coordination. If you are losing altitude, increase your back pressure somewhat and hold it there. Look at the point again. If it is drifting ahead of the wing, reduce your angle of bank by perhaps five degrees; but make a mental note of the amount by which you reduced it. Look forward again; check altitude. The increase in back pressure last time around should have reduced your loss of altitude. Perhaps you have now begun to climb. In that case, reduce back pressure by a fraction of the amount by which you previously increased it. Check coordination (if the ball is off center, the wing will move with respect to the point; what you are looking for, a motion of the point with respect to the wing, will be masked). Look again at the point. It will either be drifting farther ahead of the wing, in which case you are still banking too steeply; or it will have stayed where it was the last time you looked, or will have drifted backward.

You now have the necessary basic information to make judgments. The two things you want to control, angle of bank and altitude, have varied and you have made corrections; all future variations will be corrected in proportion to these first corrections.

If, for instance, the point is drifting farther ahead of the wing at an apparently undiminished rate, reduce bank another five degrees and see what it does. If it then is standing still, temporarily reduce the angle of bank still more, watch the point drift backward, and then return to the correct angle (the one at which it stood still) when it is off the wingtip again. If it has begun to drift backward, again increase the angle of bank, but by a lesser amount than the five degrees by which you first reduced it.

The same approach applies to altitude. It is absolutely necessary not only to react to undesired changes, but to react in proper proportion to their magnitude. When you first learn to make steep turns, your instructor will inform you that the target performance is to get around the circle without your altitude changing by more than a hundred feet. You begin the turn and your altitude begins to decrease; the instructor says, "Altitude!" You increase back pressure and suddenly you are shooting back up through the target altitude; you push forward; matters quickly get out of hand.

I can imagine a good device for training students to maintain altitude in turns, but it doesn't exist. Perhaps someone could make it and become rich. It would consist simply of a control yoke attached to a spring scale, nothing else; and its purpose would be to accustom the student to perceiving the relations of different amounts of back pressure. The instructor would say, "Pull back with a mild force," and after the student had done so, he would say, "That's five pounds; now try to double it." The student having done this, he would say, "Well, that's twelve pounds; but now give me seven pounds, which will be about two thirds of the way back to the force you started with." After a half hour of this, the student would perhaps have developed an awareness of control forces and some kind of an ability to remember the magnitude of a force, and to return to it after applying a different force.

Whether or not this device would make anyone rich, or even make anyone a better pilot, I hope it at least makes the point that in any steady flight condition, you are looking for a steady control condition to maintain it. One's tendency at first is to chase the needles: constantly move the controls about in pursuit of altimeter pointers and airspeed and rate of climb needles that refuse to stay put. One of the absolutely essential skills that has to be learned is that of abandoning the "hunting" reflex and thinking in terms of steady control input.

Steadiness, at least at first, is more important than accuracy. If you get away from your altitude in a turn, first stabilize where you are. Get the rate of climb to zero. Then increase or decrease back pressure by a small amount, remember that amount, and keep an eye on the rate of climb back to the target altitude. When you reach the desired altitude very gently change the back pressure to the value at which you had it stabilized before.

One of the many reasons for the usefulness of this approach is that not only do some instruments, notably the rate of climb indicator, lag several seconds behind the airplane, but the airplane itself lags behind the control inputs. If, for example, you have lost some altitude in a steep turn and want to regain it, and you apply a slight back pressure, the first effect will be to produce more of a climb than the back pressure really corresponds to. The reason for this is that the loss of altitude was accompanied by a slight increase in speed, and the back pressure needed to produce a positive rate of climb will also be producing a reduction in airspeed. The excess airspeed will at first carry the airplane upward at a misleadingly high rate, which will then diminish, in a few seconds, if the back pressure is held perfectly constant. Often a student will note the brisk rate of climb and relax the back pressure just applied, thinking it excessive; whereupon the gain just made is lost.

Not only must control pressures be steady; they must also be gradual. When you are a novice, your attention tends to jump by fits and starts from one thing to another, and you sometimes get an unpleasant surprise: you look at the airspeed, say, for the first time in fifteen seconds, and you find you're way too fast. You tend to react abruptly, not because you really think that is the right way to fly, but simply because the surprise of discovering a bad indication startles you into a quick response. It is better, however, to discipline yourself to make all control inputs very gradually, almost in slow motion, and always at exactly the same rate. It is helpful to use the same rate consistently because in some maneuvers, such as turns to a heading, you will have to anticipate your arrival at the chosen heading and begin leveling the wings five or ten degrees before you reach it. If you use the same roll rate all the time, you will more easily learn to anticipate accurately; and the same is true of rates of pitch, when you are leveling out of a climb or a descent.

The same practice of taking cuts at a final steady value will serve you in navigation. Suppose you are flying with a crosswind along an airway. The crosswind will carry you away from the airway; you will have to hold a correction into the wind in order to fly a ground track along the airway. Suppose, now, that you have been carried to the left of your desired track, and the OBS needle is to the right of center. First, make sure that the reason for your drift is not something inside the cockpit; you may have let your heading wander, or you may have forgotten to set the DG to the wet compass. If you have been holding the airway heading and have drifted nevertheless, then you know that you will have to find a wind correction angle that will hold you on course.

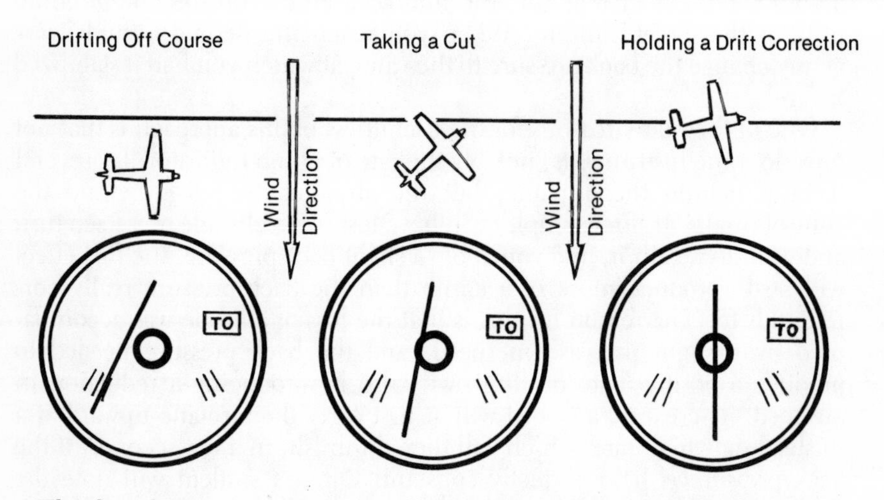


The first thing in your mind now should be that you are looking for a heading—a number. You are not simply trying to get the OBS needle centered; this you could do quite easily by simply turning sharply to the right; but you will not keep it centered that way for long. Suppose the airway heading is 100 degrees. Turn right ten degrees to intercept the airway; your heading is now 110. If the needle does not move back toward the center after a time—the closer you are to the station, the quicker the responses of the needle should be—then you have to take yet a larger cut; but let's say, for the purpose of this example, that within a minute or so the needle is centered.

Now you know that if you fly a heading of 100 degrees you will again drift left of course; so you turn to a heading of 105 degrees and wait and see what happens. Gradually, you observe the needle wandering off, this time toward the left. You now know that 100 degrees is too little, and 105 degrees is too much; so you turn to 103 degrees. The needle now stays still, but a little to the left; so you turn to 100 degrees, the needle centers, and you return to 103 degrees, which was the heading at which you were able to keep the needle still. You have bracketed your drift correction at three degrees. Notice the analogy between this case and the two others I have described. In the turn around a point you first stop the progress of the point with respect to the wing, mentally note the bank and back pressure needed to do this, and then make a temporary change to get the point moved to where you want it; finally you return to the correct attitude that you noted before. In trying to maintain altitude in a turn, you first, after drifting away from the desired altitude, stop the drift; you note the back pressure; then you return to the desired altitude and end up with the back pressure previously noted. The case of the drift correction on the VOR radial is the same.

In navigating as well as in maneuvering, you are normally seeking steady states. These states will be represented by certain sets of numbers (headings, speeds, rates of climb) and certain control positions or pressures (back pressure, right rudder). When you are trying to get the airplane "set up" on a certain track or in a certain turn or on a circle around a point, you are looking for the steady state that will solve your problem. Always try to be aware of the bracketing process; try to make a series of progressively smaller corrections until you get things just right, and then keep them there. Don't let yourself get tricked into chasing needles and numbers; you'll never catch them.

Of course, there is more to flying than that. Many maneuvers involve states that are not steady but constantly varying; many of the commercial license maneuvers, such as lazy eights and chandelles, are so to speak artistic idealizations of constantly varying states. You may ask yourself, as you practice lazy eights and chandelles, just what the point is. It took me years to understand why I had bothered. They are maneuvers without any significance of their own; but they represent—rather arbitrarily—the distillation of certain sets of actions and sensations that occur again and again in flying. Some bureaucrat, asked to dream up a set of requirements for licensing pilots, hit upon these maneuvers as symbolizing, in compact and easily measurable form, a much larger and vaguer category of maneuvers.

The problem with them is that when you set out to learn them, you are unconscious of the abilities they seek to develop. Years later, when you find yourself doing a lazy eight—that detested, tense, anything but lazy maneuver—for the fun of it, you may realize that what was involved, really, was just flying ability in the abstract. Now you no longer worry about the precise but constantly varying relationship between pitch angle, airspeed, bank angle, and heading—a relationship requiring a rather sophisticated computer for its most perfect formulation. Without conscious effort you make the continuous back-and-forth excursion from past to future, oscillating as it were within an extended volume of time, flying the airplane not only as it is now, but as it was and will be over a range of several seconds. There is nothing mystical about this process; it is exactly the same one you use when performing one of those elegant but ordinary maneuvers that files your car away in its proper slot in a crowded parking lot. Your judgment—spatial, kinetic—flows around your action in time, anticipating, correcting, evaluating. The first time you do a chandelle you grab an attitude that looks promising, cling to it, then suddenly abandon it for another when it loses its promise. You transition suddenly, by starts, from one "solution" to another. As you repeat the maneuver, you smooth your performance until you squeeze by your check ride, and then you forget about chandelles. But years later you make a climbing course reversal, not even thinking about how you do it, and it dawns on you that this was a chandelle. Then, perhaps, you realize that while you were practicing the maneuver, you were always wrong in imagining that there was some ideal, correct chandelle that you had to capture and imprison. There is no "correct" chandelle. A check pilot realizes this; that's why he will pass you on a maneuver that you consider botched, or fail you when you think you had all the numbers lined up. The check pilot is sensing your feel. Hands in his lap, he is flying the airplane with his immobile body, and his sense of your performance is the sum of his discomforts and reliefs as you do, or fail to do, what his body wants. Most check pilots take the FAA guidelines more or less seriously, and so it would be an exaggeration to say that you pass or fail on the basis of what your unconscious mind and body are doing while your conscious person struggles with the maneuvers you have learned by rote. But the check pilot's satisfaction with your performance, and his willingness to forgive a technically imperfect performance, depend on his feel of your feel; the process is basically intuitive.

This fluid and complex feel, however, is of the same kind as the feel of steady states that you were seeing in the more basic maneuvers. What is different in the advanced maneuvers is the intrusion of a complicating element of time. Rather than seek a steady state in which nothing changes, you seek a certain—you could call it a "steady"—*rate of change*. In the chandelle, for instance, you begin rolling from your banked attitude to a level attitude halfway through the 180-degree turn, and you should end up level when you complete the turn. There is a certain steady rate of roll that will bring about this result, and each angle of bank will require its own unique rate of roll to nullify it in exactly 90 degrees. You cannot, within the time normally allotted to getting a commercial license, learn the exact rate of roll by heart for a certain bank angle—say, 30 degrees—and so instead you perform the maneuver by constantly assessing your progress and making small, bracketing corrections as you come around the turn. The task is complicated by the fact that as your airspeed diminishes, more and more aileron deflection is required to produce a given roll rate; and so the student's chandelle usually involves a slightly dishonest flourish at the end, where he takes advantage of the imprecision of the concept of minimum speed to get his heading and angle of bank together in the last few moments of the maneuver. In the lazy eight, similarly, rate of roll is coordinated with rate of heading change and rate of pitch change—these are all *rates*, mind you, not fixed values—so as to produce, on graph paper, an elegant and symmetrical braid. They are good training maneuvers because they do not even permit hunting or chasing the needles; in a completely fluid maneuver, there is nothing to hunt or chase.

The most difficult private license maneuver is probably the turn around a pylon in a wind; it falls conceptually somewhere between the static geometry of the 360-degree turn and the unceasing flow of the lazy eight or chandelle, combining the fluidity of the latter with the fixed reference of the former.

Suppose, to begin with, that the circular track on the ground that your turn should follow were not an imaginary circle drawn in your mind about a visible point but, in fact, a real circle—a circular race track, for instance. To fly a circle you would simply have to stay right over the track at all times. In still air this would mean that you would get over the track, bracket an angle of bank, and then hold it, and you would have the problem licked. Suppose, now, that the wind is blowing quite hard. If you hold a constant angle of bank, you will describe a path that will resemble a penmanship exercise, and you will soon be nowhere near your race track. When you are flying into the wind, you will be turning at the same rate, but moving forward less rapidly, so you will turn inside the desired ground track; when you are flying downwind, on the other hand, you will be turning always at the same rate, but moving forward more rapidly, and so you will turn outside the desired track. The effect will be, in the sum, that after one turn you will have drifted downwind as much as if you had been hanging in the air at the starting point, like a balloon, all the while.

The thing that people find hard to comprehend is that the way to correct is to constantly vary your angle of bank, and that the minimum occurs when you are flying straight upwind (so that you spend the most time flying upwind) and the maximum occurs when you are flying straight downwind (so that you spend the least time going in that direction).

What people intuitively want to do is use the maximum angle of bank when they are at the downwind side of the circle, and the minimum at the upwind side of the circle; this, however, will not serve the purpose. In fact, it turns out that the angle of bank on the upwind and downwind ends of the circle is the same. Another mistake is to try to make more than one complete cycle of changing bank angles per turn, as though there were several maximums and minimums around the circle. The easiest procedure is simply to begin the maneuver with the wind at your side—not in front of you, as your instructor might suggest. Roll immediately to a moderate angle of bank (say 25 degrees) and then as you turn (let's say you are turning upwind to start with) diminish the angle of bank to 15 degrees in the first 90 degrees of turn; increase it to 25 again in the next 90 degrees; increase it to 35 in the next 90; and decrease it to 25 in the next 90. The reason for starting in the crosswind position is that this is the position in which your angle of bank is at its median, "reference" value. You begin by making a mental note of this angle of bank, and henceforth measure your corrections in terms of it.

In this maneuver you have to do two things: you have to pick your angle of bank correctly in the first place (as though the wind were nil) and then you have to vary it by the correct amount around the circle. As you recall from when I talked about flying a circle in no wind, you start off by bracketing your angle of bank to match your speed and distance from the pylon. When there is a wind, however, you can't really do this, because the target speed is constantly changing.

What you in fact do is take a stab at the correct angle on the basis of experience, and then try to bracket the *changing rate*. This sounds like quite a trick, and it is; when I got my private, I doubt I was ever less than 45 degrees behind the plane, and I must admit that this maneuver comes as close to obliging you to hunt and chase, rather than to bracket, as any. In practice, you end up flying a series of corrections, which you fair smoothly together so that it appears (you hope) as though you had the whole thing planned from the beginning. Later, when you are an experienced pilot, you will be able to circle a pylon unconsciously, and the main trick, you will come to see, is starting the bank angle changes soon enough.

Turning around a point with no wind, you could assess your progress by the position of the point with respect to the wingtip. In a wind, you will be crabbing into the wind on the crosswind portions of the circle, and the pylon will be behind the wingtip on the upwind side and ahead of the wingtip on the downwind side. And since the angle of bank will vary constantly, the height of the pylon with respect to the wingtip will also constantly change. The basic reference for the pylon turn will be distance from the pylon, not relation of the pylon to the wingtip. Changes in distance will occur on the crosswind quadrants, and they are initially quite difficult to discern. The novice finds himself suddenly carried in toward the pylon, or out away from it, before he thinks to change his angle of bank. The only recourse is to anticipate and guess. Think of the circle as divided into four quadrants—two crosswinds, an upwind, and a downwind. The transitions are on the wind axis, and at right angles to it. Try to be aware of leaving one quadrant and entering another, and anticipate the bank requirements of each, so that you begin to change your angle of bank before you see that you have to (at which point it is already too late).

In this maneuver as in most that involve a lot of turning, you cannot really change your angle of bank continuously and at a sinusoidally varying rate throughout the entire maneuver; that would require preternatural delicacy. Instead, you check your distance from the pylon between quadrants, you make a gradual change of bank angle at each change of quadrant, and smooth them over in between. Your stream of consciousness is something like this: "Okay, starting downwind, increase the bank. Keep it smooth . . . really moving—tighten up a little more, off the wing now, it'll be reducing, reduce the angle, don't overdo it, there's the reference angle, not quite abeam, finesse that, hold it a little, coming about, level gradually, don't rush it, god this is taking a long time, don't get too flat, cripes turned inside, keep it shallow, not too tight, have to bank more now, coming crosswind, too close to the point, it'll take a really tight turn next time, oops! Three hundred feet too high!" By this time your shoulder muscles are like bundles of steel cables and your armpits are steaming.

Well, it gets to be fun later.

But before it gets to be fun you also have to learn stalls. I used to hate stalls; for the most part, I still do. Except in airplanes about whose behavior I am quite certain, they frighten me. There is no reason that they should—there is nothing dangerous about stalls; but there is something rather unnerving about them—the sense that the airplane has stopped doing what it is supposed to do, and that it has suddenly gotten clumsy and helpless in the air, so that it is almost no longer an airplane but just a tin box in which I am falling through the sky. Somehow I got off on the wrong foot about stalls, and I have never recovered the lost ground. Perhaps it was because I learned to fly in a Comanche 250, a relatively fast and heavy airplane that I am sure was not approved for spins and whose behavior was probably not altogether familiar to my instructor; so she may have communicated to me, by an excess of caution, a feeling of apprehension during stalls which I would not have gotten if we had been doing them in a Cessna 150. Indeed, when after I got my private she took me up in a 150 to show me how to do spins, I felt quite comfortable doing them, and, paradoxically, I feel more at home doing spins now than doing stalls. But perhaps that is simply because spins involve certain control inputs and certain predictable responses, whereas stalls traverse, if only for a moment, an area of uncertainty and uncontrol. You *put* the airplane into a spin; but you just sit there and wait for it to stall.

My mistake, I suppose, has always been that sitting and waiting. The best way to practice stalls is to fly right up to them and beard them, not to lie in wait for them and then to flee the moment you detect a hint of their arrival. Any trainer has been stalled more times, in more ways, than you can imagine, and you need not worry that you will uncover some bizarre behavior that no one has ever encountered before. What is more worrisome, I suppose, is that you will encounter unpleasant sensations, principally that of the seat falling out from under you (although it will never do this so drastically that you will be floating around in the cockpit like an astronaut).

In a stall the airplane becomes, momentarily, not uncontrollable, but uncooperative and unpredictable. Normally pulling back on the yoke brings the nose up; the stall changes matters, and pulling back produces no such result. Pulling back, in fact, makes the nose go down. Some airplanes can be flown with aileron control through the stall; others cannot. This is a design choice, more or less; it is considered desirable that the ailerons work throughout the stall, but certain performance compromises must be accepted in exchange, and some designers have been unwilling to sacrifice everything to a docile stall. With good reason; even in a trainer a very gentle stall is not a very useful trait, since it will not give the student a well-rounded introduction to the maneuver. In airplanes other than trainers, stalls are normally avoided, and so designers are reluctant to compromise performance—which is a real selling point—on their behalf. Most airplanes behave more or less predictably and controllably in the stall, when correctly flown; any of them, however, may display undesirable characteristics, like a sharp wing drop or an excessive loss of altitude during the recovery, when improperly handled.

The main emphasis is on coordination. Pitch attitude is of course what produces the stall in the first place, but rudder-ailerons coordination is what determines the airplane's behavior after the wing has stalled. To familiarize you with the effects of different control positions on the stall, your instructor will take you through straight-ahead stalls with power on and off; turning stalls level, climbing, and descending; and stalls with "crossed controls." These last, in which the airplane is kept level by balancing rudder against aileron, re-create the most critical situation for real-life inadvertent stalls, the situation most likely to produce a spin. The turning, climbing stall, done with full power, is called a departure stall because it might naturally occur during a steep climb out of an airport; the descending, turning, power-off stall is called an approach stall. In each case the airplane will behave in a characteristic way. In a power-on, straight-ahead stall, you will find that the airplane gets to a steeper nose-up angle than with power off, and that it stalls at a slightly lower indicated speed; in approach and departure stalls you will probably observe a tendency of a wing to drop to the inside or the outside of the turn. With crossed controls there will be quite a definite tendency of the wing on the side toward which you are holding rudder to stall first and to drop.

In every case, recovery will be effected by some combination of the same steps: lower the nose, add power, stop the turn with rudder, keep the ailerons neutral.

Because the stall occurs at a certain speed called the stalling speed, and because power appears to delay the stall by blowing air back over the wing, and because your instructor will warn you not to let the airspeed get too low in slow flight, you will probably succumb to the temptation to identify the cause of the stall as insufficient speed. This would be incorrect. The essential precondition of all stalls is an excessively great angle of attack. The delaying effect of power is due not to the increment of air velocity supplied by the prop, but to the deflection of the relative wind near the fuselage, particularly over the wing roots, where the stall normally begins. (The stall should begin at the wing roots and move outward, so that it is well progressed before the ailerons are affected.)

In banked turns, the wing supplies not only the lift necessary to maintain altitude, but also that necessary to overcome the centrifugal effect of curving flight; the greater the angle of bank the more lift is necessary, whence the increase of stalling speed in a bank. But the increase of stalling *speed* is not the reason for the premature stall; it is simply a by-product, along with the stall itself, of the higher angle of attack necessary to produce more lift at the greater angle of bank. In a 60-degree bank, for instance, you need twice the lift you would need to maintain altitude in level flight, because half the lift is being directed inward, not upward against the pull of gravity. At a given speed, then, you will need a higher angle of attack—one closer to the stalling angle of attack—to develop that lift.

Approach stalls highlight the difference between angle of attack and "deck angle"—the angle of the fuselage to the horizon. If you do them with flaps down, so that the deck angle is already diminished (since the stalling angle of attack is diminished by lowering the flaps), and with a healthy rate of descent, you can easily bring it about that the wing stalls with the nose well below the horizon. Similarly, you can trigger a "secondary" stall by pulling too vigorously out of the shallow dive by which you recovered from the first stall; again, the nose will be below the horizon, and the airspeed indicator may show a speed above the "stalling speed." You will still stall solely because of an excessive angle of attack. The moral: even though *most* stalls occur at a low speed and in a nose-high attitude, don't be fooled into thinking that they can't occur under other conditions.

Since stalls can occur at a wide variety of speeds and deck angles, they cannot be anticipated solely by those cues. At best, you can be aware that you are in a situation—a tight turn at approach speed, for instance—in which a stall *might* occur. The airplane will give some kind of warning—bell, whistle, shake, or rumble—and the purpose of your stall training is to teach you how to react to that warning. You cannot anticipate every stall. There may be situations in which you could not even anticipate that a stall might occur; suppose, for instance, that your airspeed indicator developed a problem and indicated consistently high without your realizing it. A stall would occur at a higher than normal indicated airspeed, and you would have to recognize and avert it instinctively, in spite of the "safe" airspeed indication. Not all instructors practice stalls with the airspeed indicator covered, but it would be a good idea to do so.

In military aircraft, in all jets, and in some smaller aircraft whose owners have made the investment necessary to obtain one—as little as $500—an angle of attack indicator or "lift indicator" takes the place of the airspeed indicator as a primary low speed altitude reference. I have one of these in my airplane, and I have been impressed many times by its value. That it is not universally used is puzzling. Flying angle of attack rather than airspeed, you immediately become aware of the effect of weight on stalling speed, the effect of turns, of turbulence, of wind shear, of slight accelerations during the approach, of flap deflections, and so on. The normal approach speed, 1.3 times the power-off "dirty" stall speed, includes a fudge factor to cover all these variations; with angle of attack, you can fly much more precisely and safely. Yet, for some reason (perhaps because they are electronic, fairly complex, and.so not perfectly reliable), these instruments have not been widely adopted in light aircraft.

In stall recoveries as in turns and in simple navigation, remember the rule that you want to find steady states, not chase needles. Flying into the stall, look for a steady rate of airspeed decay—*not* for the stall itself. In other words, *fly* into the stall, don't just go up and nudge it. As soon as the break occurs, firmly (not spasmodically) reposition the yoke, keep it there, and apply rudder as needed to stay on the right heading. Don't push the yoke forward into a screaming dive the moment the wing shakes; what is needed is a firm and proportionate response, not a sudden and violent reflex. In many airplanes you can fly right at the edge of the stall, controlling heading with the rudder; slightly more back pressure will bring the bobble-rumble of disappearing lift, and slightly less will restore smooth flight. The thing to notice here is that forward *pressure* is not necessary to stop the stall; all that is needed is a slight relaxation of back pressure. The other thing to notice is that the stall is not necessarily immediately arrested by a small forward motion of the control, but it is eventually. In other words, once you have recognized a mild stall and relaxed back pressure somewhat, the smoothest recovery will occur if you simply hold the controls in that position and let the airplane fly itself out of the stall. If, on the other hand, you push the nose over too forcefully, you will lose a great deal of altitude to no purpose. Losing a minimum of altitude is important because if a stall creeps up on you unawares, it is likely to happen in the traffic pattern, close to the ground. Your instructor will show you how much is enough to stop the stall and reattach flow to the top surface of the wing, and how much is too much. Sometimes instructors will say "move the nose down toward the horizon," as though the absolute attitude of the airplane were important. It is not. The horizon is a convenient reference in some stalls, in others it is not. What is really important is to relieve the back pressure on the controls that caused the stall in the first place (in other words, lower the nose a few degrees, regardless of the position on the horizon), and to stop rotation with rudder. These two steps can be taken even if the airplane is pointing straight up or straight down, or is on its side, or upside down; but in training for a private license you will not see any of these exotic positions.

Crossed controls, back pressure on the yoke, and a banked attitude all exacerbate the stall; it is least severe in a level, unaccelerated attitude. In recovering from a stall you should try to get the airplane into level flight reasonably soon—as soon as the proviso (which applies more strictly to some types of airplanes than to others) that you not use the ailerons permits. The pitfall of too drastic a forward movement of the yoke, with the dive that it produces, is that by requiring back pressure to recover from the dive it exposes you to a secondary, accelerated stall. A shallow dive, is, however, the only resource you have available to put some distance—in the form of a margin of airspeed—between you and the stall; it is the only one because, by being at the minimum airspeed at which you can fly, you have no surplus energy available in the form of airspeed; your only surplus is in the form of altitude and engine power, with engine power representing a rather small contribution. On the other hand, the stall rapidly steals away energy because it is accompanied by a rapid increase in drag. To the extent that the stall has been permitted to progress far enough that the airplane has decelerated to a speed noticeably below that at which the stall began, altitude will have to be sacrificed to recover. Altitude, in this case, is being converted to speed by a dive. Incidentally, the immediate reduction of angle of attack that recovers the wing from the stall corresponds to a loss of lift, and is felt by the occupants as a reduction in G-force, or gravity; they feel themselves float upward in their seats, as though on a roller coaster. When the airplane is flying in this condition of diminished G, it can be at an indicated airspeed below the "stalling speed" and not be stalled, just as, conversely, it can be above the "stalling speed" but pulling more than 1 G, and stall. In an extreme case, an airplane could be flown on a ballistic trajectory corresponding to the parabolic path of a free projectile; at the top of this trajectory it could have a vanishingly small airspeed, no airspeed at all if you like, and still not stall, *because the angle of attack is small;* the wing is "unloaded," in the jargon of pilots.

# 7

# *Landing*

When you begin practicing landings, you may have your mind full of abstract notions of energy, rate of descent, flare, momentum, and angle of attack; but you will immediately find that the experience of landing an airplane is quite a different matter. It is, with other airplanes around you and your instructor helping you along, more of a social experience; and, as when maneuvering an automobile in traffic, you can find yourself devoting as much attention to the protocols of arrival and departure as to the technical feat of getting the airplane safely and more or less smoothly onto the ground.

The immediate vicinity of an airport is obviously a place of greater than average hazards; airplanes congregate there, all intending eventually to pass through the funnel that leads to the end of the runway. In order to provide order and safety around airports, we have a traffic pattern; it is a rectangle perhaps half a mile longer than the runway, with the runway located on one of its long sides. Its short dimension is always the same—about 2,000 to 3,000 feet—but its length depends on the length of the landing runway.

Traditionally, you fly the pattern in left turns—in pilot's jargon, you "make left traffic." The reason for this is rooted, but not buried, in antiquity. Early airplanes had stick controls and left-hand throttles, and required, sometimes, quite an effort to maneuver them. It is easier to apply force with your right hand to the left, across the body, than outward, to the right. The right hand being on the stick, it is easier to turn the airplane, and also to turn your shoulders, to the left than to the right. And from this combination of circumstances comes the fact that normally, when you fly in a traffic pattern, you keep the runway on your left.

Modern airplanes are easy to maneuver, and they are generally controlled with the left hand, not the right; but we still sit in the left seat, and so make left traffic *except* when there is some reason not to; for instance, a hill, tower, or a group of houses on one side of a runway may cause the pattern always to remain to one side of the runway, regardless of the direction the traffic is landing. The pattern direction is indicated most of the time by a symbol, usually assembled of painted auto tires, ordinarily somewhere near the middle of the runway, in the open space alongside it. L-shaped arms indicate the direction turns are to be made for each runway; in the center of the symbol is the mast with the windsock.

Wind normally determines the direction of taking off and landing; the only exceptions are runways with steep slopes or a big obstruction at one end, where one may always take off and land in certain fixed directions regardless of the wind.

Normally, you always take off into the wind, and land into the wind as well; or at any rate you take off and land as nearly into the wind as the alignment of existing runways permits. If there is only one runway and the wind is blowing at a right angle to it or is calm, landing direction may be up to the pilot's discretion. He may base his decision, for instance, on the location of the fueling and parking area; if it is at one end of the field he will approach from the other end in order not to have to taxi back after he has landed.

Uncontrolled airports may have a landing direction indicator, called a wind tee or a tetrahedron, to further clarify or obscure the preferred direction of landing. The wind tee is intended to represent a conventional airplane, wing near the front; you land in the direction this stylized airplane is heading. The tetrahedron, on the other hand, is a pointed, pyramidal thing, whose small end corresponds to the nose of the airplane; it points in the direction it wants you to be going when you land. Lest this seem too comprehensible, however, a windsock points downwind; its small end points *away* from the direction you should land. Most windsocks are calibrated, more or less (if years of exposure have not reduced them to tatters), so that the more straight and stiff they appear, the harder the wind is blowing. A fully extended windsock means a wind of 20 knots or more. But now there is a new gadget called an approach fish (produced by a Christian organization as it happens), which is long and wavy like a Japanese *koi nobori* and from overhead appears to be straight out even in a light wind.

Often several of these devices will be present. Sometimes they will give conflicting information. For instance, the tetrahedron may point one way and the windsock be blowing another. If the tetrahedron is of the free-swinging type, it may be stuck. Sometimes, however, operators on the ground set the tetrahedron or wind tee to indicate the active runway, and do not change it every time the wind swings briefly around. In this case, the wind tee or tetrahedron takes precedence over the windsock. If, however, you see a tetrahedron or wind tee pointing one way, and a windsock pointing straight out the other way, and you feel sure that there is a stiff wind blowing (streaks on a body of water, flat-blowing smoke, waving trees or grass, blowing leaves or papers might tip you off), you should ignore the tetrahedron. But in such a situation—which will occur rarely—you should take particular precautions to make sure that other traffic is not making other decisions: call on unicom frequency, look around very carefully, and be sure that taxiing aircraft are not heading out to take off against you.

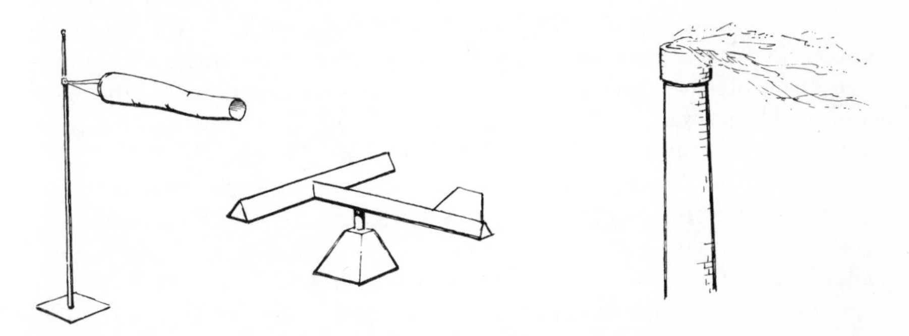

*Wind direction indicators (left to right): windsock, wind tee, and smoke from chimneys*

It also happens in some places that windsocks are placed at both ends of a runway, or in the middle and either end, or all over the place, and that they give conflicting information. Again, in such a case the runway is up for grabs; but be ready for some turbulent winds.

At your home airport you'll know where the wind indicators are, which way the traffic is going, and you might learn to anticipate the wind changes at certain hours of the day, or with certain seasons or sorts of weather. At strange airports, when you're preflighting your airplane you should take note of the direction and strength of the wind, which way airplanes are going as they land or taxi to takeoff, and where the wind indicator is and what it's saying. It's mainly when approaching a strange airport, without a control tower, that you will have to locate the wind indicator and the traffic direction symbol (if there is one), note the lay of the surrounding terrain and any obstructions, and the movements of traffic on the ground, all from the air, in a fairly short time, at an altitude of 2,000 feet AGL or so, where you are clear of traffic in the pattern, before entering the pattern to land. If there is a segmented circle with pattern direction indicators, by flying overhead and mentally enlarging the symbols to correspond with the runways, you can tell which way to fly. Failing that, a blinking orange light is supposed to indicate a right-hand pattern; but I have never seen one in my life. Failing everything, simply fly a left-hand pattern so as to land as nearly into the wind as possible.

The four sides of the pattern rectangle have the following names. Upwind leg is the one parallel to and overhead the runway, and you don't always use it; so it is not so much a part of the landing pattern as a way of reporting your position. The crosswind leg is at right angles to the runway and beyond the departure end; so it is the leg onto which you make your first turn after takeoff. The downwind leg is normally the initial leg of a landing pattern, and it is parallel to the runway and a quarter to a half mile to the side. Finally, the base leg is at right angles to the approach end of the runway, and about a half mile away from the threshold. When you turn onto the upwind leg from base and are descending to land, you are no longer said to be on the upwind leg; now you are on final approach, or simply "on final." The British say "finals," by the way.

The FAA recommends that you enter the pattern at the middle of the downwind leg from an entry leg at a 45-degree angle to the downwind, and that when you leave the pattern you do so by making a 45-degree turn after takeoff rather than a 90 onto the crosswind.

This system is not without its merits, and it has at least an equal number of flaws. But many pilots disregard the FAA recommendations anyway, and their recalcitrance is, in my opinion, a sign of good mental health. The trouble with the official system is that it forces people to fly hither and yon all around the airport trying to see the wind indicator first; then they position themselves for a unique 45-degree entry leg, a procedure which, if they happen to arrive from certain awkward angles, may involve them in a lot of maneuvering. If uncontrolled fields really are hotbeds of crowded flying and foci of accidents, then a lot of maneuvering around them should be discouraged; I think it would be better to

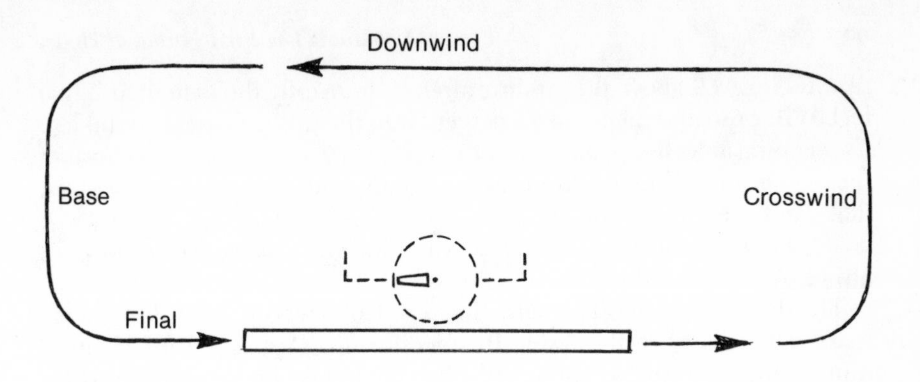


*The landing pattern*

overfly the field, scan it for a wind indicator, and then enter the racetrack pattern on whatever leg you can with a minimum of fancy maneuvering, so long as you do not enter on base or final. You want to minimize your times of blindness; so you would like to make few steep turns in high-wing planes, and to make as many left turns as possible in ones with low wings. You would not want to make a steep left turn onto the downwind leg from the runway side, for instance, because the right window of your airplane would be pointing upward and you wouldn't be able to see an airplane inbound on the recommended 45. Always enter the pattern from the outside; but while you may wish, in order to please the instructor or in order to comply with the recommendations of the FAA, to use the standard pattern, don't feel compelled to use it at all times; it is only a recommendation. It is based on certain desiderata, and if you feel that you can better comply with those fundamental principles by abandoning the consecrated method, abandon it.

The busier the pattern is, the more desirable it is to eliminate needless maneuvering. If there are several airplanes practicing touch-and-goes, all talking on unicom, you don't need to look for the wind indicator. You will hear calls such as "Whiteman traffic, Musketeer three four seven seven Juliet, downwind for one two." Three or four miles out you will be able to see the airplanes in the pattern, rolling on the runway, or taxiing; you don't need to overfly to look at the windsock, unless you are particularly concerned about the wind speed. Better to observe the traffic pattern from a distance, pick a point at which to enter it, and enter without more ado.

Upwind and crosswind entries are safe; those legs are usually devoid of airplanes at pattern altitude. Downwind is recommended, and may be safely entered from a 45, straight in (looking carefully for conflicting traffic on the crosswind), or at some shallower angle between straight in and 45 degrees. The one place where an entry is very inadvisable is the base leg. If you arrive from a direction that makes a base entry desirable, either stay well wide of the base and make a slightly angled entry to the upwind leg well above the landing aircraft, or overfly the pattern at 2,000 feet AGL or so and then make a descent into the upwind or crosswind leg. Descending into the pattern is not considered good practice, because of the danger of settling down on top of an airplane that you can't see and that can't see you; if you have to descend into the pattern, do it at an angle, or while turning in such a way that you can scan the airspace ahead of you for traffic.

The downwind leg is normally flown at 1,000 feet AGL, unless clouds make it necessary to fly lower. In uncontrolled airspace, VFR weather minimums are 1 mile visibility and clear of clouds. These minimums are very generous; they mean, among other things, that if you can see a mile, you can do pattern work at 200 or 300 feet under a 500-foot ceiling, if you feel like it. I have never known anyone who flew touch-and-goes in a mile visibility with a 300-foot pattern altitude, and I have a dim sense that it wouldn't be a very good idea, but it could be done. The 1,000-foot normal height for the pattern does not have legal force; it is simply a guideline. Incidentally, it used to be 800 feet, but for reasons of noise abatement it was recently increased to 1,000.

There have been collisions between aircraft arriving on a 45-degree entry leg and those departing on a 45; in theory the two courses should be separated laterally by a space of several thousand feet, but in practice people neither arrive nor depart on courses of precisely 45 degrees. There are several reasons for this. So far as arriving traffic is concerned, to arrive exactly in the middle of the downwind leg at an angle of precisely 45 degrees is quite a navigational trick; so, since in fact most of us can't mentally add 135 degrees to the runway heading anyway (which would give the entry leg heading for a left-hand pattern), we simply aim for the middle of the runway at a big angle. Similarly, those departing do not hew precisely to a certain angle; instead, they may be influenced by the universal spirit of approximation, or by a desire to aim more in the direction of their destination, or by having failed to set their directional gyro before takeoff, or by having learned to fly a few years back when they used to have you turn left crosswind first, then right 45—a pointless joggle that had the effect of putting you even closer to the incoming traffic.

At tower-controlled fields, you get runway information and direction of traffic before you arrive; depending on your direction of flight, the tower may give you a straight-in approach, a base entry ("Report two miles base, over the May Company"), a straight downwind entry, or, implicitly, a 45-degree downwind entry ("Report downwind for runway two four").

Runways are identified by one or two digits painted at the approach ends, which represent the compass heading that you will be flying on final, divided by 10, plus or minus 5 degrees. Runway 3 may have a magnetic bearing of anywhere from 26 to 35 degrees, runway 26 (said "two six") from 256 to 265, and so on. There is no runway 0; it would be runway 36.

When you are approaching a field with a tower and they tell you when you are seven miles out, "Two Mike Uniform, make right traffic runway seven, report downwind," you may find it difficult to figure out which runway runway 7 is.

There are several ways of figuring it out. One is to look at your directional gyro, if you have the vertical card type, and find the number of the runway on it; this will show you the runway alignment in relation to the direction you are now flying. Alternatively, you can add or subtract 18 (meaning 180 degrees) and get the desired heading for the downwind leg. If the airport is big enough, a diagram of its runways may be shown on the sectional chart, and you can compare it with a nearby omni rose, or with a mental compass rose, to decide which one is 7: it is the one running a little bit north of west-to-east. Then visualize your position on the chart and try to make sense out of what you see through the windshield.

There used to be little plastic calculators for sale that showed you the orientation of the runway with reference to your flight path; they were a help to people who had trouble visualizing things. You can get the same effect by drawing a map on a scrap of paper. The tower normally expects you, when they tell you to report downwind, to enter the downwind leg at some angle between 0 and 90 degrees. If you must enter with a 90-degree turn, make the turn gradual, so that you look as though you really intended a 45-degree entry, and so as not to catch other traffic by surprise. If you sketch runway 7 thus, with its downwind leg and entry quadrant, and then look at your own heading and find that it is, say, 140 degrees,

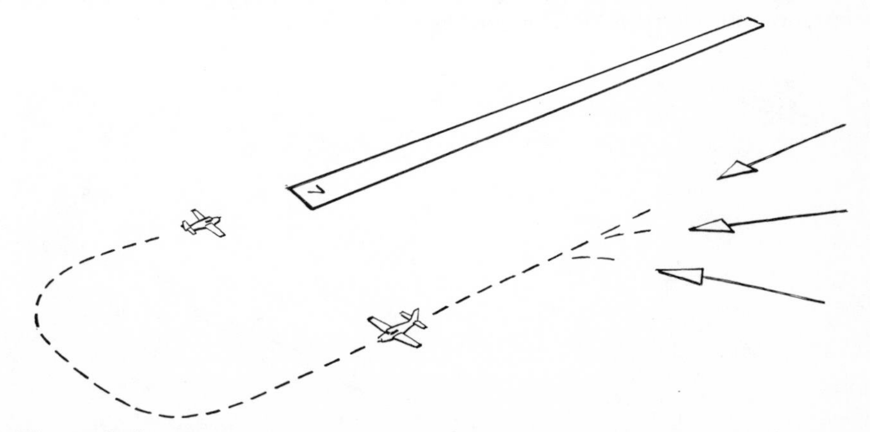


*The standard pattern entry*

and you are still far away from but in sight of the field, say, seven miles out, then you look like this:

*The view of the pattern from a distance*

This isn't very convenient.

If you have the chutzpah, you might call the tower and say, "Mike Uniform, can I get a left base entry for seven?" If they say okay, you're in; but if they say, "Unable, make right traffic, report downwind" (and it is likely that they will say this), then you ought to turn eastward, fly around the approach end of the runway giving it a wide berth, and then swing around and enter the downwind like this:

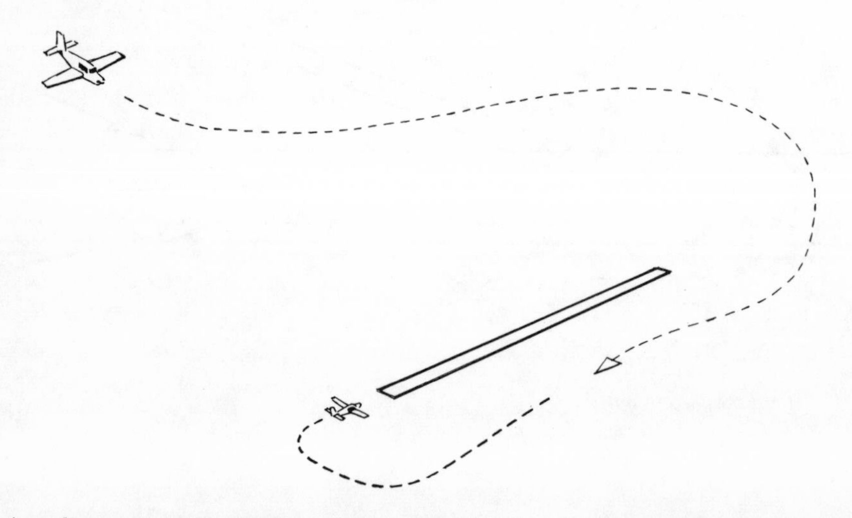

*A circling entry to lose altitude and to gain the proper downwind entry into the pattern*

But you might prefer more bargaining: "This is Two Mike Uniform, request a midfield crossing at one thousand feet with a right turn into the downwind." Chances are the tower, which realizes the inconvenience of your situation, will come back with something like this: "Mike Uniform, that's approved, traffic a Piper Tomahawk making touch-and-goes runway seven, report one mile north of the airport." This last part is to give the tower warning of your impending arrival, so that he can make sure that your unorthodox swing onto the downwind from inside doesn't coincide exactly with that Tomahawk's arrival on the downwind leg.

These sorts of modifications of standard procedure are so common that no one is shocked at their use; but a beginning student is forced to use much less imaginative, more regimented, and unvarying procedures, partly in order to encourage in him a sense that flying is an important activity in which one should not violate the rules at random, and partly because it greatly simplifies the lot of the student, the instructor, the tower, and the other pilots in the area if students refrain from investigating bizarre new ways of doing things each day. The variety of improvisation used in flying may give the impression of random disregard of conventions, but actually it arises out of a shared sense among the participants of how things work, what works well, and what is likely to be approved and what denied. This is a sense which develops with experience; and while it is good for a novice to realize that flying is a creative and individual activity, he should not be in too much of a hurry to set his own personal stamp on the air traffic control system.

Part of the importance of the 1,000-foot pattern altitude, apart from its being a convenient height from which to land an airplane, is that by putting all airplanes at the same altitude it makes them easier to spot. In theory, at least; in practice, they turn up at various altitudes, and even when you know where they are you sometimes have trouble spotting them. Contrary to expectation, a little smog, fog, or haze is helpful in this respect; by obliterating the background clutter, it makes the nearby airplanes appear more sharply defined. Perfectly clear weather over uneven terrain and the mingled textures and colors of a city are two of the most difficult conditions in which to spot other aircraft. At least by putting everyone at more or less the same altitude, you minimize the risk of planes descending upon one another—though this still happens comparatively often, usually on final approach.

Lateral position remains a puzzle. There seems to be very little unanimity among pilots as to the proper distance from the runway for flying a downwind leg. In general, slow aircraft fly tighter patterns than fast ones, the whole evolution being subject to the same laws of scale as all maneuvers. The thing that ought to remain constant is the time spent in the pattern, not the distance covered. However, the problems with this notion are many. For one thing, beginning students and their instructors seem to enjoy flying immense patterns, which defer the inevitable moment of landing, give the most time for corrections, and permit the instructor to get in a lot of instructing. But on the other hand these patterns displease, when they do not render absolutely apoplectic, pilots arriving in twins or fast singles. The heavy airplane wants to fly its pattern at 100 mph, or perhaps 90; the trainer is chugging along at 70 mph, or perhaps 60. Behind the trainer is another trainer, and another. And all of them are flying a mile past the runway threshold before deciding to turn base. If the fast airplane manages to insinuate himself into the downwind leg, he will have to fly for ages in order not to overtake the airplane ahead of him on final; but if he goes too far, the airplane behind him, thinking that he is departing on a cross-country, may turn and cut him off.

This situation, which is not uncommon, can be alleviated in several ways. One is for everyone in the pattern to use a unicom frequency, normally 122.8. Let's say a fast airplane, Aerostar 48PA, enters the pattern and finds that the Cherokee ahead of him is extending his downwind. "Cherokee on downwind at Mudlark," he calls on 122.8, "do you read Aerostar four eight Papa Alfa?"

Chances are the Cherokee, even if he does hear the transmission, won't realize that it's for him, and won't answer, because it is a little unusual to have strangers calling you on unicom. But if it happens that he hears, understands, and answers, the Aerostar pilot can say, "I'm behind you on the downwind and going quite a bit faster than you are. I'd like to turn inside you to land. I'll be out of your way by the time you're on final."

Either the Cherokee will have a scratchy radio and not understand most of the transmission, which is not one of the few cut-and-dried communications one is used to understanding; or he will understand and undoubtedly agree.

If the Cherokee is sufficiently far ahead of the Aerostar and shows no sign of turning base, the Aerostar can reasonably turn a short base inside the Cherokee, even though it is improper to cut off another airplane in the pattern, if he feels the Cherokee couldn't catch him if he tried. He does this with a radio call: "Aerostar four eight Papa Alfa turning base at Mudlark." He keeps his speed up, flies a tight pattern, and stays out of the Cherokee's way. If questioned, he says he never saw the Cherokee.

Traffic permitting, the Aerostar might chug along behind the Cherokee, fly a mile past his base leg, and then turn in, all the time calling his position out on unicom in hopes that the airplane behind him won't lose sight of him in the distance and turn inside him.

The best solution, however, is for everyone to fly a tight pattern, and to keep his speed up until short final.

Now, what is a tight pattern?

Since most of the guidelines for patterns are handed down by word of mouth and learned by experience, let's try to work out a rational model of a pattern.

The purpose of a base leg is to permit the pilot to inspect the airspace to his right (assuming a left-hand pattern for the moment) and make sure no one is coming straight in or flying a base leg outside his. Military procedures omit the base leg, because all the airplanes landing are making the same approach out of a formation; so there is no reason, other than traffic or perhaps the student pilot's need for a breather, to fly a base leg. In any case, there is no reason to fly a very long base leg.

It is the base leg that gives the pattern its breadth. Without that period of level flight, the pattern would only be as wide as the semicircle flown from downwind to final.

When I learned to fly, the pattern was 800 feet high, not 1,000, and one thought of the average rate of descent during the approach as 500 feet per minute. However, it was more than that, and it should be, because one should, in principle, always be prepared to land in the event of an engine failure from any point in the approach. Realistically, most pilots do not fulfill this requirement, since so many other considerations shape their landing approaches. No light airplane glides at a rate of descent of 500 fpm, and a more realistic glide would be 800 fpm; but since in the case of an engine failure one can take a shortcut to the runway from anywhere but the final turn, it will be acceptable to be below an 800 fpm profile for most of the approach.

It is always said that the trick of a good landing is a good approach; you shouldn't have to be making last-minute drastic corrections on short final. The trick of a good approach, in turn, is being at the right height at the right time. Idealizing the pattern, it appears that we get rid of about 250 to 300 feet between key position and turning base. The same between rolling out on final and touchdown, and the remaining 500 feet or so in the turns and the base leg. If we lose 180 feet in each turn, the rule for the pattern will be to start the descent at the key position; turn base after 250 feet of descent; and begin the turn to final about 450 feet above the runway threshold.

I have flown with a former military pilot of great experience who used exactly this method to fly a traffic pattern. Granted that the airplane we were in was unfamiliar to him, and that memorizing some key numbers helped him to bracket the right rates of descent, still I was astonished to find a pilot of his years so dependent on numbers. Personally, I don't believe in by-the-numbers flying, and I have reduced the traffic pattern to a calculation only to show that it has, ideally, a symmetrical and rational form, in which a certain amount of height is dissipated steadily over a certain amount of distance. The trouble is that one is so often called upon to fly a wide pattern, or a short one, or a high or low one, because of traffic or obstructions or dwellings below, that the idealized pattern has almost no real-life application. Nor should it. When we learn to walk, run, swim, or drive, we do not learn numbers and geometrical patterns; we learn a certain feeling, and we develop an instinct that permits us to ramify, infinitely, the essential principle of the method.

That essential principle, in the traffic pattern, is a sense of the point toward which we are moving. This point is visible ahead of the descending airplane as a stationary area from which all other points seem to be slowly fleeing. The sensation is familiar enough from driving a car, except that in a car the space in which the event unfolds is two-dimensional. As we drive down a road we think of the road as standing still and of ourselves as moving through a landscape of buildings, trees, signs, or what have you. But if you forget this version of events for a moment and simply stare like an idiot ahead of you as you drive, you will perceive that what you see is objects moving away from a point directly ahead of your car. The house on the right side of the road retreats to the right; the billboard above the road on the left moves upward and to the left. The road ahead seems to slide downward beneath you, disappearing under the nose of the car.

A gliding airplane produces a similar set of impressions, but they are less striking because everything is farther away from the airplane, and the displacements produced by its movement are relatively small. However, as you align your airplane with the runway on final approach, you gaze fixedly forward, and in a few seconds you will perceive the point from which all other points are spreading outward. It will be dead ahead (unless there is a fierce crosswind); but what interests you about it is its height. It is called your aim point, and it is the point at which you will touch down if you don't change anything. If it is above the runway threshold, you have to reduce power (keeping speed constant), which will in a moment cause the aim point to move downward. If it is below the threshold, you have to add power. Different instructors have different ways of going about things, but you might ask to make several approaches followed by go-arounds, so that you don't have to worry about actually landing, until you have thoroughly mastered the technique of perceiving the aim point. It is quite a bit cheaper, however, to practice it while walking or driving, since the trick is not the flying but the way of seeing. To try it in your living room, hold some object—a pencil, your thumb, this book—out at arm's length ahead of you and walk at a normal pace across the room. Notice how things move away from the object ahead of you in all directions. If you don't see it this way, try holding up both hands in front of you to make a frame. Using your hands as a frame, you will see how objects starting out inside the frame move out of it as you move toward them, while objects at the aim point remain within the frame, unmoving.

This is simply the technique that you always use, without being aware of it, to aim yourself in the direction you want to go. In theory it ought to be simple to aim an airplane, since the technique is no different from that used in walking; but the unfamiliarity of the surroundings, the relatively small scale of the displacements, and the notion that it ought to be done "by the numbers" all combine to prevent beginning pilots from aiming instinctively. Most commonly, they arrive high—a reflection, no doubt, of their reluctance to face the moment of having to flare and touch down.

The aim point technique is easy enough to learn for final approach; it is more difficult to use on base, when the point of intended landing is ahead and to one side, and on downwind, when it is behind you.

To dispose of downwind immediately, I'll say that in my opinion, no one judges his descent on downwind by reference to the runway. Everybody just sets up a rate of descent that looks right, and turns base when *that* looks right. This process may have something in common with the use of an aim point, but it is a learned technique. When you've flown a few hundred landing approaches you begin to know what they should look like. But for the beginner's purposes the descent on downwind consists simply of reducing power and adding flaps, when abeam the landing point, to produce a 600–700 fpm rate of descent, and waiting until the runway is about as far behind him as it can be without his having to turn his shoulders to see it out of the corner of his eye.

The turn to base is simply a turn—more than standard rate, perhaps 35 or 40 degrees of bank, letting the nose down a little to keep up airspeed. (You'll find that you lose altitude a little more rapidly in the turns than in the straight portions of the approach, and adjust accordingly. The turns are, in fact, a good time to make small adjustments in height.) As you roll out on base, you check for traffic and then take a look at the runway.

The late Bob Blodgett, who wrote for *Flying* magazine for many years, had a notion that you could look at the landing point, watching it move backward along the window, until you saw it hook upward; when it began to hook upward, you made the next turn. This system, he said, worked for both the downwind-to-base turn and for the base-to-final turn. I tried it a few times and I believe that for a while I convinced myself that I saw the aim point hooking up. But then sometimes it didn't, or I felt that I ought to turn before it hooked; and eventually I abandoned my experiments. I have never heard anyone else refer to this method. Something that would work just as well, once you got the hang of picking out your aim point easily and quickly, would be to mentally swing the runway threshold out in front of you on the base leg. This is necessarily an approximate procedure, since you can't displace the threshold with precision; but if you're sinking fast, or floating too high, it will be obvious right away that the aim point is outside the approximate vicinity of the rotated threshold.

But I ought not to put too much emphasis on these handy hints, because when you finally have pattern flying completely under control, you won't be using any tricks at all; you'll just be judging, unconsciously, your progress on a familiar trajectory, just as, when taking a freeway exit, you are always viscerally aware of your position, speed, and rate of deceleration, without relying on mental questionnaires to ensure a correct performance. Beginners need handy hints, perhaps to give them some hold on the slippery cliff of skill, and perhaps only to distract them from the unconscious process of learning, which grows best sheltered from the light of analysis; as you gain skill, you can drop your training wheels. That was why the reliance of my air force friend on numbers surprised me so much; it was as though you saw a grown man pedaling around on a tricycle.

It's really only when you turn final that you begin to make an accurate stab at the aim point. With a little practice you'll feel before you roll out on final whether you're high or low, and by how much. You can bring in full flaps as you roll out of the final turn, and now concentrate your attention entirely on the aim point.

The aim point will have to be somewhat below, or short of, the point where you want to land, because you will have a little excess speed to dissipate before touching down, and you will dissipate it in the flare. Because flaring and floating down the runway will do more than anything else to make you land long—in other words, beyond the aim point—speed control on final approach is of great importance. You will always be encouraged to keep speed under control throughout the entire pattern, since your instructor will assume that if you can't keep your speed under control as well one time as any other, you can't be relied upon to have it where you need it at the critical moment. So it is important to control speed carefully throughout the approach; but you can recover from an error easily on downwind or base, whereas a wide deviation from the desired speed on final may make it impossible to land where you want to.

However accurate your speed control, and however facile your perception of the aim point, there is a blurred area immediately prior to the touchdown. It is the flare. The flare is the most delicate part of the landing, for which all else is only a preparation. It is separate from the rest of the landing; the aim point ceases to be of concern, and speed control no longer matters either. It is a continuous, transitional motion in which the surplus speed of the approach is converted into energy which is used to arrest the descent, in such a way that the minimum speed of the airplane, a rate of descent of zero, and contact with the ground all occur at the same time.

There is debate as to the importance of getting the airplane down to its minimum speed. Generally, the faster and heavier the airplane, the less emphasis is placed on a minimum speed or "full stall" landing. When you find a pilot or writer urging that full stall landings are unnecessary, you will discover that he makes his living flying jets. The reason is that the higher the stalling speed, generally, the more powerful the airplane's braking systems, braking effectiveness being required in proportion to the square of the speed; and the greater the distance the airplane would cover along the runway while bleeding off speed in the flare. Heavy, fast airplanes stop in less distance when they are placed on the ground and braking—wheel brakes, spoilers, thrust reversers—is applied. Braking can't be applied while the plane is still airborne, so the emphasis is on getting it onto the ground.

Lighter airplanes are in less danger of running off the far end of the runway if the flare is prolonged, and in greater danger of landing on their nosewheels if it is not; and so in lighter airplanes a full stall landing, or the closest thing to one, is desirable and, for that matter, not difficult to accomplish, since such airplanes stall gently and with ample advance warning. Landing on the nosewheel first is dangerous; it can set off a series of bounces from which the only recovery may be to abort the landing entirely, or it can produce the condition known as wheelbarrowing, in which the rear wheels are off the ground, the nosewheel on, and the airplane impossible to control.

Airplanes with tailwheel gear—or, as it is often called, conventional gear, although that type of gear is no longer conventional at all—can be landed either on the two main wheels or on all three wheels at once. The landing on all three, the three-point landing, is the model of the full stall landing in the tricycle gear airplane. The reasoning for it is quite obvious in a taildragger: if you hit the ground hard in other than a fully stalled, three-point attitude, the tail drops, increasing the angle of attack and causing you to lift back into the air. A "wheels" landing in a taildragger—the type in which the airplane is brought down in a level attitude and planted on the two main wheels, the tail still up in the air—requires a delicate touch to prevent this kind of bouncing. Large taildraggers—Beech 18s, DC-3s—are normally landed on their main wheels and slowed down by braking; light ones are landed three-point at minimum speed. The reasoning is the same here as for tricycle gear airplanes; heavier ones are more effectively stopped by braking than by aerodynamic drag.

Pilots seeking the ultimate in short-field performance from a light taildragger land tailwheel first. They feel for the ground with the tailwheel as though it were an arresting hook. When the tailwheel hits, the mains come down shortly afterward, and since the angle of attack of the airplane is thus diminished, there is no chance of its bouncing back into the air with renewed lift.

Tailwheel gear was superseded because its geometry is naturally unstable. Like a car in reverse, it does not want to track straight of its own accord; instead, the tail tends to swing around in the uncontrolled gyration called a ground loop. Some tailwheel airplanes are docile and easy to manage; others are notoriously tricky and require extremely swift reactions from the pilot the moment the airplane touches down. Those that are particularly treacherous are usually landed mainwheels first, so that the tailwheel does not touch the ground until the airplane is moving along quite slowly. Control is poor in most taildraggers as the tail comes down, because the wing and fuselage obstruct the flow of air over the vertical tail and reduce the effectiveness of the rudder. Because of the comparative difficulty of handling tailwheel airplanes, those who have mastered the art, or imagine themselves to have mastered it, sometimes display bumper stickers to the effect that "Real Pilots Fly Taildraggers" or "Taildragger Pilots Keep It Straighter"—a piece of self-congratulation tantamount to announcing to the world that one has mastered the stick shift.

If you arrive "over the fence" at the proper airspeed—which, for most students, means not too fast—the principal problem of the flare is to level out just above the runway without ballooning back up into the air. Some instructors spend an hour having the student fly along just above the runway, not landing but simply trying to maintain a certain height and speed, to instill the feeling. Runways that can be so casually used are not to be found everywhere, but the principle is a good one. It's important to know where the wheels are. You can, for instance, accelerate to takeoff speed and then reduce power, manipulating the throttle so that the wheels just skip along the runway; a little more power, you rise off, a little reduction, you settle back on, always keeping the angle of attack—that is, the stick force—more or less steady and the nosewheel off the ground. Aside from the practice that this exercise provides in delicate manipulations of attitude and power, it forces the student to look elsewhere than down at the runway in front of him. Looking at a nearby spot on the runway is tempting, but inimical to good landings. It is better to look out at the far end of the runway, or to lean against the left side of the cockpit and sight forward along the side of the airplane. Leaning to the left increases one's peripheral perspective; but the attention should still be directed to a distant point. The movement of the airplane as it lands is, in the vertical plane, almost exactly analogous to that of a car pulling over to a curb and stopping; what complicates the handling of the airplane is that the same control that provides the curving transition from descent to level flight is the one that diminishes speed—the elevator. The throttle has been chopped at the beginning of the flare, and it normally won't be used during the landing unless a stall at too great a height seems imminent and thrust is needed to recover the situation.

Getting the flare right is a matter of practice; the most helpful single trick is always coming over the fence at the same speed. Coming over the fence at the same height is important too, and at the same rate of descent; but once you have the aim point under control the pivotal element is speed. Given a speed, you can flare at the same height, with the same movement and force, each time, and produce the same roundout. If you come over the fence too high, forget about landing on the numbers and concentrate on getting the flare right; for the purposes of the student pilot, landing is more a matter of flaring at the right height than at the right point along the runway—though, obviously, consistently landing long (or, what is much less common, short) has its dangers.

What makes landing difficult, I suppose, is the limitations of space, time, and speed that encompass it. You have only so much runway; you have only so much room in which to execute the flare; and you have only a certain band of speed, between the approach speed and the stall, into which to sandwich the maneuver. It is a sufficiently complex combination of events to defy rote learning, and I fail to see how, even if you fly your pattern "by the numbers," you could manage to flare and land gracefully by the numbers too. At some point, instinct has to take over, and the instinct has to be developed by practice. Don't feel discouraged if it takes you a long time to get a knack for landing. You are not in a contest with other students, and each individual comes to flight instruction with his own set of strengths and weaknesses. Sometimes an instructor fails to perceive the root cause of a student's difficulties, and even when you pass your private license flight test you are still a beginner.

# 8

# *Radio Communications*

Everybody experiences stage fright when learning to fly. It is difficult not to divide one's attention between the arriving collision with the runway and the equally imminent pride or humiliation it will bring. But at least the instructor is a familiar and, one hopes, friendly figure. Your first episodes with the radio will bring you into contact with unknown ogres, the magnitude of whose contempt you can only tremblingly imagine.

At first the radio seems useless, since you can't understand anything it says. The language is unfamiliar, the delivery rapid and clipped, there is sometimes quite a bit of interference, and at the same time as you feel surrounded by professionals, you cannot disguise your own amateurism. As a result, you may stumble all over yourself delivering the simplest messages. Matters are not simplified by the habitual reliance on hand-held microphones in trainers. Professional pilots wouldn't think of using a hand mike; they use boom mikes or tiny mikes held in front of their lips on arms attached to headphones. But students have to use hand mikes, and so the problem of fumbling for the mike is added to that of figuring out what to say into it. (To say nothing of the problem of which side of it to speak into, which has caused quite a bit of confusion.)

Aviation radio communication is so highly formalized that once you get the knack of it, you practically know everything that is going to be said before it is said, and the only purpose of communication is to fill in certain vital blanks with times, speeds, or directions.

There are a few basic rules. Be brief. Use the accepted language. Speak evenly and clearly and know what you are going to say before you say it. Listen before you speak, so that you don't cut people off. Keep communication to a minimum; find out what you can without calling people to ask. Don't supply people with useless information.

Arriving at an ordinary tower-controlled field, for instance, start listening on the tower frequency five or ten minutes before you enter the pattern. Perhaps nothing will be happening, and this will not help; but in that case at least your requests will not be taking up too much of other people's valuable time. Most likely, you'll hear how many airplanes are in the pattern, whether any are doing touch-and-goes; if there is an arrival while you're listening, you'll hear the runway and wind information, or you may be able to get it on the ATIS (Automated Terminal Information Service) frequency that is listed beside the airport on the VFR chart, if the terminal is busy enough to have an ATIS. ATIS is a loop recording that is changed whenever conditions change; it gives the wind, sky condition, temperature, runway in use, and any other information an arriving airplane needs. The current ATIS is identified by a letter of the phonetic alphabet: Information Hotel, Information Mike, and so on. When you call the tower, you tell them you have Hotel, Mike, or whatever. You're not supposed to say "with the ATIS," because you might be lying; you're supposed to say *which* ATIS. Ten miles out you call: "Archduke Tower, Grumman five four seven three Quebec, ten northwest with Hotel, landing." Note the order: first, whom you're calling; second, who you are; third, the message. The closing "Over!" beloved of movie aviators has fallen into disuse, except when it isn't clear that you've finished your transmission—for instance, when you have been transmitting a great deal of information. "Over" means "over to you," or "your turn." The tower will say, "Roger, seven three Quebec, make left traffic runway three three, report downwind." And you say, "Seven three Quebec, Roger" or simply, "Seven three Quebec," or, if you want to sound as though you've been at this a long time, you might try "Three Q," although this approach sacrifices clarity for the sake of casualness. But plenty of old salts will call their airplane Sixty-nine Sugar Daddy rather than Six Niner

Sierra Delta, and most controllers will follow suit. On the other hand, you would be unlikely to get far with One Nameless Beast in place of One November Bravo.

The function of the tower is to provide orderly traffic flow, make sure pilots see each other and don't get into the same place at the same time, and to clear airplanes to land. In effect the airport belongs to the tower controller, and he is the one who says who does what when. Here as elsewhere in flying, however, you have to learn to resolve the apparent contradiction between the authority of the controller and the "ultimate authority" of the pilot. In practice this is a simple matter; you do what the controller says to do, and if he steers you into an imminent collision you take evasive action. Perhaps you could later look up the controller and talk it over with him. Far more of these post-game shows arise, however, from the pilots' mistakes than from the controllers'. More often than mutiny, the problem is the pilot's failure to obey commands because he failed to hear them. Careful attention while in the pattern, both to traffic and to radio communications (your own and others'), is important.

A perfect example of a situation in which a pilot might overrule a controller is one involving the possibility of wake turbulence. The location of the invisible tornado behind a heavy airplane can be guessed at as well by a pilot as by a controller. If you are cleared for takeoff too soon behind a departing jet, or for landing behind an arriving one, you can refuse the clearance. No one will complain. Or, for that matter, suppose you call ready for takeoff, the tower clears you for immediate takeoff, and you discover that the door is unlocked or that one of your fuel tanks is indicating empty; you should call the tower: "Seven three Quebec, unable, stand by." The tower will realize something is wrong, and say something like "Seven three Quebec, hold short," and then clear somebody else for takeoff, if somebody else is waiting. He may then say, "Seven three Quebec, what are your intentions?" This question, which sometimes has a slightly condescending sound, should not alarm you. You reply, "Three Quebec will advise when ready for takeoff," and that gets you off the hook.

If you look at the radio glossary in the *Airman's Information Manual*, you'll find that all these phrases, and many others, are consecrated, cut-and-dried ways of saying what you need to say. The listener only needs to hear part of your transmission, certain key words, to understand your message. The use of rote phrases has two undesirable effects. One is to make matters difficult for the beginner, who confuses his idioms, the way movie scriptwriters always do, and says something like "Archduke Control Tower, this is etc., etc., I'm coming in for a landing," borrowing from the language of 1950s science fiction. The other is to make it quite difficult to transmit messages that are not covered by standard phraseology. A clear radio is a great help; clear diction helps too, and a good microphone position and the right pace of speech; shouting into the microphone does not help at all. A normal, in fact a quieter than normal, tone of voice should be used, and the microphone held just clear of the lips, so that they brush it lightly at times. You should speak in the front of your mouth, not back in your throat, although men may be tempted to speak in the back of their mouths because their voices sound deeper that way.

If you have a lot of trouble getting a message across because of distance or poor radio quality, pick your words carefully and always repeat the same words; don't change the message each time. If you can't get your meaning across, say "Disregard" and forget about it. Usually you will be able to receive better than you transmit, because ground stations are generally more powerful and better maintained than the radios in rental and training airplanes; sometimes you may be able to hear a ground station perfectly clearly and not be able to contact him.

When after several tries you get no response from a ground station, review your radio setup to make sure you are in fact transmitting (you may have tuned one transmitter to the desired frequency and then transmitted on the other), that you have the receiver properly selected and the volume turned up, that the mike is facing the right way (you may be talking to the back of the mike, especially with some of the stylishly designed, ambiguous models), that the mike is properly plugged in, and that the frequency you have selected is the correct one. Sometimes a ground station may use a number of different frequencies, and occasionally he may be talking on one while you are listening on another. Usually, with a Flight Service Station for instance, you hear the station transmitting on any of his frequencies; but sometimes you will hear him on some and not on others.

Sometimes you will get radar traffic advisories from approach controllers, normally in certain busy terminal areas. This practice, which in some areas is mandatory and in some optional, is opposed by many as an unnecessary encroachment of ground control on the authority of pilots; but nevertheless you will sometimes find yourself getting traffic calls from the ground. They sound like this:

"Seven three Quebec, traffic two o'clock, four miles, southeast bound, altitude unknown."

Or, "Seven three Quebec, traffic twelve o'clock, one mile, eastbound, unverified altitude readout five thousand six hundred."

The first call is not very urgent; there is an airplane off to your right, a little ahead of your right wing, quite far off (at four miles you might not spot him at all), and he could be at any altitude, so you probably won't be able to see him unless he is above you and visible against the sky. His direction of flight is important, however, because if you are southbound, it is possible that in a minute or two your paths may converge. If this is the case, the controller will probably call the traffic again. If you see him, you can say "Tallyho," which I have always had difficulty bringing myself to say; but if, as is more common, you don't see him, you say, "Roger, seven three Quebec, no contact." You should not say "contact" if you *do* see him, however, because the controller might think he had failed to hear your "no."

In the case of twelve o'clock traffic at one mile, this call may be more pressing if you also happen to be at 5,500; the altitude readout from the other airplane's encoding altimeter could easily be off by 100 feet, and he could actually be at or near the standard altitude of 5,500. Twelve o'clock means dead ahead. If you are westbound, you have only a few seconds in which to spot him. You reply, "Seven three Quebec, looking." You can say "looking" any time you don't see the traffic, but it seems to me most logical in cases where traffic is an immediate factor, because it implies a continuing search and invites further advice from the controller. "No contact," on the other hand, suggests less urgency.

Half the time, you never see the traffic; the controller may at some point say, "Seven three Quebec, clear of traffic," and you say "Roger" and forget about it. Sometimes the controller will say, "Traffic at such and such, not a factor," which makes me wonder why he mentions the traffic in the first place. This system is riddled with flaws. For one thing, one gets a tremendous number of calls on traffic that is not a factor, and will never be a factor, such as traffic eight miles away and headed away from you, or a jet already above you and climbing. On the other hand, controllers are sometimes too busy to give traffic, and you may have a jet come screaming close by you from behind. Presumably he is talking to some other controller and was warned of your presence; but suppose you, ignoring his presence, had suddenly decided to demonstrate a steep turn to a passenger?

En route, your radio communications will usually be limited to position reports on VFR flight plans. A flight plan, as you will learn when you begin to plan cross-country trips, is a way of letting the authorities know your intentions so that if you fail to turn up at the end of a flight, they know over what area to begin looking for you. Periodic position reports are used to reduce the area of the search; if your last position report was given seventy miles short of your destination, they will look for you somewhere in that last seventy miles.

Actually, the first place they look is at the destination airport, at neighboring airports, at airports en route, and at your home, since a common reason for flight plans not being closed is not accidents but the forgetfulness of pilots. All airplanes carry a radio called an ELT (emergency locator transmitter), which is supposed to be triggered in a crash and help searchers locate the downed aircraft. If you make a forced landing somewhere off the beaten track, and the landing does not produce a 5G forward deceleration, you have to activate the ELT yourself. You can verify that it is working, if the plane is more or less intact, by tuning a Com radio to 121.5. The ELT produces a characteristic wavering tone, a series of short upsweeps like rapid "whoops."

Filing a VFR flight plan is not mandatory. I haven't filed one in years. But I used to file them all the time, and I think it was a good idea if only because it gave me a lot of practice in radio communication.

When you give a position report, it sounds like this: "Passavant Radio, this is Grumman five four seven three Quebec, on a VFR flight plan from Pilar to Post, currently over Passavant at seven thousand five hundred." The "Radio" to which you report is the Flight Service Station serving the navigational radio station over which you are passing. Of course there is no law that says that you have to fly airways; you could as well file from town to town, or even "direct" from origin to destination, and then report "thirty-one miles west of Passavant" or "over Presque." You have to use readily identifiable reporting points, however; even though you may use the intersection of the river and the railroad near the turkey farm as a checkpoint, you cannot use it as a reporting point, because it is too difficult for the FSS person to understand and record.

Often the FSS person will give you some free information: the weather along your route, a pilot report, and, normally, the altimeter setting at his station. This information comes to you because of the courtesy, friendliness, and boredom of FSS personnel. You can request it, if you like; but more and more you request your weather on the frequency of 122.0 on the nationwide network of Flight Watch stations. You give them a position when you call, but it's enough to say, "Argus Flight Watch, Grumman five four seven three Quebec, VFR over Presque, request current Post weather and the Post forecast for two hours from now."

"Two hours from now" is a handy way of getting around the official custom of giving times in Zulu time, as Greenwich Mean Time is called. Conscientious aviators know the Zulu time; the rest of us don't and come up with convenient substitutes. Everyone, however, has to learn to use a twenty-four-hour clock, like a European timetable, saying, for example, seventeen hundred hours for 5 P.M.

When en route you may feel like giving somebody a pilot report. Pilot reports, or Pireps, are a way of warning or reassuring other pilots with firsthand information about conditions on the route. When the weather is forecast clear and it is clear, you don't give a pilot report of clear weather. If, on the other hand, clouds are hanging low over the mountains and some of the passes are obscured, you might report that you were able to make it across by a certain route, or you might say "Unable VFR" from one point to another, meaning that you could not get there while remaining in VFR conditions, and others may as well spare themselves the trouble. Turbulence reports might help other pilots choose comfortable altitudes: you say, "Moderate turbulence west of the Sasquatch in the vicinity of Undine, but now smooth at niner thousand five hundred over Northborough, a Grumman Tiger." You identify the type of aircraft because different aircraft are differently affected by turbulence, and other pilots will judge the applicability of the Pirep to themselves by knowing the type of airplane that gave the report. Severe turbulence to a Cub may be imperceptible to a Learjet.

For the novice pilot, the categories of communications I've mentioned—tower, radar advisory, Flight Service, unicom—represent the entire spectrum. Flying helicopters, on instruments, over oceans, at high altitudes, in formations, you use different procedures, talk to different stations on different frequencies, say and ask different things. To a beginner a process like hearing, copying, and reading back a long IFR clearance, with its puzzling intersection names, three-digit airway identifiers, its welter of frequencies, transponder codes, headings, altitudes, and times, may seem as inconceivable as understanding the vast instrument panel of a jet airliner. But the simplifying key is the same: only certain nuggets of information are essential, and they are placed, always in the same sequence and context, in a matrix of familiar but less essential items. Be it the three or four cardinal instruments that tell you in an instant what you want to know, or three or four names or numbers that get you started on your route of flight, the pilot's trick is to isolate them from the clutter of background material. When you first fly, everything seems to be clutter and foreground; in a few hours, however, you begin to separate the wheat from the chaff, and not long afterward you begin to learn the rhythm and the tune yourself. The funny expressions—negative, say again, unable, Roger, no joy—start to feel natural. In fact, you have to stop yourself from using them in normal conversation, where "negative" and "say again" may sound to you like perfectly natural alternatives to "no" and "what?" while to the uninitiated they sound a bit affected at best, and at worst as though you might have joined Scientology.

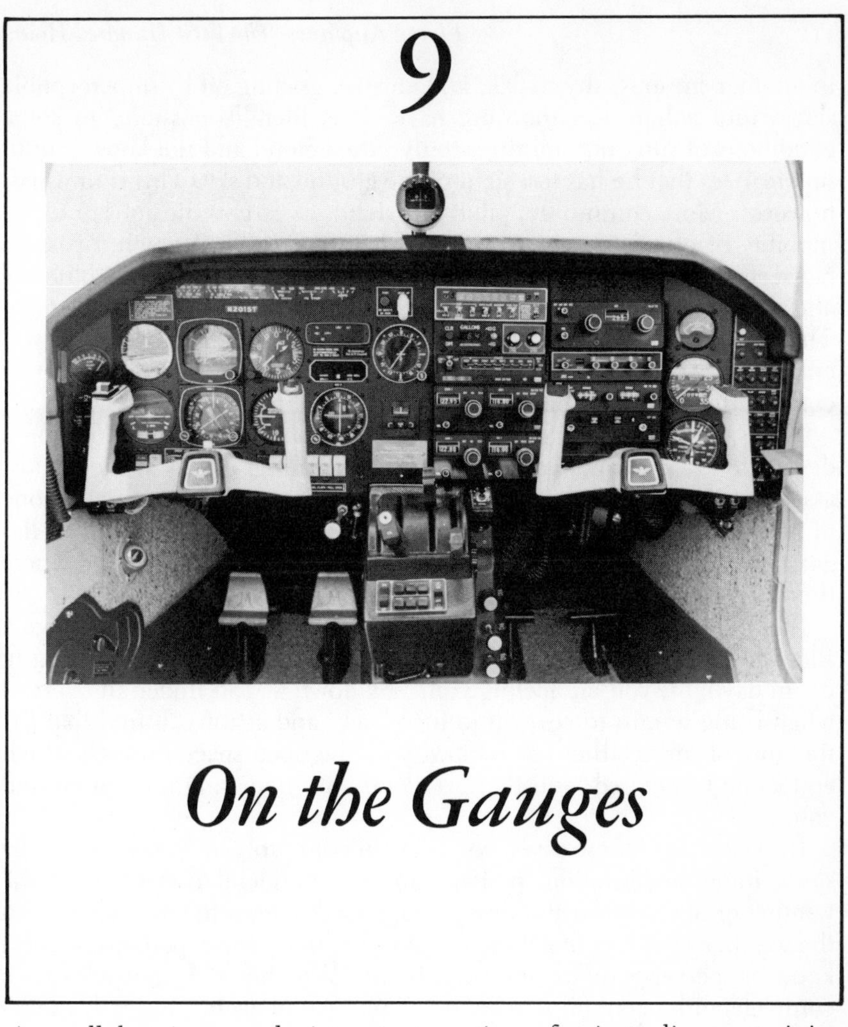

# 9

# *On the Gauges*

A small but immensely important portion of private license training concerns flying on instruments. This used not to be required, since flying on instruments was forbidden to pilots without instrument ratings, and training new private pilots to do so was thought to be tantamount to encouraging them to break the law. However, as it was obvious that many pilots who got killed could have lived had they but known the fundamentals of instrument flight, basic instrument flying was inserted into the private flying curriculum.

It is perhaps hard to imagine how a pilot could get himself into instrument conditions who did not want to. A cloud is a cloud, either it is there or it is not, and either one flies into it or one doesn't; so where is the inadvertence? But clouds are in fact rather cloudy entities, of uneven solidity, in one manifestation almost as rigid and palpable as mountains, in another sinuous, shy, fickle, and elusive, grading off by imperceptible stages into a harmless morning haze. It is literally possible, in some conditions of sun and moisture, to fly into a cloud and not know it until one realizes that he has lost sight of the ground and sky. This is unusual, however. More commonly, pilots fall victim to certain illusions or to the mobility of cloud masses. You can, for instance, fly through a passage between two building cumulus clouds toward a patch of clear blue sky ahead of you, only to have the patch shrink before your eyes and vanish. Then, trying to turn back, you can find that the notch through which you entered has also disappeared, or that you cannot turn in the narrow corridor down which you are flying without plunging into its walls.

More culpably, and perhaps more commonly, you take off for a destination that is reported to have a broken ceiling; you fly above clouds, assuming that when you get there you will simply drop down through one of the breaks in the overcast. Getting there, you find that the overcast has gone solid. You do not have enough fuel to go somewhere else where there are breaks; and so you have to descend through the overcast.

In another possible scenario, you take off under a low overcast to go a short distance, perhaps at night, and fly into cloud without realizing it; or, in daylight, you are feeling your way down a road under an overcast when rising terrain forces you to turn back, and again you find that the mobility of the weather has trapped you: the open space through which you came has closed, and there is cloud and increasing rain all around you.

In every one of these cases, you brought your problem upon yourself by some initial indiscretion: perhaps an overconfident assessment of the weather or of your own abilities; perhaps a willingness to take a chance on the weather's holding or getting better rather than worse; perhaps, for all I know, a perverse desire for excitement. Whether it is possible for a completely innocent pilot to be forced into cloud against his will, I don't know, but I'm sure that, giving pilots the benefit of the doubt, it must happen.

At any rate, once you are in cloud it doesn't much matter how you got there. You have to get out, and that is what instrument flying is for.

In instrument flying, you take all your information from the instrument panel. It is very unwise to keep looking at the windows hoping for a clear spot to appear; if there is a clearing big enough to be of any use to you, you'll see it even though you're staring at the instruments. As a precaution against vertigo and spatial disorientation, you should not move your head rapidly about; if you have to turn your head, turn it slowly, and if you have to bend over, do that slowly as well. Similarly, you have to avoid rapid, spasmodic movements of the controls; everything should be done as though in slow motion. If you act hastily it is too easy to overcontrol, and rapid rolling motions will bring on sensations of rolling or plunging that are hard to combat. Above all, you must put perfect faith in your instruments; regardless of the most compelling sensations of banking, if the artificial horizon tells you that you are level and the compass does not show a turn, you must obey the artificial horizon.

The artificial horizon is the primary instrument for IFR flight; you can do without it, but when it is working it is the centerpiece of the panel. But you cannot allow yourself to become fascinated by it, and look at it and nothing else. Instead, you look all around the panel in regular, leisurely, and more or less rhythmic glances or "scans," checking the status of all the instruments. The artificial horizon is the point through which your scan always moves in passing, and from there to the compass or directional gyro. Thence you might go to altitude, to airspeed, to the engine instruments, to the clock—anything you like, so long as you keep looking at everything.

Airplanes don't take a great deal of flying. Once you have one trimmed up and pointed in the right direction, it is barely necessary to keep your hands on the controls; if it wanders from its course, it will wander gradually, and you will catch it the next time your scan comes around to the horizon and DG. A fluid, steadily moving scan is more important than quick reactions to the instruments; quick reactions only become necessary when you allow your scan to linger and do not discover a bank or a drifting heading until it is well advanced.

In basic instrument flying, you climb by increasing power or, if you are already at full throttle, by trimming the nose up gently. You descend by reducing power. You keep things simple: one input at a time. Speed will stay more or less constant. If you have to turn, you can set up a standard rate turn—that is, three degrees per second—with the needle and ball, and then check the angle of bank on the artificial horizon. Thereafter a glance at either instrument will tell you if you are holding the proper angle of bank. An airplane that holds banks, level flight, and speeds well is said to be a "good IFR platform," and most light airplanes are not bad. Most of them, too, are going so slowly that you have plenty of time to figure things out.

Figuring things out is, in fact, the big problem in flying on the gauges. Stuck in cloud, you get frightened; until you're used to it, that's automatic. Frightened, you do not perform at your best. The situation is intrinsically confusing. Whereas when you can see the world around you, you can see yourself making turns and each new heading seems to bear a certain logical relation to the last and to the surrounding world, in cloud you can't see a turn. There is no sense of turning, and so there is no sense of having turned. You always are facing the same direction, which is no direction at all. The task of navigation becomes absolutely abstract. A simple notion like "turning back," which in clear skies involves a visceral sense of turning and of heading in an opposite direction that is so powerful that you don't need any instrument at all to tell you that you have done it, in clouds is not persuasive at all, and you have simply to absorb, from the reading on your directional gyro, the abstract, purely intellectual datum of having turned.

Similarly, there is no feeling of forward progress. If your airplane has that delightful piece of equipment called DME (distance measuring equipment) aboard, you can at least see the tenths of a mile clicking off as you approach and move away from VORTACs; but otherwise you feel as still as though you were in a closet. You don't feel that you are anywhere or that you are going anywhere.

Given this uprooted state, it is easy to experience a kind of navigational despair, like a baby who finds himself in an empty room and begins screaming for his mother. I for one used positively to pine for some sense of my location when I flew IFR; a glimpse of hills, trees, and roads through a rift in the fog seemed heavenly, and restored my sense that all was well. But now I have spent hundreds of hours in clouds, sometimes many at a stretch, and I have gradually weaned myself of that reliance upon the sense of space, though I still feel, I must admit, a profound pleasure when the earth and the sky re-establish themselves in their proper places, and the runway appears at a certain bearing and distance, and possesses color, size, and proportion and all the accidents of reality. The runways of my mind, toward which I roam the directionless and claustral clouds, are never so beautiful as the first glimpse of even the homeliest of real runways, rain-wet, laced with lights beginning to glow in an early twilight, and trailing an addendum of parked planes.

IFR navigation is simply a game. There is no use, unless you possess what to me seems like awesome powers of visualization, in trying to keep a steady track of your progress. You are simply given instructions, as in a treasure hunt: proceed on a heading of such and such for 13 miles, then turn to a heading of such and such until passing this beacon, then descend to such an altitude. You do these things one at a time. Between steps there is time to plan your next moves, get ready, anticipate problems. No feel is involved, none required. Only on an ILS (instrument landing system) approach can you begin to imagine how the runway would look in front of you, were it visible, because all ILSs look pretty much the same.

Not that any of this is of much importance to a new private pilot; but it is what lies ahead. The instrument rating is the logical next goal for any new pilot who is serious about his flying. Not to get it is on the one hand to court unnecessary risks, and on the other to cut yourself off both from much of the utility of an airplane and from a profound sense of satisfaction and accomplishment. The IFR part of the private license, however scanty, is one part that I recommend that you attack with particular fervor. Learn it. Half of aviation is there.

# 10

# *Navigation*

A few years ago I drove to the edge of the Sahara at Rissani in Morocco. Here the paved road ceased. Would-be guides fell upon arriving travelers, as they did everywhere in Morocco, in this case not to show them the secrets of the medina or to take them to the excellent rug shop of their father or uncle, but to lead them to the Great Dune at dawn.

It was necessary to be led to the Great Dune, though it was only a few miles from the oasis at which the paved road ended, because the desert tracks formed an incomprehensible network of which only a tiny part was visible at any given moment. Bifurcations gave no hint of the eventual direction of alternative paths. In the heaving emptiness of the desert the shadow of a cloud appeared exactly like a field of dark stones. A stranger would have to navigate by keeping the sun in a certain quarter—if the sun had risen—and by looking back, when he was upon high ground, at the shrinking blur of the palms from which he had come. The dunes would, no doubt, be impossible to miss; the Sahara Desert is no small target. But the danger to the uninitiated tourist was that he would involve himself in a series of culs-de-sac, reversing his path, feinting right and left, until, exhausted and impatient, he permitted himself to attempt a particularly boggy stretch of sand, and got stuck. Then he would have to walk back to the palmerai under the hammerblows of the sun, engage an exorbitant savior, and suffer the humiliation of discovering that he had been, after all, only a hundred yards from the proper path.

Guides and guidebooks hinted at much more dire outcomes, just as they hinted that one could not penetrate the medina unguided at Fez or Marrakesh, most particularly not in darkness, lest one sink into the quicksand of its mazy alleys, be assaulted, dismembered, left to die, never found. (In fact, one was far more likely to be robbed, though not dismembered, in broad daylight in the shop of the guide's uncle.)

To a new pilot the sky is like that desert. Its unposted expanses seem to spill off in all directions into a vastness which even seems, as miles-deep ocean sometimes does to a person swimming beside a yacht, to exert a subtle and perilous suction. He has the sense that except for the narrow line between origin and destination, which is like a single thread stretched across an immense gulf, everything is error, disorientation, catastrophe. Even with the earth a mile below him, he feels lost in space.

The essential trick of aerial navigation is psychological. It is to abandon the sense, useful on solid ground and perhaps at sea, that certain roads lead, like elevated viaducts, across the forbidden places, and that to wander from these roads is to risk, in a way, falling off the edge irrecoverably. For the purposes of learning, the sky should be considered entirely available to the pilot. He should think of himself as possessing the whole of three-dimensional space. Insistence upon plotted courses, airways, departure routes, checkpoints, has for its pernicious by-product the unfortunate prejudice that "good" navigation consists of the best imitation the pilot can give of a railroad train, although it does have, on the other hand, the good effect of forcing students to know at all times where they are.

The underpinning of all navigation is dead reckoning (DR). The "dead" here is said to be an abbreviation of "deductive"; it has nothing to do with death, one hopes. Dead reckoning is the type of calculation that runs, "I have been flying north from point A for ten minutes at a hundred twenty miles an hour; so I must now be twenty miles north of point A." This is really all there is to it; it is so simple that one goes right by it without paying it any attention. Yet it is tremendously important; it is what one falls back on when all else fails or is not available; in other words, when one is off the beaten track. It is also the test that must be applied to all the directions given by electronic navigation devices, in the form, "Does this sound reasonable?" In other words, does it sound like what dead reckoning would require? What you read from your instrument has to make sense; if it doesn't, the instrument may be inaccurate, you may have set it up incorrectly, you may be interpreting it incorrectly. Dead reckoning supplies the measure to which everything more precise and more convenient is compared.

It works not only deductively but projectively as well: "If I fly north for ten minutes at 120, I will be there." We almost never use dead reckoning exclusively, except on overwater hops or on a certain kind of short flight where you take off, fly in the direction of your destination for twenty minutes, and then expect to catch sight of some landmark to zero in on. But it is always the underpinning of other kinds of navigation, because in the most basic way it proceeds from a known point. Radio navigation makes points as yet unreached known, nevertheless, as a lighthouse is known, though not yet reached. Dead reckoning proceeds from what we know with certainty: where we have been. It requires that we keep a certain track of heading and time. Speed is a constant; wind may be known, guessed at, or ignored, depending on the circumstances. Heading and time are the essential things. The compass and the clock sit in most panels like a couple of antiques retained only for their sentimental value. But a pilot who ignores them finds himself one day waking up, figuratively at least, from a navigational slumber and not knowing, within a hundred miles in any direction, where he is.

So you either write down or mentally note the time you take off, the time you leave some known point, the time at which you strike out over a blank space. And you look at your compass and know what it means.

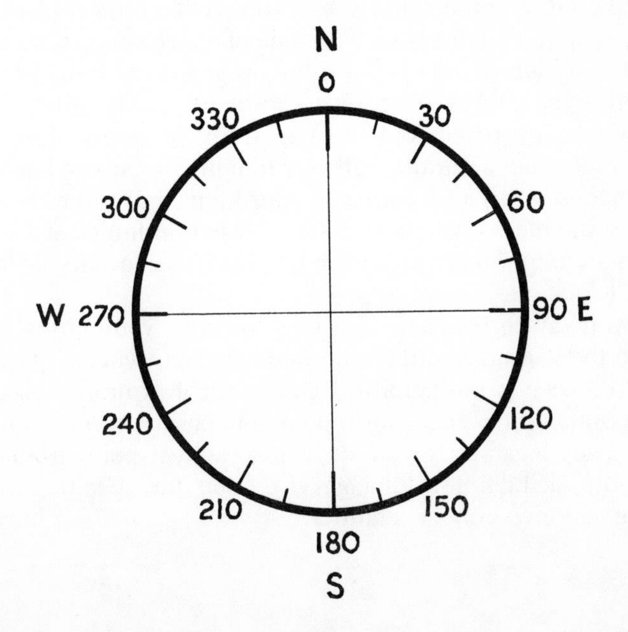


*The compass rose*

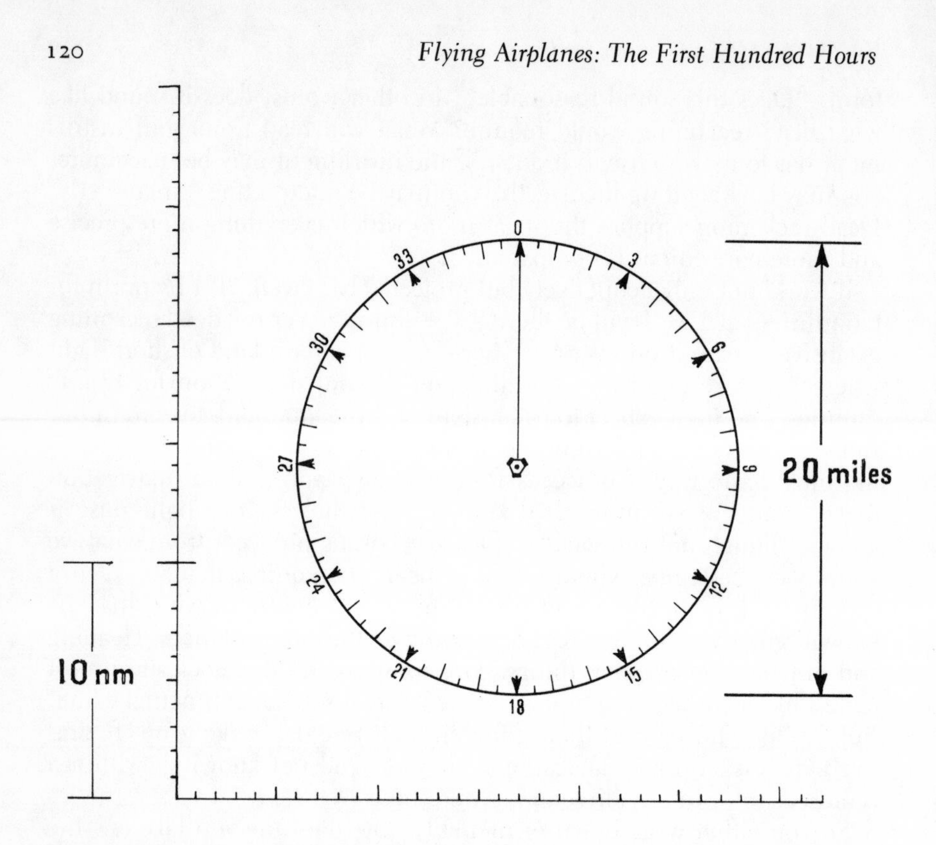


Knowing what the compass means takes a little practice. Eventually you see 240 and you think "lower left" automatically; 137, lower right; 360, up. You look at the compass and you see the little airplane crawling along the map in that direction. The rate of crawl works its way into your head too. The one-minute ticks on the up-and-down longitude lines are about a mile long; the VOR compass roses are twenty miles in diameter on Sectionals, thirty on WACs. You think in terms of two miles a minute, three miles a minute—all very roughly, because it has to be done almost unconsciously in a corner of your brain, but carefully enough to give you some idea of where you are. "Twenty minutes at 130 degrees, 115 miles an hour—that's about two compass roses toward the lower right of where I took off."

Then you say to yourself—no need to move your lips—"That little town with the stadium should be around here somewhere." That is called pilotage. Pilotage is the empirical complement of dead reckoning. DR takes you outbound from a known point; pilotage recognizes a new point, confirms your location, gives you a new known point from which to resume your deductions. Pilotage gives you the specific, while dead reckoning can give only generalities.

Pilotage contains a salting of dead reckoning. You leave the place where the railroad tracks cross from the south to the north side of the road, knowing that in a few minutes the small river will come into view. You know you are beside the railroad, but you don't know precisely where except by dead reckoning, until the landmark appears, which, in effect, cuts the line of your flight with another line and makes your position a precise point.

Basic navigation, as learned when learning to fly, begins with a chart. A destination is chosen on the grounds that it is a suitable distance away, and involves a navigational task of the right degree of difficulty and little risk. You are not at first sent into a muddle of mountains to locate a hidden strip among identical valleys.

A line is drawn on the chart and measured out. You know the speed of the airplane and its range—they are published in the operating handbook—and you see right away that the flight is possible and that it will take so and so much time; say, an hour. From notations on the chart you see the highest elevations of the terrain over which you will be passing, and select a cruising altitude. Selection of an altitude is a complex task if you care to take every variable of aircraft performance, wind, and weather into account, but for educational purposes it is sufficient to pass at least a thousand feet above obstacles and to be at least two or three thousand feet above the general terrain so that you can see a fair distance and don't get lost because of the myopia of low altitude. If you get four or five thousand feet above the ground, details begin to get harder to distinguish; sometimes, for instance, a road, a railroad, and even a buried pipeline begin to look much the same. In practice you will often fly higher than that, because you no doubt will be using radio facilities for navigation, and the higher you go, the better you receive them. As a beginner, you will probably not make much use of radio facilities, because your instructor will be trying to instill in you a proper concern for the basics to which you will have to return when your radios aren't working, as is all too often—despite their cost—the case.

Your instructor will tell you that you ought to have a good checkpoint every ten minutes, or every ten miles, or that you should be able to see your next checkpoint before you leave your previous one. It depends how conservative he is, how competent he thinks you are, and also upon the kind of terrain over which you'll be flying.

Now you study the sectional chart and try to locate a landmark every ten miles, for instance. It's not usually very difficult to find something or other, but some landmarks aren't much good. If you're flying over one of those midwestern scenes of section lines and small towns, a town is not much use in itself. There are towns all over the place, and they all look much the same. Their shapes are sometimes helpful, but it only takes a

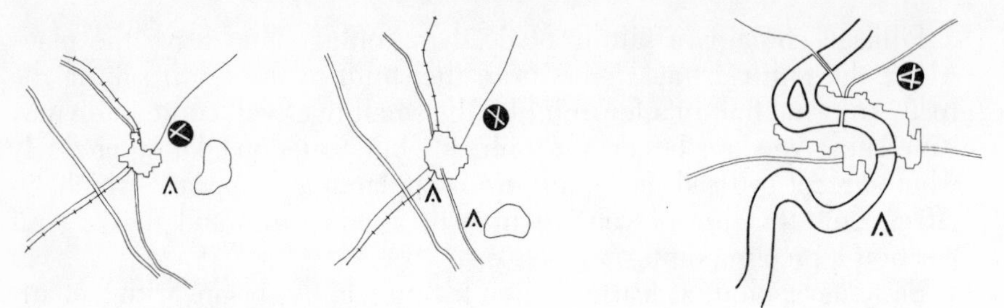

*Locating landmarks from the air can be difficult when town features such as highways, railroad tracks, airport locations, etc., are similar, as in the left-hand and center diagrams. Although the airport in the diagram at right is again to the northeast, the distinctive curve of the river and the large egg-shaped island make this city easy to spot and identify.*

developer to change the shape of a town, and cartographers are often years behind the sweep of time, tide, and real estate. You need a town with a detail. Now, the most common ones are lakes, stadiums, drive-in theaters, towers, airports, and distinctive confluences of roads, rails, and rivers. Lots of towns have these features in nearly identical combinations, but generally there is only one town in the vicinity with a stadium at the northeast side, an airport three miles west along the road with the tracks beside it, and a diagonal road heading southwest that has a funny joggle in it about two miles outside of town. Those are the sorts of marks that make identification positive; the only danger of confusion is in mistaking the compass directions, failing to grasp that if you are heading west toward a town, its north side will lie on your right. Some people have a lot of trouble relating what is on a map to what is on the ground. It's usually a problem of IQ, but with enough hard work such people may yet become innocuous pilots.

Many terrains are much more difficult. The "featureless," level Midwest is actually very easy to navigate over compared with the parallel ridges of the Appalachians, the wooded mountains of the Northwest, or the swamps and woodlands of the South. The southwestern desert, for all it may appear unpromisingly featureless, does not really present a difficult problem, so long as you are willing to follow roads and rivers and not always strike off in a straight line. Straight lines, still, are possible; sometimes a long stretch of nothing leads to a single mountain or a dry lake of particular shape, sufficiently large that you can't miss it.

In unpopulated, wooded areas, you must depend heavily on dead reckoning and on large, unmistakable landmarks—huge, oddly shaped lakes are common enough in the Southeast, for instance; you attend carefully to heading and time and fly high enough to see your landmarks even if you happen to drift askew by a few degrees.

Planning your first cross-countries—the term is generic for other than local flights, and does not imply a trip from San Francisco to Boston—you pick landmarks close together and impossible to mistake, avoiding ambiguities. Dead reckoning plays an important supporting role. If your landmarks are only five minutes apart, you can pick a certain confluence of two rivers with safety, even though there is a similar confluence twenty miles away; after a certain time, you can only have reached one, not the other. But you have to make every second or third landmark first class, unmistakable, so that you do not find yourself wandering through a series of plausible but incorrect identifications into an impasse of total non-recognition.

After a little practice with baby pilotage, you will be capable of more dramatic leaps across larger spaces; and you will also have begun using radio.

Radio navigation has a baneful, alienating effect upon the experience of flying. It makes the earth unnecessary. It is as though children (in some future world, bizarre yet no more bizarre than the present one) were provided with robot guides and audio-visual training in coping with life situations, and were thus relieved of the complication of parents. Because I would like to preach flying grounded in sensory awareness—awareness of distance, space, perspective, height, texture, time—I find myself appalled at the implications of radio, as a mother might feel appalled by ill-defined but ghastly inevitabilities when seeing her child gaze, enchanted, at a television set. Radio moves flying into the cockpit, like some egotistical mania that makes a person so self-satisfied that he never considers, or even wonders about, the thoughts of others. When you have a wire through the sky to which you can hook your airplane like an aerial tramcar and be guided effortlessly to your destination, you can turn up your nose at the earth. Even if you idly gaze out the window at the remote landscape, it means nothing to you, because you don't need it. The radio, powerful, certain, simple, unambiguous, is better than mountains, rivers, and towns. It is easier and more dependable. I inveigh against it from the position of firsthand knowledge; I am one of the fallen, and have long since ceased to regard the earth as much more than a decorative diorama in the middle of which I perform my automated tasks of radio navigation.

There are many types of radio aids; they may be divided, broadly, into those used for en route navigation and those used for instrument approaches. There is some overlap between the two categories, and there is nothing to prevent a VFR pilot from using any existing facility to help him find his position, except, of course, lack of the necessary receivers aboard the plane.

Radio terminology is full of initials. The two principal kinds of en route radio aids are VORs and NDBs. NDB means nondirectional beacon; VOR means very high frequency omnidirectional range and is often called omni. Their use is basically different, and while VOR is the more versatile and more frequently used, I'll talk about NDBs first because they are the simpler to understand.

ADF—automatic direction finder—is the cockpit receiver that is used in navigating by NDBs. An ADF needle points in the direction of an NDB or commercial broadcast station whose location is charted. In the earliest days of commercial aviation, transport companies put up strings of lights to guide their pilots across the country at night. NDBs are the radio equivalent of those lights. They operate in the frequency band just below AM radio, and in fact the AM radio band is also accessible to the ADF, so that you not only can listen to the ADF for news or entertainment while flying, but can also home in on any AM broadcast antenna whose location you know. Many of the powerful ones are charted; some are so powerful—KFI in Los Angeles, for instance—that you can pick them up hundreds of miles away, much farther than most of the strictly aeronautical beacons will carry.

NDBs radiate in all directions, like a bare light bulb, and appear the same to an ADF receiver from all sides. The receiver drives a panel indicator with a stationary symbol of an airplane and a rotating arrow; when you tune in an NDB, the arrow swings around until it points to the NDB with respect to the symbolic airplane. If it points off along the right wing, the station is off your right wing, in your three o'clock position.

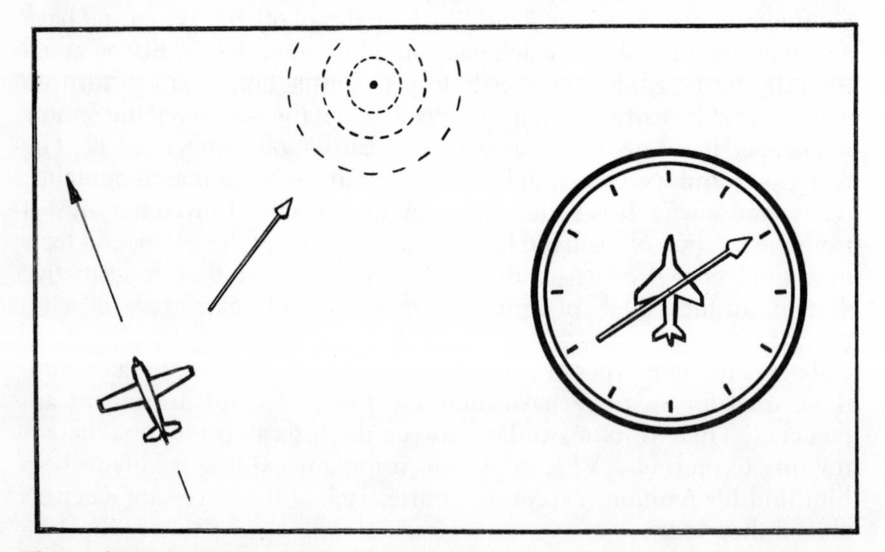

*The nondirectional beacon–NDB*

Now, if you fly in a circle and watch the ADF needle, you'll see it rotate, because it is always giving you the bearing to the NDB with respect to the nose of your airplane.

By a simple deduction, you can discover your position with respect to the beacon. Suppose you are heading due north and the ADF needle points 90 degrees to the right. The NDB is due east of you. Therefore you are due west of the NDB. You may turn about any way you like, and the reciprocal of the needle indication will be the bearing *from* the station *to* you. All you know, however, is that you are somewhere along a line radiating from the station in such and such a direction; you don't know how far away from the station you are.

To reduce your position to a single point rather than a line of possible points, you perform a "triangulation." To triangulate by ADF alone you need a second NDB, preferably located in one of the two quadrants adjacent to that in which the first NDB was located, as you will see presently. Suppose again that you are flying due north, one beacon is due east of you, and another is due south of you. If you draw a line on your map radiating due westward from the first, and due northward from the second, the unique point of their intersection is your location.

Now, it so happens that beacons are rarely ideally located, or that the indication of the ADF needle is solid and unambiguous; so if you have to find your location with ADF, you will do well to try to find three stations at least, rather than two, particularly because unless your bearing lines from two stations intersect at nearly a right angle, your position may remain somewhat uncertain. Hence the preference for beacons in neighboring quadrants. If you pick two beacons in reciprocal quadrants, or in the same quadrant, the angle of intersection of your two position lines will be so shallow that it will not give an exact position.

Normally, what you do with ADF is fly toward or away from a beacon. At least within the contiguous United States there are so many more convenient ways to determine your location than by ADF triangulation that the system is almost never used. But since a beacon is often located close to your destination or to a checkpoint, you may often find yourself turning to the direction the needle is pointing, or turning exactly away from it, in order to fly toward or away from the beacon.

The matter of tracking outbound from an NDB is a little tricky to grasp. Suppose you cross the station southbound and then want to track outward on the westbound, or 270-degree, radial. As you cross the station you make a right turn. Because you don't know you're at the station until you cross it and the needle swings around, you necessarily overshoot. So you turn right to a heading of 280 degrees (for example). The needle will point at first toward the right rear of the airplane, and then as you move away from the beacon the needle will swing closer to an indication of dead behind you. When the needle hits the point ten degrees to the right of straight backward, you turn ten degrees to the left. Your heading is now 270 degrees, as desired, and the station is directly behind you, and so you are tracking outbound on the 270-degree radial of the station.

At first the principle may seem difficult to understand, and once you have understood it on paper it's hard to put into practice, because you have to juggle a forest of bearings—your bearing from the station, the station's bearing from you, your desired bearing, your desired heading, your intercept heading, and your intercept angle. The intercept angle is the difference between your intercept heading and your desired heading; it will be suddenly canceled by a turn at the proper moment. Most private pilots don't have the faintest idea of how to track outbound from an NDB, and they never miss the information, so there is no cause for alarm if the whole subject seems dark as night.

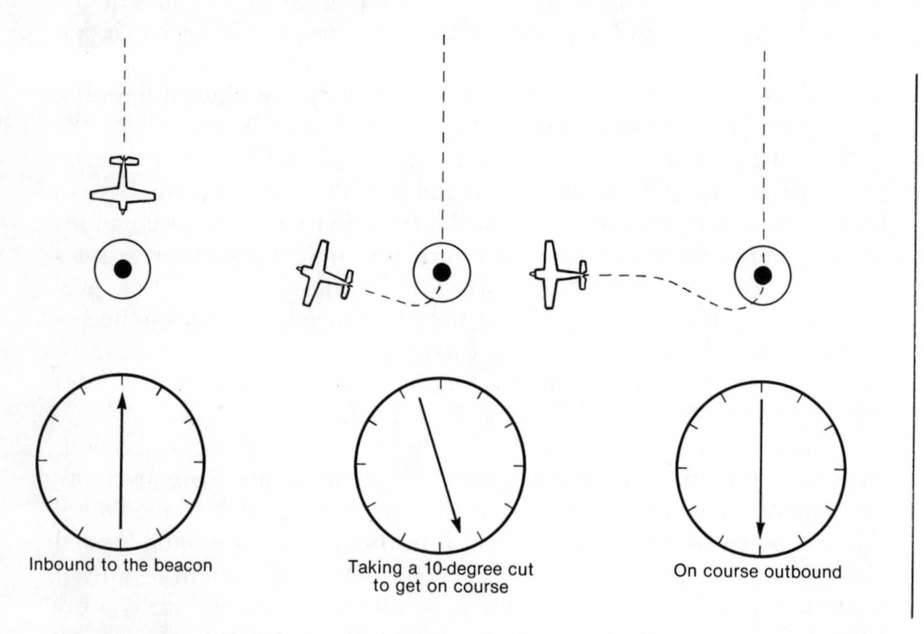


*Navigating with the ADF*

What is more necessary, and requires that you bring it at least to a twilit understanding, is the operation of the VOR. It is the universal navigation system today, and will be for a long time to come; it is very precise and comparatively immune to the distortions of night and landscape that can make ADF an uncertain proposition. It has nothing much in common with ADF, so don't try to understand it as a variant of ADF. It works quite differently, and to understand it, start from scratch.

Think of a huge flat space, paved (this should be easy), with markings painted on the ground. The markings consist of lines radiating, like the spokes of a wheel, from certain points. The points are quite far apart, and the radiating lines are only of a certain length, after which they die out. Imagine now that each point's lines are of a certain color, different from the others; and finally, imagine that each radial line has its compass bearing from its point of origin written all along it, so that no matter where you stood along that line you could read which radial it was, and from its color tell from which point it was coming. There are enough of these points of origin, and the radiating lines are long enough, so that at any point on this huge parking lot you can see lines of at least two colors crisscrossing at your feet.

Suppose, finally, that you have a map reproducing the arrangement of the points of origin, and telling you their identifying colors. Now, to find your location, you have but to look at the ground and pick out two lines of different colors that intersect at your feet. One, let's say, is red and marked "331-331-331-331"; the other is blue and marked "28-28-28-28-28." You look at your map, find the 331-degree radial of Point Red and the 28-degree radial of Point Blue, and where they cross is where you stand.

In the sky all this takes place in the invisible reaches of the electromagnetic spectrum, but your VOR receiver is able to distinguish all the

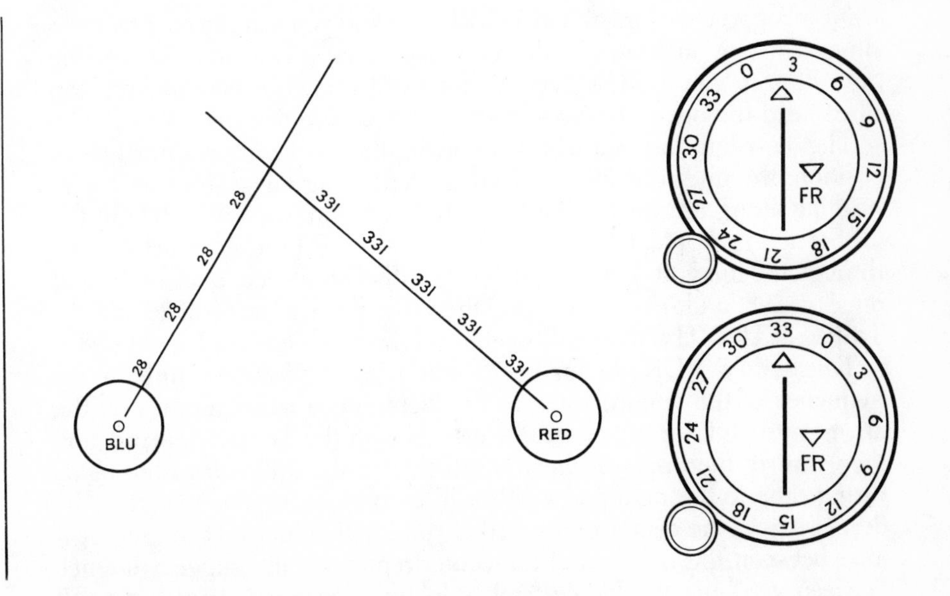


*Navigating by VOR*

radial lines of ground stations from one another, and to separate one station from all others by means of its frequency, just as your car radio tells one broadcast station from another.

The VOR display in the cockpit consists of a window with a vertical needle that can move side to side like a windshield wiper. There is a knob called the OBS (omni bearing selector) that you turn to select radials; when you are in fact upon the radial that you selected the needle is centered.

The needle can also tell you whether the selected radial would be to your right or to your left if you were moving either directly toward or directly away from the station.

That's the tough part. What you have to get through your head, and it isn't easy, is that the needle indication refers not to your actual heading, but to either of two reference headings, namely, To or From the station. There's a so-called To-From flag on the instrument face to tell one from the other.

Let's go back to that parking lot for a moment. You can stand at a certain point—Red 331/Blue 28, for instance—and you can jump up and down or turn around in circles, and you will still be at the same point. The instrument indications won't change; unlike the ADF needle, which points to the station from the airplane, and so turns when the airplane turns (but in the opposite direction), the VOR needle, in effect, points to the airplane from the station.

Now suppose you are at Red 331/Blue 28 and you want to go directly to Blue. You are on Blue's 28-degree radial. That means that the bearing *from* Blue *to* you is 28 degrees. So for you to go from here to Blue you must head the opposite way—28 plus 180, or 208 degrees.

The To-From flag is a way of resolving the ambiguity of your line of position; the line runs 28/208 degrees, depending on which way you're heading along it, and the To-From flag lets you know which way the OBS reading would take you. If you rotate the bearing selector knob through the full 360 degrees, the needle will center twice, once on 28 and once on 208, and, in our example, the From flag will be up at 28 and the To flag at 208. The flags will switch at OBS readings of 118 and 298.

To go to a VOR station from your present position, tune in the frequency of the station, listen to the identifier to make sure it's on the air, turn the OBS until the needle centers with the To flag showing, and then turn to the displayed heading. If the needle drifts off to the right, turn a little to the right and wait for it to come back. The needle is the desired track, the center of the dial is you. Remember that the space, if any, between the needle and the center represents the angular distance between you and the desired track. Making a heading correction won't immediately move the needle, but the needle will swing back toward the center as you close the space between you and your desired track.

If you are at a station and want to fly away from it in a certain direction, turn the OBS to that direction with the From flag showing. If the needle is on the left, turn to a heading that will carry you toward a track to your left with an intercept angle of 30 degrees or so (the choice of angle is a matter of experience) and wait for the needle to swing to the center.

You might have noticed that neither ADF nor VOR provides you with cross-track navigational ability—what is called area navigation ability, for lack of a more descriptive term. In other words, you can only track to and from stations, but not along randomly chosen lines. For quite a few thousand dollars you can buy a device called an Rnav, which is no more than a computer programmed to triangulate constantly on VOR stations and display your position on a normal VOR indicator in relation to a fictional VOR station that you put wherever you want it. Suppose, for instance, that you want to fly to a certain airport which is 38 miles south of one VOR station on the 187-degree radial, or is at the intersection of that radial and the 043-degree radial of some other VOR. You program the computer with that information, and by processing the signals it gets from the reference stations it synthesizes an imaginary station right at your destination, and makes the OBS needle behave as though it were guiding you there.

Even without this rather costly navigation aid, however, you can more or less do the same task yourself by falling back on your old and long neglected helpmate, dead reckoning. You don't have the convenience of a needle to show you the way; but you can take a series of triangulations off convenient VORs and make course corrections accordingly, dead reckoning as you go. The task is in itself simple, and is complicated only by the inconvenience of doing plotting chores in the cockpit where there is no room to unfold a chart nor a desk top upon which to draw lines and take bearings.

Apart from understanding the significance of the VOR display, and appreciating the difference between it and an ADF display, you have to know how to fly the display. You don't fly the needle; you fly the airplane toward or away from the needle. This is important, because there may be a long lag between your making a heading correction and the needle's starting to center, especially if you're far away from the station. Turning to intercept a radial is colloquially called "taking a cut" at the radial. The angle of interception depends on your distance from the station and how much of a hurry you're in. The deflection of the needle from center represents an angle, remember, not a distance. Close to the station a large deflection may represent a distance of only a few hundred yards; fifty miles from the station, the same deflection represents miles. If, for example, you have determined from your map that the place you want to go is 17 miles from Zorro (ZOR) VOR on the 071 radial, and you are now five miles southeast of Zorro, you needn't fly to ZOR and start outbound from there. From inspection, as we used to say in geometry class of things that were self-evident, if you fly northward you will pass east of ZOR, but intersect the 071 radial somewhere less than 17 miles away from the station. You tune your OBS to 071 From; the needle will go over to the left side of the indicator, because if you were going away from the station, the radial would be on your left. (That is one way to think of the To/From flag: "If I were going To, or From, the station, the radial on the OBS would lie to the left, or right.") In this case the intercept angle does not concern you at all, but it will be about 70 degrees—an unusually sharp cut. Suppose, on the other hand, that you have arrived at ZOR on a heading of 100 degrees, passed the station, and then belatedly started your turn to intersect the 071 radial. You are a mile or so past the station, and the needle, when you reset the OBS to 071, swings over to the left. Now you would take a shallower cut at the radial, because you are not far away from it, and you have about 16 miles in which to reach it. Obviously, if you have flown a mile past your intended turning point on a heading 30 degrees to the right of the proper one, you can't be more than about a half mile to the right of course. You turn left past 071 degrees to perhaps 040 or 050 and wait for the needle to move in from the left edge of the indicator, which it will start to do in a short time.

Geometrically speaking, you could take a smaller cut, say 10 degrees, and the intercept would take a little longer but still occur in time. However, for everyday purposes a cut of 15 or 20 degrees is a reasonable minimum because of the cumulative error that can be introduced by wind, compass error, directional gyro precession, and VOR error. In other words, while a two-degree cut would be adequate to make a half mile course correction in 16 miles, such precise aim is nearly impossible. In real life, nonfanatical pilots might remain unaware of 5 degrees each of wind drift, compass or DG error, and VOR error, and there is a chance—one in sixty-four—that they would all be cumulative.

Ordinary day VFR navigation in the United States is done with heavy reliance on VOR, which is made irresistible by its convenience. Since VOR radials are geometrically straight lines, they relieve the pilot of having to concern himself with wind drift and, indeed, even with his heading; if he has a very simple autopilot, as many airplanes do, he can couple the autopilot to a VOR and leave his hands in his lap; the airplane will fly along the radial as though on rails.

The charts used for instrument flying present no topographical information to speak of; they show only the locations and frequencies of radio facilities and those lines connecting them in an irregular web which have been consecrated with the names of airways. But since these charts are smaller and easier to handle in the cockpit than so-called VFR charts, many instrument pilots use them when flying VFR to the exclusion of the cumbersome Sectional and WAC charts. Various private publishers offer compromise chart systems intended to combine VFR and IFR information in a manageable format; many state aeronautical departments publish charts of their state, usually giving more comprehensible relief information than the official charts.

Alternative chart systems exist because WAC (world aeronautical chart) charts, which are drawn on a scale of 1:1,000,000 (about 16 statute miles to an inch), are too cramped to contain topographical information sufficiently detailed for low-level nonradio VFR navigation, and Sectionals, at 8 miles to the inch, have the information but are tremendous things, monumentally difficult to handle gracefully in the cockpit. Thirty-seven of them are required for the contiguous United States alone. Whence the duty, made incumbent on all novice pilots, of plotting their intended route in pencil upon the chart, marking headings, distances, and times—recording, in short, a superfluity of information. Once all this work has been done, the chart can be unfolded in the cockpit a bit at a time, disclosing each portion of the route as one reaches it.

When they teach you, a student pilot, to mark up your charts and fill out dozens of squares on a flight log form, they may neglect to add that few experienced pilots do the same. A few do; I know one fellow whose accountant suggested that he keep a detailed log of every flight to help him write off his airplane as a business expense, and who had printed up a fantastically detailed form which he fills out on every flight, recording not only the details of his route but also all the engine instrument readings, fuel consumption, weather en route, and so on. He is a calculating sort of a person, however, who may get more pleasure from spinning numbers out of his calculator than from tuning in a rock station on his ADF. Most pilots determine the distance and approximate heading to their eventual destination, grab the necessary WACs, Sectionals, or IFR charts, take off, and then start planning the flight.

This may seem like "poor preflight planning," but it's real life. All the instruction in detailed trip planning is simply intended to make you aware of navigational problems. Rough solutions to all of them can be gotten in the cockpit. Headings, for instance, do not have to be calculated by measuring the course line against a meridian with a protractor and then adding or subtracting the magnetic deviation; you can simply visualize the course line, mentally move it sideways on the chart until it passes over a VOR compass rose, and read the heading from the rose. The magnetic deviation will be taken care of automatically. Distances yield to similar shortcuts; instead of measuring a crinkled map half collapsed across your knees with a ruler, just figure that one minute of arc—one of the ticks on the north-south meridian lines—is equal to one nautical mile, and using the span of your fingers, or a pencil, or the edge of another chart as a comparator, measure the distance you want to know against the meridian. IFR charts are convenient this way; they have all the distances between VORs printed on the chart. You can pick up discarded IFR charts easily, since they are constantly being updated and replaced.

You will discover in your early navigating that aviation operates on a confused double standard of statute and nautical miles. The nautical mile, which is equal to 1.15 statute miles, is used as a standard for IFR flight, and along with it the unit of speed called the knot, which is equal to one nautical mile per hour. (There is no etymological connection between "knot" and "naut," but both derive from the maritime world, as does the word "navigation." Furthermore, it is incorrect to speak of "knots per hour.") Advertisers of airplanes dislike knots because speeds in knots are numerically smaller than the same speed expressed in miles per hour, and they would rather advertise their 200-mile-per-hour than their 174-knot airplane, albeit the same machine. Many pilots never escape the tyranny of the mile per hour, so familiar from everyday life; only years of IFR flying make knots equally familiar, though it seems to me, still, that the words "miles per hour" still slide by me in a blur, slanted, as though on whirling wheels, while "knots" lies before me like a sodden heap of rope on a ship's deck.

From snobbism, magazines like *Flying*, after interminable discussion, have adopted the knot as a standard, after going through some grotesque periods of adjustment in which fixed-gear airplanes flew in miles per hour and the rest in knots. The knot, because of its association with instrument flying, is considered professional, and since most magazines hope by sloughing off every scrap of amateurism to best court the advertisers' dollars, they lean to the more professional, but boring and confusing, unit. Some fleeting mention is always made of the golden age to come in which we will at last convert to the metric system, and that same 174-knot, 200-mile-per-hour airplane will suddenly spurt ahead at 325 kilometers per hour. In truth, however, because of American leadership in air traffic control, even European countries now use the knot (which European pilots laboriously convert into kilometers per hour when they want to *feel* a speed).

The bottom margin of VFR charts is given over to three distance scales (statute miles, nautical miles, kilometers), which because of their contiguity are endlessly confusing. The comprehensibility of plotters—the short-lived plastic rulers you use to measure off your courses on charts—is similarly sacrificed to the multiple standard, though kilometers are here mercifully omitted. Between two kinds of miles and two scales of charts, VFR plotters contain so many possibilities of error that they resemble those swinging doors, both marked "pull," one of which is always locked, so that you make three vain attempts to open them for every one that succeeds.

Between their cumbersome size and the wealth of opportunities for error that their scales offer, VFR charts cannot be very handily used for plotting a course in the cockpit. They can be used, but not *handily*. If you have VORs to show the way, then you don't have much to worry about; if you have to strike out across open country for any distance, it can be very helpful to have drawn a course line across the chart. When you have to go from one chart to another or, worse, from one side of a chart to another, you have to do an elaborate little song and dance, explained on the margin of the chart, which is nearly hopeless in flight.

However, one should not succumb too completely to the tyranny of straight lines. Zigzags and jogs may not be the shortest distance between points, but they are not so much longer as you might think. A trip executed entirely in 15-degree jogs back and forth across the straight route is only 3.5 percent longer than one flown optimally along the divine straight line. On a 300-mile trip, to put it another way, you can go to a point 40 miles to either side of your straight route, and only increase the trip length by 10 miles. So there is very little reason to shun small doglegs that offer the convenience of unmistakable checkpoints or VORs. Most instructors appreciate this point, if only because they are reluctant to have students disappear in search of an invisible landmark that happens to lie upon a straight line. We are not rulers, after all; there is no reason why we should not fly crookedly.

A well-developed tolerance for crookedness comes in handy when weather complicates your navigational task, as it all too often will. Weather presents several problems to the VFR pilot. One is its uncertain nature; another is the lack of clarity of the boundaries between passable and impassable weather; a third, and the simplest and most obvious, is that it obscures visibility and, one way or another, interferes with basic pilotage. Weather does not, of course, interfere with radio navigation; and many pilots, forgetting or ignoring the fact that a VFR flight has to end with a VFR arrival by pilotage, not radio guidance, have flown hundreds of miles over the tops of clouds, to find that the holes they had counted on finding at their destination were not there.

IFR pilots use a set of rather simple procedures for dealing with weather, the simplicity of the procedures increasing in proportion to the pilot's dedication to instrument flying. When they encounter scattered clouds they usually climb over them, their general commitment being to radio navigation and therefore to the higher altitudes. If the weather begins to look quite doubtful, they air-file IFR—a remarkably simple procedure that enables you to continue straight on as though the weather were not there. If the weather clears later, they cancel, most likely, on the general principle that VFR is slightly more expeditious than IFR.

If you don't fly IFR, you have to wage more of a war with the weather. You can't just ignore it. It is an adversary whose forces you must measure, and which you must then outwit, or to which capitulate, as your judgment dictates.

IFR pilots, who have on the whole forgotten the days of hedgehopping along roads and rivers in rain under a low overcast, have the impression that half of all VFR flights must be abandoned because of weather. Not at all. VFR pilots will tell you that they don't cancel more than two or three flights in a year because of weather. The truth is probably somewhere in between; not that VFR pilots are consciously lying about their cancellations, but they unconsciously don't plan to make flights on which success is doubtful, and forget to include those flights that were canceled days in advance, with other plans conveniently made. It is only the trip canceled in the middle of nowhere, when you have to spend a day or two in a small town where you don't know anybody, that impresses you as a cancellation due to weather. (The loneliness and nostalgia of those motels and coffee shops, the remoteness of the waitresses, the void of those streets, the rain in the lamplight and the weather posters on the TV before which a narcotizing camera slowly shakes its head in disbelief! What curious longings arise in the expanded time of strange places; what a pallid blend of restlessness and despair.)

A beginner has to set himself some fairly narrow limits, or he will sooner or later scare himself and his companions badly. Or get killed; weather is one of the most popular excuses for getting killed in airplanes.

A person with only the ordinary sublunary understanding of the weather is liable to think of it as congealing and evaporating out of thin air. Flying, you quickly come to see that while weather does form and dissipate, it much more often simply arrives and departs. Storm tracks across the United States almost always run from the northwest down, then swing eastward and leave the country toward the northeast. They may make excursions into a million different subroutines in this process, but the general direction of motion, like that of a pendulum swinging across the country, appears again and again. Oregon gets the storm, then California, then the mountain states, and so on; or else it swings down out of Canada across the Great Plains or, worse, across the Great Lakes, picking up moisture as it goes. Weather is produced by differences of moisture content and temperature, and propelled by differences of pressure. As stop-motion satellite film sometimes shows, the swirling motions of the weather are quite similar to those of eddies of water in a stream. There may be layers and masses at different temperatures which are reluctant to mix, and instead overrun one another; at their surfaces of contact, condensation and precipitation occur. The mechanisms of weather are simple enough, but the combinations in which they occur, particularly with the admixture of terrain effects, are fantastically numerous. An extremely seasoned pilot might expect to foresee, down to the position of individual clouds, the weather in areas through which he has flown regularly for years; but send him a few hundred miles away with a weather report, and his prefigurements will be nothing but the wildest guesswork. For every time that a gap magically appears in the clouds over the airport of our destination, there will presumably be another when the only fog bank for miles settles right upon that same airport (although often airports are located with a certain regard for local weather, above the fog line or in the place that clears first in midmorning). The VFR pilot, deprived of the almost universal solvent of instrument capability, must navigate through weather as though the weather itself were part of the landscape—a treacherous part that cannot be charted.

It may be clear where you take off and cloudy fifty miles away; so good weather at the point of departure can never be used as an excuse for not getting a destination and en route forecast. If the destination is reliably clear or scattered, you can fly on top of an overcast while en route, relying on radio or dead reckoning for your position. If the destination has broken clouds, you have to know the trend before taking a chance by going on top: are the clouds building or dissipating? Sometimes the answer is simple: coastal stratus decks break up as the day goes on, and postfrontal broken conditions tend to be stable or, at any rate, not to go solid for long periods.

In moist postfrontal weather, clouds will form on the upwind side of rising ground and ridges, sometimes building up twenty or thirty miles ahead of a ridge. For navigation by pilotage, therefore, you would want to plan a route on the lee side of mountains after a frontal passage, even though it is likely to be the more turbulent area.

Flying under cloud decks close to the ground is in some ways quite easy, and usually enjoyable. Your view of the ground is least like what the map shows, however, and you must be particularly careful in selecting checkpoints that will be recognizable from all sides and perhaps at a distance, without ambiguity. Checkpoints that lie athwart your route of flight are best; if you are somewhat to the right or left of your intended course, you will still cross them. Attention to distance and time is particularly important. You can usually make some estimate of the wind direction and intensity by scrutinizing trees, bodies of water, smoking chimneys, and the direction of slanting rain (the wind is blowing in the direction toward which the *top* of the column of rain is leaning); fudge your guess at the wind into your groundspeed estimate, and time your checkpoint passages with care until you have a consistent groundspeed. Then estimate your time for each upcoming checkpoint. They will march into view with a regularity and predictability that is both gratifying and encouraging.

Low flying in bad weather is best done along roads or rivers or rails; considerable excursions from a direct course are justifiable for the sake of following an unmistakable path.

What happens, however, if the path leads into worsening weather?

If you are flying across an area of showers and low ceilings toward a destination that you know for a fact to be experiencing fair or fairer weather, you can reasonably go on flying right through heavy rain if you are sure of the terrain ahead, or if it is flat and undeveloped enough not to present major obstacles. It is better to follow a planned course straight through rainshowers than to be led off course toward areas of brightness and apparently better weather. It is nearly impossible to dead reckon on a randomly wandering course, and a bright area is not much use to you if, once you reach it, you have to turn back to a dark area to resume the direction toward your destination.

It is acceptable to fly between hills whose tops are in cloud, but only if you know the way intimately or the other side is bright and offers good visibility over descending terrain. What you want to avoid is flying into a cul-de-sac and then losing your way out. This is most likely to happen when you are flying across a line of weather that is moving toward you, because if you turn around you are now flying back toward an area that was in good weather when you passed through it, but which will have worsened since. This situation does not require a grand stage for its action to unfold; in a couple of minutes you can fly into a dead end among hills and rain, turn around, and find your escape blocked by more hills and rain. Remember that a given piece of weather might look passable when you head through it in one direction, and impassable when you turn and try to get through it in the opposite direction, merely because of different angles of illumination or perspectives upon the surrounding landscape.

There is, finally, among the already difficult hazards of navigating through heavy weather, the additional and particularly treacherous one of man-made obstacles—paticularly treacherous because, very often, they are hard to see. Transmission towers, which are normally studded with flashing lights, are supported by guy wires that are not illuminated and that will slice an airplane's wing right off. Narrow valleys are occasionally crossed by high-tension or telephone lines. Most obstacles are charted, but I would hesitate to trust my life to the reporting and charting procedure for new obstacles, whatever it may be.

The great difference in VFR weather flying is made by your knowledge or ignorance of the terrain. If you're flying 75 miles across a stretch of familiar land to a destination whose landmarks you know so well that you never even need a compass, let alone a chart, to find it, any more than you need a road map to find your own home, then you can make the trip in horrible weather with perfect ease. You could fly safely, albeit illegally, below VFR minimums, without even feeling uneasy. But exactly the same flight might be too much for a stranger to the region, even in much better weather. When you *know* the landscape—and pilots get to know the magnified landscape that lies open to an airplane just as hikers know the trail from the cabin to the stream—navigation becomes unconscious. You do not measure, time, take aim, consult charts; rather, from the moment you take off, you feel the destination, its presence is known to you as you know the direction from which a sound comes, without the intervention of thought or reasoning. You select a heading without knowing why, and, always to your surprise, you emerge over the last line of hills pointing directly at the airport.

If you have to fly a zigzag course over unknown terrain—making a series of deviations around rainshowers, for instance—the chances of getting lost are excellent. You can restore a semblance of order to your wanderings by remembering the following highly compressed table of sines: if you turn 20 degrees to your intended course, you will fly one third of a mile away from your plotted course line for every mile you go; 30 degrees, one half a mile; 40 degrees, two thirds of a mile; and 50 degrees, three fourths of a mile. A 60-degree deviation takes you almost seven eighths of a mile from your course for every mile you fly, and you may as well consider any greater deviation than that a right angle. If you have any knack at all for mental mathematics, you can convert these figures into miles per minute. For instance, if your airplane flies at 120 miles per hour, and you make a 40-degree deviation to the left for four minutes to get around a shower, your cross-track distance will be 4 × 2 × ⅔ (four minutes, two miles a minute, two thirds of a mile per mile) or just over five miles. A 40-degree turn to the right will make you parallel your course; another 20-degree turn to the right will let you intercept your original course in about 8 minutes.

The miles-per-minute approximation of your airplane's speed is extremely handy for rough navigation; but a speed that does not lend itself to mental arithmetic—135 mph, for instance—can still be set into a pilot's computer and the mile values of times flown read off immediately. If this rigmarole of cross-track distances and times seems excessively pedantic, it is because you have not experienced the ease with which one can get lost in the air, and the awful feeling of helplessness that comes over you when you do. You may be only a few miles from some recognizable point; but if you can't locate it, you may as well be on Saturn. I flew for many years—twelve, to be exact—and covered a hundred fifty thousand miles in the United States and Mexico before my turn came to get lost; and I know that prior to that experience I would have rolled my eyes in condescending intolerance of anyone who had suggested to me that in making course deviations around weather, I should keep a running tab of my position, and even turn in increments of 10 degrees (20, 30, 40, 50, etc.) and fly those headings for certain numbers of whole minutes, eliminating fractions in the interest of a precise knowledge of my whereabouts.

I was flying my plane Melmoth from Flores, Guatemala, to Guatemala City with Nancy, my perennial companion; it was in the late summer of 1974. We had taken off in the afternoon. Probably I could have gotten a thorough weather briefing, but did not because of the language problem and because the farther you get into Central America, the more you begin to regard the formally consecrated aeronautical procedures as a lot of silly hocus-pocus, so great is the disparity between the pretensions of the flight plan filing system and the reality of the broken-down runways, the disintegrating DC-3s that serve them, and the capricious radio beacons that tell the way. The weather was good at Flores and good at Guatemala City; so we took off. There was a VOR at Guatemala City, and a couple of NDBs along the way; but since the airplane had no ADF at that time, the trip would have to be made by dead reckoning until we picked up Guatemala City VOR.

Now, for some reason I had a chart that extended halfway down Guatemala, but only a tourist office road map for the bottom portion of the country; and an IFR chart that provided the frequencies and headings I needed, but no relief data.

As we flew southwestward over the jungle from Flores, we soon found ourselves over a layer of scattered stratus clouds of a grayish, nondescript sort; and a thin, high overcast cast a shadow over everything. Scattered layers in cool, moist weather are suspect; they may convert themselves rapidly into broken layers and solid overcasts.

It seems to me now that I had no idea, or only the vaguest inkling, that Guatemala City was ringed with mountains about thirteen thousand feet high; but as we flew toward that fortification it was quite obvious that we would not be able to cross it: towering cumulonimbus buildups rose to twenty or thirty thousand feet, burying the entire ridge.

It seemed that we might swing around the western edge of this wall, and I kept deviating more and more to the west as we got closer and closer to the cloud barrier; finally I realized that we were flying northwest, not southwest, and would never reach Guatemala City at this rate. More or less all at once, I realized that we were not going to reach Guatemala City, that it was getting pretty late in the day, that we were getting low on fuel—just a couple of hours left, and the gauges were very imprecise—and that I did not know where we were.

I turned back northeastward toward Flores. But where was Flores, and where were we? The meandering rivers below did not correspond to those on my touristic road map; for that matter, there were no roads, only virgin jungle, for a hundred miles in all directions, so there is no reason why the map should have troubled itself about this region at all. It may as well have shown a breaching whale and said, "Here there be dragons."

The jungle was vast, undifferentiated, featureless, except for its serpentine rivers which, for all I knew, might change their courses every year. The thin overcast had thickened and, worse, the little wisps of stratus that had pebbled the sky below us on our outbound course had grown now to a half-broken condition. Such a sky impedes pilotage; you can see well enough close to you, but at an angle the gaps between the individual clouds diminish and disappear, and you can see the ground no better than you can see the sidewalk in the distance as you look down a street crowded with pedestrians. Not that there was anything to see.

It would be dark in an hour; we would run out of fuel in two, unless I reduced power so that we could crawl around in the dark over the jungle for three or four hours before sputtering down into the trees. Without the ability to receive Flores NDB, we could only find the airport by finding the big lake that lay beside it.

Not having kept any record of angles and times during our progressive divagations from the desired track, I could only gaze at the map with the same blank surmise as an aborigine who has never seen a map before and does not know its function. I traced a curving line from our last known position hooking to the west and then the northwest—how far to hook, how sharply, I didn't know, but I had some idea—twenty minutes, perhaps half an hour, forty, fifty degrees off course, then ninety degrees. Picking almost at random a position that I posited to be our present one, I took a heading from that point toward the lake, and started the forty-minute wait for the lake to come into view between the clouds.

I explained the situation to Nancy. We had parachutes in the airplane; it was new then and I was still afraid it might fall apart in the air. I said that if worse came to worst we could always bail out. This was like telling someone that if worse came to worst, we could always amputate from the waist down. She began to scrutinize the jungle for landing places. Surprisingly, there were a few—a clearing on the bank of a river, a sandbar, the river itself, an occasional unexplained gap in the trees. She thought it would be better to make a controlled landing and hope to be rescued than to jump out in semidarkness at the last moment, and risk injury and separation. Her reasoning was impeccable; in fact, unknown to her, it was the classical reasoning of books on air-crash survival. Naturally, however, I was not in a hurry to crash the airplane, which I had just worked five years to build, in some trackless jungle if there was the slightest chance of getting back to safety in it. Nancy suspected my motives. She knew that I nourished puerile fantasies of survival and that in some corner of my mind the idea of parachuting into the jungle with a handy-dandy all-climate survival kit clutched in one fist was seductive to me. It would certainly solve forever the problem of what to talk about at parties.

She did not persuade me to dump the airplane, and in forty minutes Flores hove into view. We were heading right toward it.

In aviation, anticlimax is welcome. The only price of my indifferent navigating was half an hour's anxiety. But if I had not made such a lucky guess of a return heading—or, to put it perhaps in another light, if I had not been aware at least to the extent that I was of how far we had gone and in what direction—we could easily have ended up crashing in the jungle.

Not all the world is jungle, and if you get lost in Nebraska you risk nothing worse than a landing in a cornfield and a few words with a solicitous or irate farmer, as the case may be. But there is almost nothing for which the modern day pilot is worse prepared than an off-airport landing, and he will go to fantastic lengths to avoid making one; even, it seems, to the length of running out of fuel while hoping to find a genuine, government-approved airport. Losing track of where you are produces a sense of yawning apprehension which may lead you to make foolish decisions, or even to panic. Best, therefore, not to get lost, even in the most hospitable surroundings.

Most instructors will tell you that you should know at all times exactly where you are. I suppose I agree in principle, but I know that most of the time I "know" only in the sense that a Ph.D. "knows" all about his field—he knows where to look things up. This is a consequence of using IFR procedures while VFR or, worse, IFR charts. An excellent argument can be made for always knowing exactly where you are; you're never lost, in the first place, and in the event of an emergency you can consult the chart instantly for nearby airports, terrain height, and so on. This consideration could be particularly important at night. In fact, however, most pilots don't fly that way, and I think that beginners should at least be aware that the seemingly exaggerated demands made by their instructors will be relaxed when they go off on their own.

For training purposes, instructors will sometimes have you spend every spare moment scanning the ground for suitable emergency landing places. This is a little like driving the freeway in constant search of a place to swerve if all your tires go flat at once or your transmission falls out. We routinely fly single-engine planes over terrain and in conditions of weather and darkness, where a forced landing would be extremely dangerous or, at the very least, extremely uncertain. So it is unreasonable, in fair weather, to torment ourselves over where to land if the engine quits. For training, however, you *do* torment yourself, since the instructor might pull the power on you at any moment and tell you to prepare for a dead-stick landing; and the effect of this is to make you think about what you would do at all times, until all the answers—and there are only just so many of them—are planted in your unconscious like the multiplication tables. Then, if you are flying along one day reading a paperback and the engine quits, you will be able to dog-ear the page you are reading so as not to lose your place, lay the book aside, give one sweeping look to the surrounding terrain, and recognize instantly the road, riverbed, or ridge that you have prepared for, in training or imagination, countless times.

That scenario does remind me, however, of one reflection that has crossed my mind many times when I was flying in Baja California or in Canada or Alaska, where rescue did not seem likely to arrive soon were I forced down. I have thought that I ought to try to keep track, somehow or other, in my mind, of the principal features of the terrain around me, always updating my observations and discarding those which pertained to the landscape fifty miles behind me, so that if I did have to land, I would know which way to travel to reach a river, a valley, a road, or a settlement. For all that it sounded easy, however, I think that it would be very hard to do. The last minute of a forced landing would be a hectic time, with turns and adjustments occupying your attention to the exclusion of other things; and when you stepped out of your crumpled plane on a brushy hilltop, I doubt that the simple map of stream, ridge, lake, and road which presented itself to you while you were airborne would reconstruct itself easily now that you were on unfamiliar ground, wondering which mountain was which, seeing the sun go down, feeling a cold wind start to blow.

Nevertheless I must repeat, first, that it would be a good idea to know exactly where you are all the time; and, second, that a lot of people don't. IFR, of course, you know, if you have a DME, "exactly" where you are. Eighteen miles east of Otto. But that information is only good so long as you keep going; if you suddenly have to land, it isn't much good unless you have been following your progress on a VFR chart, which few instrument pilots do. Without DME, positions are "known" in terms of intersecting VOR radials or estimated times to the station—knowledge also quite different in nature from that which you have when you constantly look from your map to your window and back to your map. The two ways of "knowing" your position are essentially different; the difference is like that between a name in the phone book and a face in the crowd, if you're looking for somebody to kiss.

I've been lost many times, but the only time that seemed to matter was the one in Guatemala. It gave me a new sense of the meaning, and the indispensability, of dead reckoning. Other times have been less grave. Once, somewhere in Iowa or Indiana, I had to drop down to read the sign on a water tower; another time, over Los Angeles (this will give you some idea of the size of the city), I had to drop down to read freeway signs, and another time I landed at night upon a lighted runway that happened to present itself, in order to find out where I was, and not get still worse lost. A relative of mine once landed on a road in bad weather, taxied up to a house, asked directions to the nearest airport, and took off and flew to it. This occurred during the seventies, not the twenties. Flying eastward across the Pacific, I missed my first checkpoint, Shemya, 1,500 miles after losing sight of Japan, by 150 miles; that could be considered an instance of being well lost, I suppose, although the uncertainties of oceanic navigation are such that the intervening distances between widely spaced checkpoints seem beyond such categories as "lost" and "found"; like some Heisenbergian particle, one is navigating less through space than through a cloud of probabilities. Most likely I am about here; probably in four hours I will be there; in the meantime, I will be somewhere. Put in another cassette.

Depending on the terrain, knowing your exact position may or may not be significant. You should distinguish between places it's important to be and places that don't matter. Airways, for instance, are not like roads; if you stray from the center of the airway, you are not bumping along a soft shoulder, falling into a ditch, or crossing the center divider; nor, despite vague indications from time to time that this ought to be so, is there any attempt, other than that provided by the hemispherical altitude rule, to separate airplanes going in opposite directions on the right and left sides of the airway. If you fly outbound from a VOR along an airway for forty miles and then switch to another station to begin to track inbound, and discover that you had mistuned the outbound track and are now several miles to one side of the airway, there is no reason at all to make a sidestep maneuver to get back onto the airway. Forget the airway; it doesn't exist. Simply fly direct to the next VOR. If you have strayed so far from your intended track that even the next VOR represents a significant dogleg—say more than twenty degrees, determine or estimate the heading to the next VOR beyond it, and aim for that one. Even if you can't yet receive a VOR, you can aim approximately for it and you won't in all probability be off by more than five or ten degrees when you start to receive its signal.

As a general rule, though—and this is a rule that imposes itself automatically upon one's thinking and does not need to be memorized—

the care with which one ought to navigate is directly proportional to the hostility of the terrain and weather. On a fine day over smooth country, you can be pretty easygoing, using dead reckoning, aiming at a distant cloud, and enjoying the view. Crossing mountains under a low cloud deck at night—well, find me a pilot whose finger is not pressed to the map spread out in his lap, and whose eyes are not glued to the ground.

# 11

# *Rules of the Game*

The game of flying is played on a worldwide board, in air about ten miles deep. Different players abide by different sets of rules; and as in chess, certain pieces are only permitted certain moves. The degree of regimentation for some of the players is very high indeed; and since for the general public the most visible element of aviation, the airlines, is also the most heavily regimented, it is widely believed that every flight of every airplane, however minor, takes place in an environment as controlled as that of a space shot. This is not the case; thousands of airplanes come and go without any contact whatever with aeronautical officialdom—as was the case in the beginning.

Airplanes started out as eccentric gadgets; as you do not now need a license to operate a motorboat, you did not need a license to fly a plane.

By the 1930s, however, there were enough planes, and I suppose they did enough damage, or threatened to, that the government started licensing pilots. At first, since all the pilots were already pilots, government examiners went around watching from the ground as the pilots flew and then gave them little pieces of paper saying that they could go on doing so. This act of presumption was, by the lights of many fliers fifty years later, the original sin, and ought to be rescinded.

Today in order to fly at all you have to have a medical certificate of one class or another, regularly renewed; to fly alone you need at least a student license, and to carry passengers, a private license. To fly passengers or cargo for hire you have to have a commercial license, and to fly in cloud you need an instrument rating. To carry a passenger in a multiengine airplane you need an appropriate multiengine rating. To land on water you need a seaplane rating. All of these—and they go on to include gliders, rotorcraft, balloons, anything you can think of except parachutes and hang gliders, which require no license at all—must be endorsed by means of a flight check every two years. If you plan to fly a passenger in a large, fast, and complicated airplane, you need a special rating for that specific type of airplane. Ironically, however, no matter how many ratings you have, and no matter how proud you may be of them, nobody, except when you are renting an airplane, ever asks to see your pilot's license.

In the beginning airplanes took off and landed in fields (though aerodromes were quick to come into being, with wind indicators and fuel supplies, hangars and repairmen, and places for fliers and their admirers to gather), and they followed roads and obvious geographical features between places not far apart. No special provisions were made for them. Eventually, however, as they increased in numbers and began commercial services, there sprang up around them a network of navigational facilities, airports, regulatory bodies, manufacturers of airplanes and equipment, inspectors, regulations, and formalities. Until some time after World War II, when aviation suddenly underwent an explosive growth and began turning into a big business, aviation belonged to aviators. It no longer does. It is no longer necessary to consecrate one's life and personality to the role of pilot in order to fly; you can do it in your spare time.

The rules are now very complicated indeed; but for general aviation flying they are still within the learning ability of the average adult. Everything you need to know can be found in a publication called the *Airman's Information Manual*, Part One of which contains a digest of regulations in a somewhat indigestible form. For commercial, air taxi, or airline flying, the airman's world is vastly detailed and complex, and to learn its language and gestures and be at home in its alien spaces takes years of training and practice. When you begin to fly a private plane, however, you do not have years of practice; you do not have anything.

In the United States, you can still fly freely. It is not necessary to file a flight plan, announce your intentions to anyone, report your position, or request permission to land (so long as you confine yourself to nontower airports, which are by far the majority). You just get into your plane, taxi out to the runway, take off, go where you want to go, land, and park. On the whole it is exactly like driving a car. American aviators love this freedom, they cling to it, and they have defended it, so far with a good deal of success, against efforts by the federal government to regulate what remains unregulated.

Why, apart from the proverbial need of legislators to legislate about something or other in order to make a living, is the government interested in curtailing the freedom of citizens to fly about in airplanes? Essentially, because flying is dangerous, and the Federal Aviation Agency (later Administration) was established in 1958 from the Department of Commerce Civil Aviation Authority to take whatever steps were necessary to prevent a repetition of the disastrous midair collision of two airliners that occurred over the Grand Canyon on June 30, 1956. Though no one, not even the FAA, would say so in seriousness, it is obvious that one way to reduce the danger of flying is to reduce the amount of flying. Commercial interests, on the other hand, wish to increase the flying; they want more passengers for their airlines and more buyers for more private planes. The interests of government and commerce, ostensibly contradictory, have found a compromise course, a grand historic current guided, all unconsciously, by the delicate equilibrium between Washington and the general aviation industry, in a program of selective regulation that seems to have for its essential mechanism the tactic of enveloping the dangers of flight, as though they were invading cells, with the antibody of technological sophistication. Like colliding glaciers emerging from convergent valleys, the regulators and the regulated stand, locked together in trembling stalemate, until a gaudy accident, a statistical survey, or a legislator's messianic vision produces a jolt that moves the dreadful mass a few feet further downhill.

For many years the drift of this action, which is tediously comic, like some oafish, overlong stage routine, has been to reduce the amount of airspace available to the independent, unadorned, unequipped primitive aviator, but then to give it back to him on condition that he purchase some piece of radio equipment. The effect is bad for the grass roots but good for business, because it pushes aviators into more and more expensive, more and more sophisticated equipment, lures them into more advanced ratings, and tends to make widespread the feeling that a good pilot is a "professional" pilot, and that today's substitute for seat-of-the-pants ability is redundant transponders. By raising the ante in this way, the combine of government and business, which as usual is mutually protective and instinctively hews toward an identity of interest, serves the interest of safety by limiting the number of people gaining admission to the sky, and by making the price of getting there and staying there astronomically high. Only addicts would pay such prices; and most pilots are hopeless addicts.

But because this is the United States and not a banana republic, real old-fashioned freedom has not been forgotten, and the ground floor, the airspace underlying all the other airspace, has in fact been reserved for the Little Guy. With the exception of certain chunks, all the airspace between the ground and 18,000 feet above sea level is available for general VFR flying; and that is why there is more general aviation flying in the United States than anywhere else in the world.

VFR means "visual flight rules"—the mention of rules strikes one immediately—and the rules here are, basically, that you stay a safe distance from clouds and from obstacles, notably the ground, from other airplanes, and from persons and property. These rules are quite reasonable, and they boil down to the exercise of good sense.

The reason you must stay a safe distance from clouds is that in clouds you have no way of seeing other airplanes. The radar carried by some civil aircraft is intended for helping identify and avoid heavy weather, not other airplanes, and cannot be used to prevent collisions, even ones with the ground. In the present state of airborne equipment, airplanes cannot avoid bumping into things except by following directions from ground radar and ground controllers, by relying on probability (which works quite well), or by looking out the windows as drivers of automobiles generally do. Looking out the window, which aviation dignifies as "the see-and-be-seen principle," works reasonably well so long as everyone stays out of the clouds. Now, since airplanes do—and must—continue to operate in cloudy weather, why, you may wonder, do they not simply put every airplane under the command of a ground controller? It seems sometimes that is what they want to do; but the cost would be prohibitive, the effect on the private flying and the private airplane building industry disastrous, the loss of individual freedom serious at least to some, and, in the long run, the benefit would be rather slight, since, in 1976 (for example), only forty-six people died in midair collisions. It seems as though cigarettes, automobiles, or even railroad grade crossings might be more fertile ground for life-saving legislation than airplanes. Nevertheless, the slow but general movement of rulemaking has been toward increased ground control, increased equipment requirements to interface with ground controllers, and efforts to segregate types of aircraft (airline from general aviation, jet from prop) and types of operations (IFR from VFR).

How crowded, really, is the sky? If you divide the cubic miles of air by the number of airplanes likely to be aloft at any one time, it seems that each airplane has ample room in which to wander around. Indeed, you may make a long flight and never see another airplane in the air, and not for lack of looking. But airplanes do not distribute themselves at random, like raisins in a fruitcake; more like people in a country or fish in a sea, they tend to cluster in some places and barely appear in others. The points of concentration are terminal areas around big cities and certain busy airways, and in the traffic patterns of large, busy airports on weekend afternoons. There you may be able to count ten or fifteen airplanes at one time, droning along in swarms in the traffic pattern. But never, under any conditions at all, is air traffic anything like road traffic. Most people cannot control airplanes with nearly the precision that they can cars, and the kind of situation that exists even on a lightly traveled highway, with several cars moving along in a string, or passing two or three going in the opposite direction in a few moments, does not exist in the air. Other airplanes appear as remote floating points; sometimes they float toward us; sometimes they pass close enough to allow us to identify the make or year, or to descry the occupants and see whether they have noticed us as we have noticed them. For the most part, however, and in cross-country flying nearly all the time, we are alone in the sky, and even commonly used radio frequencies are disturbed by few voices.

Given normal—not fanatical—vigilance, VFR pilots are not running much risk of midair collision. Only because collisions are dramatic, get into the press, and are easy to attribute to acts of man rather than of God, do they command the attention from the FAA that they do; and while some of the steps taken to prevent collisions (like the inauguration of an air traffic control system, to begin with) were made in reaction to actual accidents, many are made to prevent accidents that may—some would say eventually must—happen. If the steps fail and a collision occurs, more steps are taken; but if no collision occurs, we never know whether it was because of all the steps that have been taken or whether there would have been no collision anyway. That preventive measures are only partially effective is obvious from their breakdowns. The collision in March 1977 of two Boeing 747s under tower control on the runway at Tenerife was a particularly hair-raising example of the kind of breakdown that can and always will occur through human error, and that undoubtedly brings airliners and private planes (to say nothing of military airplanes) close to disaster, without actually achieving it, every day.

In brief then, despite the existence of a fabulously expensive and ever-growing air traffic control system, which might imply that simply sending uncontrolled airplanes up to take their chances in the sky would be the height of rashness, the risk of collision in most places is actually minuscule. It is further diminished by the simple precaution of looking where you're going; but since, in fact, almost all midair collisions occur in the immediate vicinity of airfields, with or without tower control, I would venture to guess that you could spend most of your en route flying time reading novels and still run almost no risk of collision. In all my flying, though I have often come close to other airplanes near airports, I have only had to take evasive action to avoid a possible collision two or three times while en route. Of course, one collision would have been enough.

Recognizing the fact that traffic congregates in certain corridors, the FAA has instituted something called the hemispherical rule—heaven knows why; "semicircular rule" would make more sense—which governs the altitudes at which VFR and IFR traffic will fly. More than 3,000 feet above the terrain, VFR traffic heading eastward—that is, on any heading from 0 to 179 degrees—is supposed to fly at odd numbered thousands plus 500, that is, at 3,500 feet, 5,500, 7,500, and so on up to 17,500 feet. Westbound traffic gets the even numbered thousands plus 500. These altitudes, like all cruising altitudes, are expressed in feet above sea level (MSL, or mean sea level, is the abbreviation). Thus, if at your location in Colorado the terrain height is 4,800 feet, you can have your choice of cruising altitudes up to and including 7,800 feet; higher, you are supposed to cruise at 8,500, 9,500, 10,500 feet, and so on, according to your direction of flight and whatever other factors might play a role in your selection of an altitude (factors about which I'll talk more later).

Layers of opposing traffic are not separated by 1,000 feet, however, because IFR traffic flies at even and odd thousands. There is plenty of IFR traffic even in VFR weather; so in principle you have a slab of airspace 500 feet thick which is sandwiched between the 500-foot thick slabs of the neighboring IFR traffic going the same direction below you and the IFR traffic going the opposite direction above you. Along airways, this arrangement ensures the vertical separation of traffic.

Unfortunately, you can still have a head-on collision, even ignoring the fact that you have to climb and descend through everybody else's layers, because if you are heading due north and your traffic is heading one degree east of true south, you will be at the same altitude. And of course you are free to collide at a wide range of other angles. Furthermore, because some airplanes are hard to keep at an exact altitude without constant attention, and some pilots don't try terribly hard to keep them there, one encounters other airplanes (when one encounters them at all) at all altitudes, approved or not; an airplane cruising at 6,500 feet according to his flight plan may at times be found at 6,200, at other times at 6,700; or, quite frequently, you may be cruising along westbound at 8,500 feet and pass by another airplane going in the opposite direction at the same altitude, whose pilot has apparently decided to ignore the hemispherical rule altogether.

And, indeed, some pilots do ignore it deliberately, whether they feel that squeezing the majority of traffic into these layers makes the intervening space emptier and therefore safer, or because they despise official meddling in their activities, or because some special circumstance, like a cloud layer, makes an altitude that for them is "illegal" more practical than any other. Like other air regulations, this one is not a "law"; so an illegal altitude is not illegal in the sense that it would bring with it a civil penalty. The worst penalty the FAA can impose is the revocation of a pilot's license. But in the case of an illegal altitude, if you were caught at one—though there is no way in the world you can be "caught" in the air if you don't want to be—you would either confidently recite the hemispherical rule backward, so as to show that you were at the wrong altitude in good faith, or you would maintain that you were climbing or descending, activities that exempt you from the rule, and as to whose rapidity no allusion is made in the regulations.

The so-called navigable airspace of the United States (whatever that means; it all looks navigable to me) is at present divided up into a fairly simple set of categories. Above 18,000 feet MSL is the high altitude route structure. Altitudes are there given in terms of "flight levels"; the flight level is the altitude in feet minus two zeros, so that an airplane cruising at 24,000 feet says that he is at FL (flight level) 240. Since that airspace is well clear of terrain, it doesn't bother with local altimeter settings; all aircraft flying at or above FL180 set their altimeters at 29.92 in. Hg. They use a somewhat different airway structure from the traffic below FL180, because, being higher up, they can receive VORs farther apart, and so proceed more directly from point to point.

Flight levels are only rarely of interest to general aviation pilots. Unturbocharged airplanes can, for the most part, barely reach FL180 in the first place. Turbocharged ones can and do, but may be deterred from using flight levels because all flights above FL180 are under positive control—that is, they are on IFR flight plans, requiring IFR equipment and instrument rated pilots. Furthermore, the pilot has to use supplemental oxygen above 12,500 feet (by regulation; physiologically, some people begin to need it lower down, others higher up), and oxygen is an expensive nuisance; so as a matter of convenience even the pilots of turbocharged airplanes usually cruise at 12,500 or below.

Finally, high-level flight involves considerations of weather on an order of magnitude more complex than low-level flight. Not that the weather up high is necessarily worse, though the problem of ice accumulation on the airframe is more common at higher altitude; but one may have to descend through all kinds of awful stuff to get back to the ground. So, to make a long story short, flight levels are of merely academic interest to the VFR pilot.

Below FL180, the airspace is either "controlled" or "uncontrolled." In uncontrolled airspace you can do anything you want, including flying IFR without a clearance.. There is a blanket of uncontrolled airspace covering the entire country from the surface to 1,200 feet above the ground, for the most part, though shafts of controlled airspace, which I will mention shortly, do drop through this blanket to the ground at many places. There are a great many places where uncontrolled airspace extends all the way from the ground to FL180; they are mostly in the western two thirds of the country, and they are not of much significance for the cross-country pilot because they are isolated fragments separated from one another by airways.

Controlled airspace is mostly indicated by a blue shaded outline on charts, and the bulk of it is within airways. Airways are specified tracks between VOR stations, and they are like a random spider web; not all stations are connected by an airway to all neighboring stations, but enough are connected to chop up the uncontrolled airspace above 1,200 feet AGL in most of the country. Airways are corridors about ten miles wide extending from a floor usually 1,200 feet above the ground up to FL180. But the name "controlled airspace," which suggests that all flights within it are accountable to someone or other, is a misnomer; it should rather be called "controllable airspace." In fact, most of the flights in controlled airspace are not controlled, and are not intended to be.

Now, there are over 10,000 airfields in the United States, most of which are open to public use and have no kind of traffic control at all. Pilots fly into and out of them in accordance with the conventions I have already described, and they avoid hitting one another, with rare unlucky exceptions, by keeping their eyes peeled and by announcing their position and intentions over a common radio frequency. But a small percentage of airports are controlled. The controlling facility is a control tower, in most cases operated by the FAA, and it has authority over operations in a cylinder of airspace called the airport traffic area, which is 10 miles in diameter with the field at its center, and extends to 3,000 feet above the ground.

Notice that the top two thirds of the airport traffic area sticks up into the controllable airspace of the airway system. This means that if an airway carries you across a controlled field, and you are below 3,000 feet AGL, you have to call the tower for clearance through the traffic area. This is routinely granted if you are at least 1,500 feet above the surface, in other words clear of the traffic pattern. As a practical matter, on the other hand, in urban areas where airport traffic areas overlap one another and where you might pass through the traffic areas of several controlled fields on the way to an uncontrolled field, you don't harass busy tower operators with transit requests. You just stay well clear of their patterns and at a safe altitude. This is not strictly legal, however, and if someone challenges your action, you say that you thought you were five miles from the airport. It is not illegal to be a bad judge of distances.

Many airports possessing published instrument approaches have in addition to an airport traffic area a control zone whose core exactly coincides with the airport traffic area; but it also may have arms extending farther outward along the instrument approach paths; and the control zone extends upward to 14,500 feet, which is the floor of something very ephemeral called the continental control area. Despite their imposing names, the control zone and the continental control area are of no significance to VFR pilots, except insofar as the control zone's extensions on the chart might signal the presence of IFR aircraft. In fact, the significance to VFR pilots of categories of airspace seems to be exactly the inverse of what is suggested by their names, with "continental control area" meaning nothing at all, "control zone" being of merely cautionary importance, "controlled airspace" being in fact uncontrolled, and only the lowly "airport traffic area" being, in fact, the one place that is really controlled.

There is one other kind of airspace in which all traffic is controlled, and that is the terminal control area, or TCA. These exist at an increasing number of major airline terminals and they come in three degrees of seriousness, named Group One, Two, and Three. Group One, consisting of the busiest airline airports (Atlanta, Boston, Chicago, Dallas, Los Angeles, Miami, New York, San Francisco, and Washington, D.C.), has the most stringent requirements, including that of a transponder with altitude encoding capability—the ensemble costing, at the very least, $1,200. In a TCA, traffic is under positive control, just as it is above FL180; heading and altitude changes must be authorized by ground controllers. For most new private pilots, flight in TCAs is not a concern; all of the busy metropolitan terminals are surrounded by smaller general aviation airports, and it is possible to get into the smaller airports while remaining outside the TCA.

TCAs are quite complex in shape; they are commonly compared to an inverted wedding cake with, in many cases, tunnels running through it.

For VFR pilots, they are portrayed on large-scale local charts, and they appear in top view divided into segments, each of which is assigned a floor and ceiling which is marked on the chart thus: 70/40. Meaning, in this instance, that the segment extends from 4,000 feet MSL up to 7,000 feet MSL; within that area, between those altitudes, you would be inside the TCA.

Circumnavigating the TCA is not very difficult, in spite of its complicated structure. Special large-scale charts are published, and conspicuous landmarks and nearby radio facilities can be used to stay clear; you can, for instance, note that the 100-degree radial of Arceo VOR passes just outside the TCA, and that if you stay on or to the left of that radial you will be in the clear. So you tune that VOR, set the 100-degree radial From on the OBS, and keep the needle to the right of center. In another case, you might be cruising at 5,000 feet and not want to circumnavigate the entire TCA; you might want to pass underneath its uppermost and largest tier. You then observed on the chart that you have to be below 4,000 feet (for instance) by the time you cross the 046-degree radial of Abajo VOR, and you might set the OBS to 046, or a little in advance of that radial just for safety, and be at or below 4,000 when you reach it.

When TCAs were first invented, the representatives of general aviation urged that climb and descent corridors be instead established for airliners, so that whole blocks of airspace did not have to be "sterilized." But since airline flights multiply without restraint, and the traffic delays that cause airliners to hold and to be vectored around in the altitudes normally most used by light airplanes are actually caused not by "private planes" but by other airliners, corridors were rejected as assuming, too optimistically, that airliners would always be able to arrive one after another in a steady and orderly parade.

In the near future we will see the TCA concept enlarged. The present system is an interim measure; TCAs generally extend no higher than 9,000 feet, while the floor of other positively controlled airspace is at 18,000 feet. Airliners climbing, supposedly, out of the top of a TCA (though many of them emerge from the sides, not the top) pass through a band 9,000 feet thick before attaining the cover of positive control again. There is plenty of uncontrolled VFR traffic between 9,000 and 18,000 feet, and the FAA may eventually drop the floor of positive control to 12,500 feet and raise the tops of TCAs to meet it, at least in some parts of the country.

From the point of view of the private pilot, the co-opting of blocks of airspace by the forces of positive control presents certain hazards. Positive control airspace is impenetrable to the pilot with VFR ratings and equipment, and TCAs would be like so many thunderstorms rising into a solid overcast at 12,500 feet. Inevitably, their presence complicates flying when any kind of real, rather than metaphorical, weather is present. If cloud layers lie below or beside the TCA, or across the altitudes of corridors running through the TCA, they make impenetrable barriers, and impenetrable barriers can become traps. Strewing blocks of impenetrable airspace around the country is equivalent to erecting hazards for the VFR pilots.

Blocks of positive control airspace, which will almost certainly grow larger and more numerous, rather than shriveling away, represent a serious navigational consideration. If the floor of positive control is 12,500 feet, then flying above an overcast layer takes on a new aspect: the limits are no longer just those of the airplane, but those of the airspace. Even in perfect weather, ground control and flight plans will become mandatory for many flights that now would take place VFR without even entering the ATC system.

There is no reason to go into a panic over this prospect, however. For me, the worst consequence of stretches of positive control is that I have to listen to ATC rather than to my stereo. That is no doubt partly because I do most of my flying in the West, where IFR deviations and delays are few. I am always amazed when in the East, especially around New York, I have to spend two hours going 150 miles. But it is partly because I have really not found positive control to be particularly onerous. Most of the time, I follow exactly the same routing as I would VFR; I get deviations around weather whenever I ask for them; and I get cleared direct from point to point, avoiding flight-planned doglegs as soon as VOR reception on a distant station is strong enough for navigation. The procedures, the conversations, and the eavesdropping on other people's conversations are often quite entertaining. Flying IFR helps the time pass quickly, and it gives you an extra margin of safety at night, because if you run into trouble somebody on the ground knows exactly where you are. The reluctance of a certain segment of general aviation to accept increased control is quite understandable; but for most pilots it turns out to be, like a traffic jam, not quite such a catastrophe as they anticipate. The problem is not the control itself but the cost of equipment, and the practical necessity of getting an instrument rating if you really want to make complete, full-time use of an airplane. But that is already a practical necessity anyway.

At present, however, despite terms like "controlled airspace," "control zone," and so on, almost all airspace is available to private pilots flying private aircraft VFR, with no controls whatever. The only exceptions are the immediate environment of airports with control towers (which are the minority of airports), the extended vicinity of a few major TCA hubs, and certain restricted or prohibited areas.

VFR charts bristle with these supplementary areas, which represent airspace that is set aside for various special reasons. Some of it is absolutely prohibited; some is restricted at certain times, days, and altitudes; some involves specific restrictions (for instance, no flight below 3,000 feet above the surface in a bird sanctuary); some only comes with warnings. Much of this airspace belongs to the military and is used for flight training or for artillery, guided missiles, and so on.

Each chunk of special use airspace has a designator, like R-496 or W-1341A, starting with a letter which tells which category of airspace it is and indicates whether its prohibition is absolute or conditional, and ending with a number which distinguishes that chunk of airspace from others. You look up the one you are interested in in a table at the edge of the chart, and it will tell you the limits of the prohibition or warning (many are only "hot" during weekdays in daylight hours, or above 14,000 feet, or what have you) and whom to call to get permission to cross, if permission is available.

Nothing is likely to happen to you if you accidentally fly into a forbidden area; nobody will come up to get you. But since you could collide with a jet fighter, stop an artillery shell, distract a guided missile, or wake up the President in his summer home, you should not take these areas too lightly. You should also bear in mind that military pilots practicing dog-fighting are not paying much attention to the boundaries of their consecrated airspace, and they are very likely to spill over its edges; you have to be just as alert flying near some of these jet training areas as flying through them.

Although VFR flight in most airspace is not subject to control, whether or not the airspace is designated as "controlled airspace," it is still subject to certain weather requirements in order to ensure that VFR pilots actually are able to "see and be seen."

In uncontrolled airspace, the VFR weather requirements are 1 mile visibility and clear of clouds, day or night. There are some weather conditions in which you could comply with these limits and really barely fly without blind-flying instruments; for instance, suppose you are at 1,200 feet AGL, can make out the ground beneath you but only just a mile ahead, and are flying in an undifferentiated mist in which you can just make out scattered clouds at your altitude; or, worse still, it is night. You will have no definite horizon, and so might have a hard time staying oriented except by reference to instruments; and you would be unable to see the terrain ahead except when you got quite close to it, and so might easily get lost, or fly into rapidly rising terrain or a tall transmission tower without realizing it. These VFR minimums are, therefore, exceedingly generous, particularly when you consider that they apply equally to the remote countryside and to urban areas.

More than 1,200 feet above the surface, but below 10,000 feet, the 1-mile visibility requirement remains the same, but you are expected to remain 500 feet below, 1,000 feet above, and 2,000 feet horizontally from clouds. Nobody knows how you are to measure these distances; so for the most part we just figure that you are supposed to stay at a distance from all clouds so that emerging IFR traffic has time to spot you, or you it. Above 10,000 feet, the cloud clearance becomes 1,000 feet below, 1,000 feet above, and 1 mile horizontally, with 5 miles visibility; and these requirements apply in controlled airspace above 10,000 feet as well. Below 10,000 feet in controlled airspace, the minimums are 3 miles visibility and, again, 500 feet below, 1,000 feet above, and 2,000 feet horizontally.

As a matter of fact, these minimums don't mean a thing. Towers use them to determine whether or not the airport is VFR: less than 3 miles visibility and 1,000 foot ceiling means the field is IFR. But pilots have to face continually changing conditions; they can't simply go back to square one if some extra clouds pop up while they are in the air. So as a matter of common practice, VFR pilots stay a good distance from clouds except when they are climbing or descending, when they often have to make their way through holes in the clouds and passages between them, and can't be sure of doing more than merely staying clear. The FAA is perfectly aware of this. IFR pilots don't like it, but they have done it too. When a pilot "comes down through a hole" in what looks like a solid overcast, you can be fairly sure that he picked a good spot and spiraled down, VFR minimums temporarily be damned. This being the case, you can see why airline pilots would like everybody at least to have encoding altimeters; then controllers could steer them around these mysterious spiraling targets. Or perhaps a special transponder code could be used, with immunity, for "VFR flight illegally in IFR conditions."

It's an interesting peculiarity of this system, by the way, that whereas for the most part controlled airspace stops 1,200 feet above the surface, IFR flight is permitted down to 1,000 feet AGL. Since IFR flight is permitted without a clearance in uncontrolled airspace, the 200-foot-thick layer between 1,000 AGL and 1,200 AGL, except where controlled airspace pokes down through it, is available for unannounced IFR flight. I wonder how many pilots use it. If most don't it is not because the terrain is too lumpy; in many places it isn't. It is probably because they have a sense that there is something too outlandish about this strange gap in the rules. It sounds like bad luck—profiteering on a rulemaker's oversight. Somehow, it just doesn't sound safe.

Flyers are imbued with a sense of risk, a kind of obsession with the idea of safety, not with safety itself. Safety is a rather abstract idea; it could best be served by staying at home, but since we are determined to fly we endlessly pay lip service to the idea of safety. This ritual worship produces in the authorities an equally mechanical concern with rules and regulations, as though by our obeying them safety can be assured. Violations of rules are blamed for accidents, but when an accident occurs despite ostensible compliance with all rules, hardly anyone thinks to blame the accident on the rules, though it would be logical enough to do so—at least as logical as the reverse. If two planes collide, someone will be found to say, "He was flying at the wrong altitude," as though if there could be anything certain in this world, it would be that flying at the "right" altitude would preserve you from collision. If a VFR pilot gets too close to a cloud and accidentally falls into it, his principal sin was not simple incaution but violation of a rule. It seems to me that there is a subtle but important flaw in the emphasis—a flaw of a kind that permeates our moral thinking in every area.

When you are driving a car, you drive on your side of the street, not the one occupied by oncoming traffic, not because it would be illegal to do otherwise, but because it would be dangerous. What is at risk is your body, not your morals. If the road is perfectly empty and you can see ahead of you, you might go over to the "wrong side" to pass or to show somebody what it's like to drive in England. If a policeman saw you driving on the wrong side of the street for no good reason, he would give you a ticket for breaking the law, although he might not argue with your contention that there was no danger to anyone. He is concerned with law, not danger; the lawmakers did all the thinking about danger when they made the laws. And so, on the principle that there might always be a policeman lurking behind a bush, you do not, as a rule, amuse yourself by driving on the wrong side of the street. When you come to a stop light in the middle of the desert at two in the morning, you look carefully in each direction and then proceed through the red light (I do; don't you?) because you feel that your eyes are a better guide for your conduct than the theories of some distant stranger.

In an airplane you have the assurance, absent in a car, that there is not a policeman lurking behind a cloud. You could therefore break rules to your heart's content. Perhaps in recognition of the unenforceability of many of its laws, aviation places a special emphasis on the importance of obedience and conformity, and much of the time spent in training is spent on learning to comply with rules. But this emphasis on rules has a destructive influence upon the good sense of pilots. Initiated into an exclusive and elite fraternity (so they believe), they leave their instincts behind and adopt the codes of the air wholeheartedly. So thoroughly do they accept the regulations that when they go to another country and find regulations not corresponding to the ones they learned at home, they are bewildered and amazed, as though it were not the prerogative of every government to invent its own version of safe flying. Americans in Mexico can barely bring themselves to obey Mexican regulations at all, and sometimes get into trouble for their independence. In Mexico, for instance, a flight plan is required for every flight, even though many airports have no facility for accepting a flight plan, so you file a flight plan after the flight, when you have reached an airport suitably equipped. Night VFR flying does not exist (Mexico being one of many countries that have transformed the obvious differences between night and day flying into regulations). Americans regard these rules with amazement, as though they could have been made only by madmen; but they fly eastbound at odd thousands plus five hundred without question, even though this proceeding seems, on analysis, to increase their risk of encountering traffic.

Rules are a substitute for experience; you have to know them and understand them, and then you can cast them aside. The best solution to every situation is the creative one which arises from the experience of the flyer and the exact nature of the situation—not from the generalized qualities of the whole class of situations as the rulemaker saw them. It is a general truth about all kinds of learning, that one first submits to restraints and limitations of the most pedantic sort in order ultimately to create one's own freedom. This is the fact that makes conservatives deplore permissiveness; whatever unthinking fear of immorality may fuel that disapproval, it has its foundation in the knowledge, which is almost instinctive, that no freedom is real that has not been preceded by some kind of imprisonment.

The rules of the air are a prison for the expression of creative intelligence, the release of energy, the explosion of temporal and spatial liberty which the ability to fly brings. It is only when human intelligence is powerless, as in IFR flying, that the rules assume, with justice, an overriding importance. They are, for the VFR pilot—that pleasure pilot whose life is ten times more at risk than that of the Sunday driver—only a temporary support. Ultimately he discovers them to be unnecessary; like the rules of the road, they are eventually forgotten by drivers who, after decades of motoring, have internalized not the rules themselves but the logic underlying them, and who, though they may drift over speed limits and not come to a complete stop at grade crossings, nevertheless have arrived at a state of skill at which their minds and bodies unconsciously direct their entire attention and capacity to the act of driving safely.

Whatever the rules may say, a pilot who makes a rational but unconventional—and therefore illegal—entry into the traffic pattern of an uncontrolled airport, looking carefully around him, and handling his airplane with unconscious skill, may be a better pilot than one who flies the FAA-prescribed entry mechanically but without understanding the reasons that led to its invention. The pilot of the Aerostar who enters the pattern behind a Cherokee, and then turns base while the student in the Cherokee is still motoring along downwind, is arguably flying quite safely, even though he is, strictly speaking, cutting the other airplane off. But experience shows us that students are prone to fly excessively large patterns; that the fast airplane will easily be on the ground and off the runway before the student arrives on short final; and that the dangers, such as they are, of the Aerostar's having to fly an immense pattern while waiting for the Cherokee to land and clear the runway are greater than those of simply turning inside the slower airplane. The student may be alarmed; this is the only problem. It is up to his instructor to teach him, or to have taught him, that a fast airplane turning inside a slow one is not a dangerous situation. To an experienced pilot this is obvious; to a novice storing rules of thumb in his mind, the ideas of "cutting off" and of violating the established precedence in the pattern make the sensible act seem dangerous.

Similarly an excess of zeal in observing the imaginary zones surrounding controlled fields is foolish; it would be better to understand the probable routes of traffic around the airport, to listen to the tower for news of inbound airplanes, and to look carefully where one is going, than to mechanically avoid the traffic area without sensing its arbitrariness, and without realizing that the gradient of traffic density at the boundaries of the ordinary traffic area is so slight as to be imperceptible.

The rules as they stand are full of omissions, inconsistencies, and flaws; but a certain amount of experience serves to make rules that are not rules but more like states of mind. Flying around the boundary of a TCA, for instance, one is aware of a perceptible increase in traffic density right at the perimeter of the "wedding cake," and particularly just beneath its lower surface, where airplanes trying to be as high as possible above the city, but just clear of the TCA, will collect. Where the bottom of the TCA is at 2,000 feet, over an urban area you can be sure of finding a great many airplanes flying at 1,900 feet. Similarly, certain alignments of busy airline runways produce shafts of heavy traffic extending far beyond the TCA, as at San Francisco (SFO), where the column of airplanes approaching the runways from the east extends far out over the inland valley on a gentle slope, so that an airplane flying well east of the TCA at 9,500 feet may pass through the inverse equivalent of a spray of bullets from SFO's gun. The same is true at Los Angeles, where strings of airliners arrive along a narrow corridor from the east, entering VFR altitudes fifty or sixty miles before they reach the TCA. These obvious areas of danger are not charted. In cases like this, the rules are inadequate; the rule to follow is the basic one, the rule of rules, which you write for yourself without help from the government; fly as though your life depended upon it.

# 12

# *Strategy*

The rules of the game laid down in the Federal Aviation Regulations and found in the *Airman's Information Manual* are quite complex. In the previous chapter I have reviewed some of the most basic ones, I hope in a sufficiently expeditious manner to permit the reader to get through them without falling asleep. If he wants to fall asleep he can always pick up the *AIM*.

Most experienced pilots have forgotten many of the complex details of the rules, though some make a point of knowing every one. Most make do with a somewhat blurred set of ideas about what may and what may not be done, ideas that experience has shown fit well with their flying habits. Every pilot I have ever known considered himself qualified to stretch or break rules when it seemed expedient to do so. They felt that they knew what they were doing, and they did what they did because it seemed to them correct, not because rules called for it. Rules, at any rate, ordinarily only told you what not to do; they did not tell you what you ought to do. That was the role of strategy.

Every flight must be planned, however perfunctorily, like a campaign. It begins with a group of choices, and if the choices are the right ones the flight unfolds routinely. There are choices of altitude, of routing, fuel load, speed, loading, time of departure, type of flight plan. Together, they are the strategy of the flight.

The circumstance that most often influences your choice of an altitude, and might even make you want to fly westward at eastbound altitudes, is the weather. But the choice of an altitude is a complex subject, and though in the long run each pilot ends up returning on almost every flight to the same favorite altitudes, and it makes little difference in time or fuel consumption where he cruises, an understanding of the subject is basic to an understanding of the conditions of flight.

So far as airplane efficiency is concerned, it is generally enhanced by climbing to the highest possible altitude. Light airplanes are so designed that their most efficient speed, the one at which they get the most miles per gallon, is a fairly low indicated airspeed, close to the speed at which they achieve their best rate of climb. They normally cruise at much higher indicated airspeeds, with some loss in efficiency. Now, one of the effects of high altitude, as I mentioned earlier, is that engine power is diminished by the diminishing supply of oxygen in the thinner air; and so the airplane flies at a lower indicated airspeed. At the same time, the thinner air produces less drag, and so, for a given amount of power, the airplane is able to move faster. The result is that for a given power setting, the corresponding true airspeed gets greater and greater with increasing altitude. Only at the most efficient indicated speed does true airspeed remain in a fixed proportion to power.

The greatest indicated airspeed and the greatest true airspeed are both attained at sea level, where the power available is at its maximum. One does not cruise at maximum power, but rather at a setting of no more than 75 percent of power, and generally even less than that. The indicated airspeed that may be reached with 75 percent of power decreases gradually with increasing altitude, while the true speed to which that indicated speed corresponds increases; but there is a certain altitude above which, even at full throttle and maximum rpm, you cannot get more than 75 percent power any longer. What that altitude is depends on the rpm at which you cruise; the lower the rpm, compared with the maximum permissible rpm of the engine, the lower the altitude at which full throttle will produce no more than 75 percent of power. That altitude may vary, from model to model, from as low as 6,000 feet to as high as 11,000 feet, but usually it will be around 7,000 feet. Let us say, for the sake of discussion, that 7,000 feet is the altitude at which 75 percent is the maximum available cruising power. The maximum cruising speed will be attained at 7,000 feet, and at any higher altitude the fuel flow will diminish, because the oxygen available to burn fuel is less, and the speed will diminish as well. It happens, however, that the diminishing fuel flow produces a diminishing indicated airspeed, and as the airplane gets closer and closer to its "ideal" indicated airspeed—the one at which it gets the most miles per gallon—its efficiency gets steadily better and better. What this means in practice, since you almost never really fly at the ideal indicated speed, is simply that if you set your mixture similarly at all altitudes you will always fly more efficiently the higher you go.

But it takes time to climb high—how much time depends on the power of the airplane—and for a short trip it may not be practical. Above 12,500 feet there is the question of oxygen. And efficiency may not be your principal concern. It gets a lot of publicity in the aviation press because it sounds like a noble and suitably scientific ideal (like quietness or cleanness), because the price of avgas keeps going up, because future shortages or allocations or rationing are on everybody's mind, and because efficiency is a more easily quantified goal than pleasure or a sense of power. All the discussion of efficient cruising and economical operation would seem a little sillier, however, if the subject were broadened to include the fact that airplane operation is to begin with so uneconomical that fuel costs—or at least the portion of fuel costs that could be done away with by more efficient flying practices—are a drop in the bucket, and that by simply skipping a trip altogether now and then you could probably effect a greater saving of fuel than by honing your cruise control to a razor edge and wiping all the bugs off your wings.

Still, efficiency is worth understanding; at least then you can defend your choice to ignore it from time to time.

In the equation that relates cruising speed to power output, speed appears raised to the third power. In other words, roughly speaking, power required is proportional to the cube of speed. To double the speed of a given airplane, eight times the power is needed; more realistically, doubling its power produces only a 26 percent increase in its speed. In general, power output is almost directly proportional to fuel flow for a given engine; so by doubling your fuel flow you will get not double the speed, but only a quarter again the speed that you had before.

Obviously, speed is inherently uneconomical; if you want to go economically, go slowly. This is, in fact, the rule given to pilots: To fly economically, fly at, say, 50 percent of power rather than 75 percent.

Now, since the highest speed for a given percentage of power is to be had at the altitude at which that power is all the power you have, this rule means that you should try to cruise at 11,000 or 12,000 feet, or higher, other things permitting.

There are still more good reasons for choosing high altitudes. One is comfort. During the summer and fall months particularly, the atmosphere is turbulent because of heating of air by the ground, which sends bubbles and columns of warm air floating upward. The warm air rises through layers of heavier cool air, since the atmosphere is normally layered with temperature steadily decreasing with altitude. But very often there is a kind of ceiling on the rising warm air, called an inversion, where rather than get cooler and cooler with increasing altitude, the air gets temporarily warmer; the layer of warm air, in which the thermals rising from below are no longer buoyant, puts a lid on atmospheric mixing. Above the inversion, the air is smooth. The same will be true above the tops of fair-weather cumulus clouds—the puffy white clouds that gather, like mounds of mashed potatoes, on the afternoons of summer days. In either case, the smooth air will begin at a fairly high altitude; in the Midwest in summer, it is not uncommon to climb to 13,000 or 14,000 feet in order to fly above the turbulence; in the Rocky Mountain states you must climb even higher, and without turbochargers and oxygen it is usually impractical to try to cruise in smooth air. Instead, you try to get an early start, flying in the calm morning air before the terrain has started to heat up.

High altitude air is not only smooth, it is also cool. And it usually offers superior visibility—the air above the mixing layer is free of airborne dust and vapor—and, simply as a product of absolute height above the surface, superior radio reception and hence navigational ability. At 10,000 feet, you will receive VOR signals of good quality from nearly a hundred miles away—more than the average distance between stations, which means that your way will be marked for you by an uninterrupted chain of VORs.

There is much to be said, then, for cruising altitudes around or above 10,000 feet; but they also have disadvantages. For one thing, a lot of low-powered airplanes can barely make it to those altitudes and, having reached them, have trouble resisting downdrafts. In a Cessna 172, for instance, with four people aboard in summertime, you may not consider altitudes above 9,500 feet worth bothering with, even though the airplane can, in a pinch, drag itself up to 13,000 feet. In summer particularly, there is the serious problem of density altitude; ironically it is in summertime, when you need the comfort of altitude most, that it is hardest to attain. With temperatures 15 or 20 degrees Celsius above standard, 10,000 feet becomes, so far as the engine is concerned, 13,000 feet or so, and for all practical purposes out of the reach of low-powered, heavily loaded airplanes.

On the other side of the coin there are aesthetic considerations. From so far above it, the earth is static and featureless. Its geologic visage, bloodless and flat, resembles a bad reproduction in a book. Even that old scenic chestnut, the Grand Canyon, looks, from high above, like a muddy ditch.

A lady who thought a lot about such things complained to me once that she objected to traveling by air because from an airplane you could not imagine what it would be like to live in a place. She was half right; seen from high above, a river, a stand of trees, a town, a hill, betray to an occasional flyer nothing of that physiognomy which, if we see it from eye level, even rapidly passing, speaks to us like a human face in a familiar language. We may be altogether wrong in daydreaming that we would be happy living at the foot of a certain hill, in a certain house—because the conditions of our happiness would be at once more complex and simpler than a certain house and a certain hill; but it is certainly one of the pleasures of surface travel to imagine that we can sense the kind of life that is led by people in the places that we pass. And also to see those people themselves: a solemn child watching our car sail by, a horse, a solitary girl ignoring us, give us momentary, inchoate, irrecoverable pleasures. In an airplane at ten thousand feet we can imagine, but we cannot smell the air, feel its temperature, hear the river or the flies or a hidden shout, sense the glare or the coolness of the sky; instead we see an unpeopled earth, a geologic panorama which at first, for the first years in fact, means nothing to our hearts. It is only after we have flown for years that the lofty view becomes touching because it is full of familiar paths and it has sweet nostalgic associations that we cannot identify, but which we recognize, like the voices of old friends.

Despite its inconvenience and possible discomfort, low flight is far more immediately interesting than high. You see more that you recognize; you are diverted and if the airplane does not go quite as fast at low altitude as at high, it doesn't matter because you are less aware of the time. Navigation is more difficult, because you cannot see far around you; but landmarks have a greater intrinsic interest. And you have a greater sense of speed and space, which is pleasant in itself. Still, most people don't choose to fly low., perhaps because they don't want to be a public nuisance or, more probably, because they feel that if they have engine trouble down low, they will have very little time to pick a landing place, whereas from a high altitude they can glide miles to any of a wide choice of spots. This consideration of safety is the most compelling reason for not flying quite low, aside from the environmental one, which is important in some places and less so in others. But this same consideration of safety does not prevent pilots from flying at night, or on top of cloud layers, when a forced landing would be just as difficult as it would be from a height of two hundred feet.

The regulations in the United States show a wonderful tolerance for flying at night—a practice that is, on the face of it, fraught with greater danger than day VFR. It has been argued, in fact, that night flying is sufficiently different from day to merit a separate classification, with a special rating on the license or, at the very least, a separate set of ceiling and visibility limitations. Whether putting such limitations into the form of rules would have much effect I don't know; certainly most instructors teach a special respect for night flying, and sooner or later any pilot discovers that weather that would be perfectly acceptable for VFR in daytime can be very tricky at night, when you can no longer see the location and extent of clouds, and the bright areas which normally signal thin spots and clear weather ahead cannot be seen. Spatial disorientation is common at night; and incredible as it may seem, pilots have mistaken the lights on the ground for stars, or lost track entirely of the horizon, or taken desperate action to avoid a collision with the rising moon. It also is difficult to preflight an airplane well in the dark. If there is some control in the cockpit whose position you don't know, you will probably not be able to find it at night. On the other hand, other airplanes are much more clearly visible than during the day, and airports equipped with rotating beacons are very easy to find. Night landings are not difficult once you get the hang of not looking down at the ground in front of the airplane, but out at the rows of lights leading to the far end of the runway. (Night taxiing, on the other hand, can be a real problem; many airports have few of the blue lights that outline taxiways, and if they are there they usually appear to the bewildered pilot as a sea of blue points without rhyme or reason.)

Many people will not fly single-engine planes at night because if the engine failed they would be unlikely to be able to make a successful forced landing. Personally, I fly single-engine at night, IFR, over water; but in saying that I am reminded of the Alaskan pilot Don Jonz, who wrote an article in *Flying* about how he had flown for years in icing conditions, and how ice was no problem as long as you knew a few tricks, which he went on to reveal; and while that very issue was on the newsstands, Jonz disappeared, with Congressman Hale Boggs, in icy weather, and has never been found. Jonz thus inscribed his name forever in the annals of bold pilots, and of people who should have kept their mouths shut. (It's not certain, of course, that icing got Jonz; but it gives the tale coherence.) I suppose that I may, after writing this, lose my engine in the dark, or in cloud, or over the water, and add my name to those annals as well. But when I fly in what are considered to be safe conditions—clear weather, daytime—I wonder how much safer I really am. There are many moments—over cities, during the climb immediately after takeoff, over mountains, even over merely rough, rocky terrain—when an engine problem might be a very serious matter; and there is always the question of how well I would handle the emergency, and whether I would, after picking a landing spot, actually arrive at it at the right speed and the right height to make a landing. Flying must necessarily involve these uncertainties and risks, and their differences are in degree, not kind. It is difficult to make a rational survey of risks and weigh them against one another, and I think it is not unduly reckless to ignore them, for the most part, altogether, as we ignore the risks of driving a car. Which one of us always drives as though his brakes might fail the next time he put his foot on them, or as though a child might suddenly burst out of the rows of parked cars? But these risks are not the subject of endless and significant discussions; they are taken for granted by young studs and little old ladies alike. Questions of risk and safety seem to have an obsessive interest for pilots. But when the pieces are picked up after an accident, it always seems as though, in a pinch, risk and safety seemed less important than impatience, overconfidence, or reluctance to spend a boring night in a strange town.

Most small aircraft do not make hops of more than about five hundred miles at a time. In meteorological terms, five hundred miles is a fairly short distance; weather systems move that far in a day, and the spaces between systems are usually that large or larger. For a short trip, spending only three hours en route, the pilot can get a fairly clear idea of his en route weather. Longer flights pose greater problems. If you are planning to fly all day in a Cessna 172, landing for fuel and a snack and covering fifteen hundred miles between sunrise and sunset, the ramifications of weather can be complex. For instance, if you are flying westbound and there is a forecast of some thunderstorm activity in the afternoon, you can expect a fairly easy job of maneuvering underneath the storms, because the light will be behind the clouds. Eastbound, the flight would be much more difficult. A line of thundershowers which, when backlit, is seen to be full of wide gaps, appears solid gray-black when viewed from the west in the late afternoon. The same is true of clouds in general. So in this kind of weather, a pilot might decide to take off very early in the morning or divide the trip over two days, so as either to avoid the storms completely or to have the sun in the right place when he reaches them.

Winds entail similar considerations. A rapidly moving weather system might bring with it a complete change in wind direction over a period of half a day. By leaving earlier or later the pilot might take advantage of more favorable winds, or the better visibilities that usually prevail after a cold front has passed through. Not that the wind in itself is a determining factor in the feasibility of a trip; it simply makes it longer and more tiring when it is a headwind, and pleasantly quicker when it is a tailwind. The slower the airplane, the greater the effect. A 40-knot headwind, which is about the worst you would usually encounter, will cut the groundspeed of a Cessna 150 almost in half, but that of a Beech Bonanza by only a quarter. Headwinds do not only mean longer flights, however; they also mean that you will not get so far on a tankful of fuel. A leg that you could normally fly without refueling might require a refueling stop if there is a significant headwind. This in turn will protract the trip much beyond its normal length, because you always end up spending longer on the ground than you think you will.

The wind normally gets faster and faster the farther you get from the ground, and it often isn't blowing the same way up high as it is down low. Usually the difference is ten or twenty degrees, but once in a while the winds at altitudes a few thousand feet apart will differ by ninety degrees or more. When you call for a weather report, you might only ask for winds at the altitude at which you intend to cruise. But if you asked for several altitudes—three, six, nine, and twelve thousand would be the choice open to most general aviation pilots—you might find that at some level the wind was sufficiently different from the others to make you change your normal choice of a cruising level.

Wind flows over the terrain like water down the bed of a stream, and it undergoes similar sorts of disturbances by obstacles. Mountain ranges are a prime example. Wind blows up the windward side, accelerates over the top, and tumbles in disorder down the lee side, just as water flows over a spillway. If you had to swim alongside a spillway, you would probably prefer to do your swimming along the upstream side, where the water was smooth; the same in flying. If you have a choice about where to fly with respect to a mountain ridge, find out the wind direction and fly along the upwind side of the ridge. Even thousands of feet above the mountain, its effects may be felt. Similarly, the turbulence generated by mountains remains in the air for great distances, and a westbound pilot crossing the Rockies begins to detect the turbulence, the thickening of the haze layer, the rising of the inversion and the disturbed quality of its upper surface a hundred miles before he catches sight of the mountains. The wind not only blows roughly over the mountains, but harder too; a low groundspeed due to headwinds over the plains will become lower still when you reach the mountains.

You can usually get a better idea of the wind patterns over large portions of the country by looking at a newspaper weather map than by asking the Flight Service briefer, if the weather map is provided with the contour lines called isobars, which map the distribution of pressure. The winds aloft blow parallel to the isobars, and the direction of the flow is, in the northern hemisphere, clockwise around a high and counterclockwise around a low. The steeper the pressure gradient, the closer the isobars are to one another and the faster the wind. The general movement of lows and highs is in an arc from west to east. Often there is nothing you can do about the weather; but occasionally you can make use of it. When, for example, you are flying across the center of a low, you would incline your route to the right of the center, because that would be the side on which the wind would be behind you.

I like to do my flight planning on a Jeppesen low altitude planning chart; it covers the whole United States, gives the major airways and distances, and makes it apparent at a glance what major towns and airports lie along my route. I almost always plot a straight course, but with certain exceptions. Flying from the east coast to Los Angeles, for instance, I like to swing somewhat to the south. Santa Fe, New Mexico, is located at the southern tip of the high Rockies, and you can often get under weather at Santa Fe or Albuquerque when you can't get through farther to the north. Once you're past that area, you can make it to the coast at 8,500 feet. Flying along the west coast toward Seattle, I like to bend my course somewhat to the west, to stay on the seaward side of the Trinity Alps. Flying up and down the eastern seaboard, I go direct, but I often take lower altitudes than I would in the west. Traffic in the East is heavy, and short-distance commercial flights are often found scurrying back and forth at 10,000 feet or less; the visibility there is also often really awful, with the air full of a brilliant moist haze that seems to have no definite top; and so by staying relatively low one at least stays in touch with the ground. But I rarely fly below 4,000 feet, because VOR reception deteriorates at low altitudes. In the West, where the VORs are farther apart, higher en route altitudes are needed. But if I'm flying a slow airplane, I sometimes forget about VORs, and follow rivers and roads instead; it is much easier to tell where you are at all times when you are following some extended landmark, and it is more interesting to watch a road than a needle.

I like to fly at night, and sometimes deliberately leave the second leg of a trip for darkness; but preferably if it is over flat country. High mountains present particular problems at night. Recently, flying from Fond du Lac, Wisconsin, to Los Angeles, I drew my customary straight line and planned a stop at Denver. We took off in the early afternoon. On westbound flights, because the time is changing in such a way as to prolong the day rather than shorten it, you can better afford to get a late start. The headwinds were pretty bad, and we took more than five hours to reach Denver. It was rough, Nancy was feeling bad, and a stop was in order. But there were difficulties. With a stiff northwesterly wind, it was obvious that the climb out of Denver to cross the mountains was going to be long and rough; the wind would be pouring down over the ridges into the plain, and we would be climbing upstream, like a salmon. Another problem was light. Evening was coming, and the IFR chart showed a minimum en route altitude over the mountains of 17,000 feet, which meant that the mountains came up to about 15,000 feet along our route. Finally, the stiff headwind, which meant that we would still be a long time flying before reaching Los Angeles, also meant that we would have to take off from Denver with quite a bit of fuel—at least 70 gallons; so we would be particularly heavily laden as we climbed out. I called Denver Flight Watch and got the current weather: 84 degrees on the ground. That made up my mind; we ought to continue, however tired and uncomfortable, to Grand Junction, more than 200 miles farther along, but on the other side of the maximum Rockies. The elevation at Grand Junction was about the same as that at Denver; but we would have a shorter distance to go from there, could take off with less fuel, and the sharks-denture mountains and violent ridge-line downdrafts would have been negotiated in daylight. We would be taking off in the relative calm of darkness, and, though we would have to climb to 13,000 feet in the vicinity of Bryce Canyon, the first leg out of Grand Junction would call for only a 10,000-foot cruising altitude.

The rest of the flight went well, just as planned, and I could look back on it with some satisfaction as an example of more or less sensible strategic thinking. It proved the value of imagining the situation as it would be in a couple of hours. On the face of it the difference between taking off at Denver and taking off at Grand Junction was not great; both fields were at the same elevation and had the same temperature. The difference was in details—we would need less fuel out of Grand Junction, and we would need to reach a lower cruising altitude with the load of fuel, and reach it less quickly than if we had left from Denver. In every way, Grand Junction made more sense; I later reflected how stupid it had been of me, when I planned the flight at Fond du Lac, not to foresee the decision I would eventually have to make. Perhaps the thought of the seven hours airborne that it took us, bucking 30-knot winds, to get from there to Grand Junction was just too much to take. It would have made better sense to leave earlier in the day and to divide the trip into three legs, stopping at Grand Junction or Hanksville or Cedar City and making up for the greater time spent en route by the more tolerable leg lengths and

strange places. Other aspects of the flight, ones that you take with you, are equally important to safety and require their own forethought. Density altitude is one of them. As I mentioned in the instance of our continuing on to Grand Junction, the same density altitude can have different implications at different times. What is dangerous is not the density altitude itself, but the density altitude plus the need to go a long distance or to carry a heavy load. (Not that there aren't extremes of density in which even a lightly loaded airplane couldn't take off; but they are so rare that they call attention to themselves.)

Another safety consideration is fuel supply. It is a remarkable thing that many accidents occur because pilots allow themselves to run out of fuel. What could be easier to foresee, or to prevent?

General aviation planes have, for the most part, crude fuel gauging systems. Perhaps because of this, some pilots permit themselves to interpret the gauge optimistically, thinking that since it is so crude, the manufacturers of the airplane must at any rate have calibrated it conservatively. Perhaps most pilots don't even bother with that much of a rationalization; they simply think, as one does in a car, "Just fifteen miles to go!"

If you lean your engine the way I have described, bringing it back to the point of roughness and not enriching any more than is absolutely necessary, you will be able to match the airplane handbook values of fuel flow and, give or take a few knots, of speed. Handbook values of speed are not important, however, because what realistically concerns us is not airspeed but groundspeed. We know from the handbook, or from experience, how many gallons per hour we are using, we know what we have aboard; the fuel gauges permit us to verify, roughly, that things are as we reason that they should be. Finally, knowing how fast we are going and how far we have to go, we should be able to tell how much we will have left in the tanks when we land.

We talk about carrying a reserve of fuel—for VFR, one hears figures like half an hour's fuel at cruise. In a Cessna 150, that isn't much—just three gallons. It would be hard to be sure that the tanks had been filled completely to start with; perhaps they were a bit low, or there was a trapped bubble somewhere, and the theoretical three gallons is really two or one and a half. But never mind; what does reserve mean, anyway? Does it mean that we want to land with three gallons unless some completely unforeseen emergency prevents us from doing so? Or is three gallons the buffer that we intend to save for the headwind that we suspect we might have? I think it ought to be the former, and I also think that it ought to be at least an hour's fuel, even for a VFR flight. Suppose you are in a retractable-gear airplane and the gear fails to lower properly; you would not want a low fuel stated added to your problems. Suppose you strayed off course and were lost for a while. Suppose you arrived at your destination airport and a disabled airplane was stuck in the middle of the only runway. Half an hour's fuel is simply not enough. Half an hour may seem long when all is going well and that is all the time that separates you from your destination. When you have problems, it's no time at all.

# 13

# *Unhappy Landings*

More than other forms of transportation, flying seems to bring to us the thought of Death. I capitalize the name because Death is here like a personality hunting the pilot, whom he, the pilot, outwits or outruns his whole life long, or until he is finally overtaken in an automobile or in a hospital where, surrounded by medicine's ministers and acolytes, he succumbs to cancers as modern and technological as airplanes are.

Fear of heights, fear of falling, they are so fundamental to our nature that it is tempting to say that the enjoyment many people find in flying is paradoxically rooted precisely in those fears; and, on the other hand, it is surprising that as many people who find no particular pleasure in flying—that is, in defying and abrading their atavistic fear—do it with an air of indifferent calm and unconcern. In flying, we forget what it is to fly. There is no sense of height, curiously enough, or what sense there is is arrived at through verbal self-assurances: "I am two miles above the ground; see, the people look like bacteria!" People sometimes wonder at the superior impressiveness of a view from the top of a hill to that from an airplane beneath which the hill itself appears insignificant; a hill gives a superior sense of height. To recapture the perception of height in an airplane it is necessary to do something exceptional. In my own experience, two procedures that come to mind are parachuting out of an airplane and flying over a cliff. No doubt there are others; undoubtedly hang gliding gives the proper sense, but I have never done it; and I cannot remember whether ballooning, which I have done but long ago, has the impact I am thinking of.

What is needed, at any rate, is something that brings the gulf beneath us back to life. Stepping out the door of a jump plane onto the little step from which we will momentarily push off into space, backward, falling face upward (an insane act; I did it thirty-seven times before fate intervened to stop me); or stepping out the door into space without the intermediate stop on the step; or, really, just riding up in the plane next to the open doorway, looking down, knowing that shortly you will have to jump—any of these acts revives your sense of height, of the space beneath as a three-dimensional emptiness with certain ghastly implications for one who penetrates it without special equipment and the normal amount of luck and divine favor. You can thus re-acquire, for the purposes of flight, the sense you have when teetering on a narrow catwalk ten feet above the ground—the sense of real height, the fear of falling. Flying over a cliff does the same thing. If, for instance, you fly toward the Grand Canyon low over the treetops of the south rim, so that you barely see the canyon before getting to it, and then suddenly it falls away a mile beneath you, you feel as though you were a projectile, fired from a gun on the rim, and about to lose momentum and plummet down, down. You experience a flood of fear and, instantly, the sublime delight that comes from knowing that there is nothing to fear.

These are, properly, the sensations of flight; doubtless they are the sensations of the aborigine when he first rides in an airplane and is uncertain that he is not being carried aloft in the entrails of a huge predatory bird. They were the sensations of the first flyers—those characters whose passing overhead filled the poets of the first decades of the century with extraordinary, and not always verisimilar, fantasies. But they are not ours. Flying rivals the utter banality of driving in its ordinary sensations, except for the rather special relationship which seems to exist between flight and fear.

Statistics, which are to our time what the pronouncements of shamans and prophets were to earlier ages, give support to the notion, not a cause of enthusiasm for the manufacturers of light aircraft, that small airplanes—general aviation airplanes—are indeed one of the most dangerous ways of getting around. Airlines are quite safe, in spite of their occasional spectacular lapses; cars are as dangerous as we all know; and general aviation is about ten times more dangerous than cars. Each year about 1,400 deaths occur in light airplanes; a rate of 1 fatal accident per 50,000 airplane-hours flown. Many people who know nothing else about aviation have somehow absorbed this intelligence, perhaps because the newspapers report private plane accidents with such monotonous regularity, and if you do not take the elementary precaution of keeping your involvement with airplanes a secret, people you meet socially will inevitably, once they have a drink or two in them, either bore you at length with accounts of their own or their relatives' peripheral experiences of small aircraft, or treat you, and perhaps the spouse whom you have with difficulty persuaded to accept your interest, to an explanation of its horrific dangers.

Apart from the dangers of the cocktail party, however, there are those of the flight; and they are the more calamitous.

What do statistical dangers mean to pilots? The answer is hard to come by, but at least it is obvious, to start with, that the statistics are least useful to individuals when they refer to large groups, unless the pertinent qualifications of the group and the individual are identical. By this I mean that each individual actually possesses exemptions of one kind or another from the fate of the statistical norm. He may be more or less at risk, but at any rate his dangers are his own, not those of the group at large. If they tell you that one out of a thousand Americans will die in childbirth, and you are an adult, you do not feel alarmed even though you are an American. Likewise, the fact that as a pilot you have, say, one chance in a thousand of being killed in a plane crash this year, need not necessarily concern you, because the group of pilots who provided the material for that statistic was a group and not you, an individual.

A breakdown of the types of accidents will show what I mean. The figures are hypothetical. Say that out of 1,000 pilots 20 will have accidents in a year. Ten of these will be fatal. On the face of it, it would seem that you have 1 chance in 50 of having an accident each year, and 1 in 100 of being killed. That would be 1 in 10 of being killed over a 10-year period. Not so good. But consider your exemptions. For one thing, you may fly only half as many hours per year as the group average; so your risk may be less. Perhaps, of the 10 who have fatal accidents, 1 dies in the crash of a twin that lost one engine on takeoff and entered a stall/spin because of pilot mismanagement of the disabled airplane; you don't fly twins, so that can't happen to you. Now your chances are 9 in 1,000 rather than 10. Furthermore, of the 9 remaining, 3 flew into adverse weather conditions without instrument capability; but you are instrument rated and equipped, so now you are down to 6 in 1,000. Of these, 1 drank a few too many before taking off, became disoriented, and crashed into a lake on takeoff. You don't drink, so you're safe from that fate. Down now to 5 in 1,000, you further find that one of the victims got lost and ran out of gas at night, and another flew into a blind canyon and went into a spin while turning to get out. By the simple expedient of never running out of gas you could disqualify yourself from one category, and by that of staying well clear of canyons, blind or otherwise, from the other; thus your risk declines still further.

And so on. Many accidents involve pilot errors which can be avoided by adhering to certain rules and procedures; others involve categories of operations—icing, thunderstorms—that are known to be dangerous and that one can, if one wishes to, easily avoid. Some may involve categories of equipment that one is not exposed to—cropdusters, homebuilts, sailplanes. In many accidents the risk was obvious at the beginning of the ill-starred flight—obvious, at least, in retrospect—and despite the bromide about twenty-twenty hindsight, it does not usually take much foresight to descry at least the possibility of what, in hindsight, looms as having been a virtual certainty.

Is it, therefore, simply that most of the pilot-victims of airplane accidents are blind, bullheaded blunderers?

I have divided feelings on the subject. One comes away from the study of some accidents with the conclusion that the pilot (out of ignorance or stupidity or the ill-advised optimism of people who have ceased to believe in their own mortality) brought the catastrophe upon himself. One feels a positive dislike, a contempt, for the heedless idiot who killed himself and his family because he could not take the hint of bad weather and postpone a vacation flight, or for the dude who ran his fuel tanks dry twenty miles short of his destination because he could not wrench his tiny brain free of the obsession that he must be *there* at a certain moment, and nowhere else. But I also feel pity for them—for the disorienting fear they must have felt as circumstances turned upon them, and as the safeguards and standby systems in which they had been trained to place their confidence proved useless; for those who, alone, far from home in gathering darkness, saw their fate come suddenly to scoop them up.

There is a kind of unfairness about airplane accidents—about all accidents, perhaps; it is that there is often no fixed connection between actions and their consequences. We have all done the things that have killed a few of us—driven home from a party at which we drank too heavily, slipped under a low ceiling in snow showers to scud-run to a doubtful destination, or stretched a tank of gas too far. But we have escaped unharmed. That is the reason why it is difficult to divorce oneself too completely from the accident statistics, and claim too many exemptions. It is quite possible that the statistic who crashed the twin had recently taken a refresher course in engine-out procedures; that the pilot who crashed VFR in bad weather was actually instrument rated, but for one reason or another thought he could make it VFR and didn't want to file; or that the pilot who got lost and ran out of gas at night was an experienced navigator, but that his compass failed in a way that the accident investigator could not identify. So that at the same time as we reflect that by our qualifications and practices we exclude ourselves from the statistical categories of those who have crashed, we must also consider that those categories are not so narrow and exclusive as we imagine, but may, in the infinite variety of chance and circumstance, expand to encompass us.

To the reader of accident reports in the newspaper, they are sometimes mysterious to the point of incomprehensibility. One of the essentials of a newspaper report seems to be some mention of the engine; whether witnesses report that it was running, sputtering, or silent, we are encouraged to believe that the engine, like some contraption of the early industrial revolution, could not be counted on to turn for a few hours without stopping for one reason or another. To the popular sense of things, a stopped engine means an airplane falling vertically from the sky, like a bird with a heart attack. The process of re-education that would be necessary to correct this widespread error is too vast to contemplate. But the fact is that the engine plays a role in a minority of accidents, and in most cases where it does play a role, its failure is due to some action or omission of the pilot. A truly magnificent example of this occurred in 1978, when a National Airlines 727 cruising at some distance from the Atlantic coast, northbound from Florida, lost all three engines at once. When I read the front-page newspaper account of this in the Los Angeles *Times*, after I had retracted my eyeballs and closed my mouth, I reflected that obviously some crew action had to be at the root of such an event; the possibility of all three engines dying of natural causes *at the same time* was inconceivably remote. Indeed, a month or so later the flight engineer fessed up; he had some fuel pumps off that should have been on, and, in combination with other actions of the pilot and copilot, they caused the engines to lose fuel feed because of vapor lock. (The engines had restarted immediately when normal restart procedures, which included turning on the fuel pumps in question, were used—another tipoff that it was not the engines themselves that were at fault.) This explanatory report also found its way into the press, but to my knowledge only the aviation press; the

*Times* did not carry it, and so all the readers who noticed the first report were left with the impression that airplane and engine design are in such a parlous state that a three-engine airliner could have all three engines quit at once more or less as a matter of course.

On the other hand, immensely detailed reports of accidents, such as those published, in the distant wake of the event, by the National Transportation Safety Board, are often no more enlightening. The risk of complete information is that it prevents us from forming convenient judgments of simple facts. We can discern the outline of the pilot's error in the bristling mass of hurried events, but we can sympathize, as well, with his action. The trouble with accident investigations is that the fact that an accident happened seems to put its antecedents into a different class from other, ostensibly identical events that occur daily without bringing about a disaster. When the famous Tenerife collision of two crowded 747s occurred because the KLM pilot misunderstood, or anticipated, his takeoff clearance and began his takeoff in heavy fog while another jet was taxiing across the runway, all attention was focused on this error. It was deemed all the more incomprehensible because of the seniority and exemplary record of the peccant captain; but no attention was given to the fact that if there had not been another airplane in the way the improper procedure would have passed unnoticed, and that, in all likelihood, pilots misunderstand or anticipate clearances every day.

The classic example of an item of information that is made to grow in importance by the popular press—whereas in fact it has no importance whatever—is that of the flight's being or not being on a flight plan. Usually the newspaper report mentions that, according to an FAA source, the aircraft was not on a flight plan, as though this had something to do with the accident. Nothing could be more misleading, more infuriating for that matter, because of the impression given that government supervision, as represented by whatever official sanction for flying a flight plan may seem to imply, somehow enhances the safety of flight, and that a pilot who evades his duty to file a flight plan is of course exactly the type of crazy bandit who would get himself into an accident. The one value of a VFR flight plan—that it may alert the authorities to a missing airplane and even in some cases give an indication of its possible whereabouts—is apparently not taken very seriously even by the FAA itself, which has proposed as an economy measure to do away with VFR flight plans altogether.

It appears, then, that capsule accident reports, or the two- or three-word summaries accompanying accident statistics, or, worst of all, the mystifying scenarios pieced together by newspaper reporters when the dust has barely settled at the scene, provide us with little genuine illumination. Lists of "don'ts" compiled by ferreting out the apparent antecedents of accidents and then telling pilots to shun them do very little to educate pilots or prevent accidents. To observe that many pilots died by flying into bad weather and then colliding with the ground, and then to advise students, "Avoid bad weather; do not fly into the ground!" will serve no purpose; for one thing, you may be certain that each pilot who flew into bad weather and crashed had, in fact, been advised not to do so, probably quite emphatically, hundreds of times.

The root causes of accidents must be sought for at a deeper level. *Flying* magazine has published, for many years, transcripts of recorded radio conversations between pilots and ground controllers that preceded accidents, originally under the title of "Pilot Error," and then under the less judgmental title of "Aftermath," when it appeared that certain heirs and assigns resented the imputation of fault to the deceased. These transcripts presented, at least to me, a keener insight into the anatomies of accidents than that afforded by most narrative descriptions. One felt that one was in the cockpit of the doomed flight; what was most impressive was the familiarity of it all. When you read in a capsule report, "Pilot, aged 41 years, 2,100 hours total time, etc., etc., lost control of the aircraft after loss of power in right engine . . ." you imagine what you regard as a "typical" 41-year-old pilot of a twin, a blend of all those whom you have known, fumbling incompetently with a rolling airplane in some typical manner which you have distilled from all the incompetent fumbling you have seen before. And thus your perception of the event becomes, without your knowing it, unreal, blurred, as though you were to create an image of a "typical housewife" by superimposing upon one another photographs of ten or a hundred individual housewives. The accident ceases to make an impression, because it has taken on the generalized, undifferentiated qualities of characters in movies made for television.

The "Pilot Error"/"Aftermath" transcripts, on the other hand, were real life, and as real life always does, they gripped the reader with the unexpectedness, the novelty, of particular details buried in the "typical," general situation. You saw immediately that the question "How could he have gotten so mixed up?" that accident reports always elicit has its simple, obvious answer in the fact that the mental processes of a frightened person in an airplane bear no resemblance to those of the reader of an accident report in a magazine, just as the mental state of a person deeply and newly in love bears no resemblance to that of his friends who are at a loss to see in what way his beloved is superior to the rest of mankind. We imagine that the mental states identified by the words "disorientation, confusion, panic" can be turned on and off just as we can turn our imagination of them on and off. But the mind of a person who is disoriented, confused, panicky is a different mind from that of the person sitting at home in his chair. Such a mind cannot simply "pull itself together," any more than a person who is drowning can arrest the process and tread water long enough to clear the water out of his lungs. Fear leads again and again in these accounts to loss of control, bad decisions, traps, stupidities. Sometimes good luck extricates a frightened pilot from his situation; sometimes his fear is out of proportion to the problems that confront him, and he emerges unscathed as a matter of course, having learned a little more than he knew before about himself and about flying. In fact, flight without fear is hard to imagine; I do, however, know one or two people who claim never to have gotten a good scare in an airplane, and who have enough time behind them now that I suppose they may already possess the sang-froid that comes with experience and which the high-time pilots in the "Pilot Error" series consistently displayed, even in the worst circumstances.

The effect of taking one's instrument capability to a strange place can be unexpectedly devastating. One new instrument pilot set out in his new airplane, with his family, on a vacation trip. I think they were going to Disneyland; they ended up in the "Pilot Error" column. The pilot planned the trip carefully, consulting his instructor. Not that the flight, starting somewhere in the East and ending up in southern California, was anything extraordinarily difficult. But it was his first big trip.

The radio transcript made touching reading. He had left Denver, crossing the Rockies in light IFR weather at 15,000 feet. His airspeed indicator started to act up; probably a little ice had accumulated in his pitot tube, and his pitot heat, if he had turned it on, was not working. Alarmed, he informed the controller of his problem, and the controller, infected with the pilot's fear, cautioned him to keep his airspeed up. This was terrible advice; if the airspeed indicator isn't working, diving to increase airspeed won't help a bit. The pilot slid into increasing panic, and eventually dove right into a mountainside in the clouds.

His plight illuminates the shortcomings of a new instrument rating. The pilot had passed the tests, but he was completely unprepared for the most routine malfunction. He seems to have forgotten, or not to have known, that sudden loss of airspeed, unaccompanied by loss of engine power or changes in wind noise or control pressures or G-loading, is simply impossible; it has to be an instrument problem. He seems also to have made an error in flight planning; given his insecurity, he would have done better to fly farther south, at lower altitude and probably in better weather. But the worst problem was that he was psychologically unprepared for IFR flying. The prospect of a long cross-country trip loomed unreasonably large in his imagination, and moved him to excessive early precautions which, as is usually the case, weren't the right ones. The simple precaution of flying farther south when you have a heavily loaded airplane and clouds over the Rockies was the one he failed to take. The rapidity with which, as the transcript reveals, terror built up in him when the airspeed went awry suggests that the terror was there all the while, waiting to get out; the very situation of blind flying was terrifying to him.

There is, indeed, something quite unnerving about the IFR environment, as there would be, had one never been in one before, in a speeding car. One steels oneself by habit. Because of the potentially devastating effect of imaginary fears on a pilot, one must approach one's blind flying step by step, gradually enlarging one's territory, and letting one kind of weather or approach become ordinary before attacking more difficult ones. One should first fly from good weather to good weather, passing through cloud en route. Then leave in bad weather and arrive in good weather. Finally arrive in weather that is bad, but with excellent alternates. Similarly one should avoid storms, cold fronts, icing, and night IFR until one has, by progressive stages, nibbled around their edges. It is wise to skirt all situations that contain terror; better to wait until the terror has drained out of them, and been replaced by habit.

Learning about flying, whose ramifications are as endless as those of the terrain and the weather and of chance itself, almost absolutely requires passing some bad moments in the air. If they do nothing else, bad moments bring you to a recognition of the states of mind—the increase of the "mental viscosity"—that pressure brings about, so that, having learned to recognize the successive stages of fear, you recognize their reversibility and your own ability to control them.

I have been in a few frightening situations; enough that I have tried to discriminate among the sorts of fears that I have felt, and to assess the power that I possessed to control them. In one for instance, I was sufficiently terrified that my teeth were chattering slightly, my legs trembling, and I could only with difficulty decipher the numbers on the directional gyro and turn to a heading called for by an instrument approach. I doubt that I would have been able to complete the approach to minimums, but fortunately the airport appeared through a gap in the clouds and I got to it visually without any trouble. That episode taught me a number of valuable lessons which I had no doubt read and heard many times before, but which had never entered my consciousness in the necessary way. Some of them were lessons about the capabilities of airplanes, certain quirks of weather, some nasty aspects of ice formation on wings; but the most important lesson, the one with the most general application, was that I could not count on myself to perform simple tasks properly once I was sufficiently frightened. I doubt that I am much different from most other people in this respect. Two don'ts followed: don't get into frightening situations, and don't let yourself get frightened if you do.

Easier said than done, obviously. There is, as I began this chapter by saying, something basically frightening about being airborne in the first place, and so one has, by virtue of being aloft, an account of fear upon which to draw. Thus it is not the icy wing or the sputtering engine, but the combination of those things with the fact of being two thousand feet above mountains in darkness, that releases the fear. It flows out more rapidly and in greater supply than one would have imagined possible. To control fear, we must control that unconscious mechanism by which we shut out, generally, our natural fear of being airborne—because it is that fear that will augment and make uncontrollable the fear arising from any given dangerous situation. One technique that I have found useful is to do nothing. A bad situation seems to call for immediate action, and the time available seems suddenly very short. One acts rashly, automatically, spasmodically, incompetently. It is better to do nothing for fifteen seconds, half a minute, a minute. If you fly into a cloud, for instance, not meaning to, and want to get back to the VFR weather that you have just left behind, the worst thing you can do is suddenly rack the airplane over into a fast turn; sudden maneuvers produce vertigo—the compelling but erroneous sense of position that is so difficult to ignore—and to succumb to the temptation to act suddenly can lead deeper and deeper into trouble. Better to sit still, hold heading, hold altitude, hold the wings level. Relax. (You can't really relax, but you can loosen your grip a little, force your muscles to relent.) Then, knowing that *you have time,* begin a very gradual bank, very shallow, forcing yourself to scan the instruments, relaxing, patiently waiting for the reciprocal heading to appear. Of course, there's a problem right there. If you're scared, you might not be able to figure out a reciprocal heading. When your mind feels as though it's sliding down a slope of loose gravel, adding or subtracting 180 is very difficult. Two hundred might be better; it will bring you out within 20 degrees of your original heading, and that ought to be good enough. As an alternative, you can read a reciprocal from an instrument: a card-type directional gyro, or an omni bearing selector. Once you get turned around, do nothing. Sit still. Relax. Breathe slowly and deeply. In a minute or two you'll be out of the cloud. You will have been on instruments for three minutes, perhaps; it will have seemed like the three minutes preceding your arrival at the guillotine, but in retrospect it will also seem an uneventful stretch of time. Flying is, in fact, uneventful. Danger, confusion, fear make us anticipate events, expect them, where there are none; and we end up by creating them.

I put a lot of emphasis on fear because I am convinced that it is more than simply an accompaniment to emergencies; it creates them, increases their seriousness, or makes them irrecoverable. Paradoxically too, sometimes in an emergency one feels not fear but an icy, stoic calm. One feels one's mind tossing out questions and answers like a card sorter. Someone who has experienced only the rigid calm cannot imagine the terror; someone who has experienced only the terror cannot conceive of the calm. Only when you have felt both do you realize that they both spring from the same ground, and that it is very difficult to tell what circumstances bring forth the one, what the other.

If you manage, by chance or by will power, to keep your senses in an emergency, you have still a further challenge: to keep an open mind. Suppose you're cruising along in the middle of nowhere and the engine suddenly starts to run roughly. You don't know the reason. Your mind begins to click. *Stay calm, stay calm,* you tell yourself, and you are gratified to see that you are staying calm, at least inside your head, because your body is suffused with tension. You review the few items over which you have control: mags, mixture, fuel tank. The engine is still rough. What should you do? The engine is developing power, so you could go on this way, perhaps for some distance; but perhaps its roughness presages a complete stoppage. Would it be better to pick a landing place and set the airplane down, even at a risk of damage, with some power at your disposal? Or would it be better to head for an airport, hoping that things hold together until you get there? The most difficult element in this decision, for many pilots, would be the idea of putting down the airplane in rough country while the engine is still running. The precautionary off-field landing, once a standard part of practical flying, has become so remote and infrequent an event these days that we are not prepared to confront it.

Exactly the same problem faces the pilot trapped in bad weather. Many accidents seem to have occurred because the pilot, perhaps goaded by an unreasonable optimism, passed up opportunities to land on a road or in a field, and instead remained airborne until he smashed into a cloud-wrapped hill. Too much time is spent telling pilots not to fly into bad weather, and not enough telling them that if they do, they should keep their minds open to the possibility of doing something unconventional, like landing on a road, in order to save their arses. What deters them? Fear of being caught red-handed in violation of VFR minimums? Fear of damaging the airplane? Fear of using their own initiative? Loss of face? Admission of error?

I started working on my instrument rating shortly after getting my private license, and so by the time I started flying into weather illegally I had enough time on the gauges to head automatically up, not down. I can remember a few times that I took off in bad weather, got far enough from the airport not to be able to find my way back visually, saw a bright spot in the clouds, and climbed up to the blue sky above, without a clearance. A lot of people do that. Instrument pilots say that there's nothing you can do if "some nut" is flying around out there without a clearance in the clouds, but actually the "nut" is just another pilot like themselves, taking another chance and, no doubt, learning something. For what it's worth, I have never heard of a collision between a legal IFR flight and a bandit sneaking up illegally to VFR on top. Once you're rated and equipped, or at least equipped, you don't need to break the laws to get where you're going; but you can still find yourself illegal from time to time for some reason or other. Things can happen quickly. But if you're not rated and not equipped, and things happen quickly, that one magnificent escape route—upward, and traffic be damned—is not available to you.

Flexibility of mind is difficult to retain under pressure because, in its anxiety to discover some solution, the mind seems to clamp with the compulsive fierceness of a drowning man upon the answer that may be its rescuer. Even when fright does not produce a sort of monomania, too rigid a state of mind is dangerous. There was in 1978 an interesting series of cases involving airliners and wind shear in which the rigidity of the rules for handling jets came under scrutiny. In these cases, pilots had not been paralyzed by fear, but by a respect for procedures. There is a speed, $V_2$, which is the optimum performance speed in case of an engine failure, and it was a firm rule that the airspeed could never be allowed to decay below $V_2$ in flight. Now, between $V_2$ and the onset of "stick shaker"—the device that warns of an approaching stall by mechanically shaking the control yoke—was a margin of 15 knots (in the Boeing 727), and between stick shaker and the actual stall another 20 knots. In a 727 accident at Tucson, Arizona, the pilot, following handbook procedures to the letter, struck utility poles after a long takeoff run when, hitting a wind shear, the airplane did not climb as rapidly as it normally should. The airplane could have cleared the poles if the pilot had made use of some of his airspeed by pulling up and converting it into altitude. Once clear of obstacles, he could have regained speed easily, since the airplane, with all three engines running, had a surplus of power. By refusing to slow below $V_2$, the pilot deprived himself of the one resource—surplus energy—that could have carried him over the obstacle. (It might be argued that an engine failure, had he gone below $V_2$, could have been disastrous; but in the face of one certain disaster, it is gratuitous to invoke a highly improbable counter-disaster.)

General aviation pilots, who are on the whole far less disciplined than airline pilots (and this is one of the reasons for their far worse accident record), have probably suffered, more often, from an error diametrically opposed to that of the 727's crew at Tucson. Confronted with an obstacle that the airplane will not clear, they forget about minimum speeds and pull up, hoping that they will not stall, or forgetting that they may. But they suffer from analogous fixities of mind, persisting in taking off when it has become apparent that the airplane is using too much runway and has too little power (to mention a case similar to the Tucson one), or, to return to the classic "continued VFR" situation, driving on into worsening weather as though their putative destination were the only place on earth that was to be spared sulphur and brimstone. The pilot of the 727 was to be forgiven because his training insisted upon $V_2$ as an absolute minimum speed, and probably, in the interest of inspiring compliance with its rules, did nothing to illuminate the area below $V_2$ so that the pilot could know that he had, in the 35 knots between $V_2$ and the stall, a resource which might some day be valuable to him. Similarly, the precautionary off-airport landing, the unauthorized climb through clouds, are resources available to the VFR pilot, but which he may regard as taboo or fraught with unimagined dangers or nightmarish consequences.

Circumstances have their momentum. A person who does not fly, asked to imagine what he would do if he found himself moving into a worsening situation—weather, night, icing, fuel—answers, "I would turn back," or "I would land right away!" The failure of so many pilots to do so, then, seems incomprehensible. But when it's really happening to you, it feels different. The situation is no longer something theoretical, objective, at a distance; it envelops you, you become part of it, and the outside world becomes saturated with characteristics projected from the psyche of the pilot. It seems hostile and competitive; one feels challenged, and automatically begins to fight back—not consciously, not with anger, but on a level at which one's reactions are shrouded in rationalizations. A light spot in dark clouds—a so-called sucker hole—seems like the beckoning salvation, the piece of overdue good luck, which you feel that you deserve and keep hoping will materialize. Furthermore you have already, in imagination, reached your destination. When you planned the flight, when you took off, you were already assuming that you would, in two or three hours, be in a certain other place. The possibility of some entirely different course of events has not entered your mind. And so now, when the rain squalls are closing around you and you're on the verge of losing your way, you find it particularly difficult to break free of your assumptions about what is going to happen in the next few hours. You keep telling yourself that if you can just get around this next shower the weather will clear up; you remember, in the back of your mind, the many previous times that you pressed on and were rewarded with improving conditions and on-time arrival. You are aware of the prestige possessed, however undeservedly, by the pilot who, despite difficulties, gets there. Conversely, you sense that if you call your destination and report that you had to land because of the weather, and the people there look up at a partially cloudy sky with twenty miles visibility, you will seem fussy, incompetent, old-womanish. Your insistence on flying your own plane will seem like an eccentric, irrational foible. And so in order to prove everything from your own competence to the viability of personal air transportation, you press on a few more minutes, a few more miles.

A while ago a friend of mine flew on airlines to a Kansas town to meet another pilot who was arriving in his own plane. The weather closed in, a blizzard began, the airport virtually shut down. Nothing was flying. And then word spread that a light airplane had just landed. General wonderment; and the awaited pilot entered from the storm.

The story was repeated among acquaintances of the daring pilot, who is himself a vocal advocate of careful flying. No moral was ever offered, because the image of his Cessna materializing out of the impenetrable snow where nothing else was flying had at once an epic grandeur and a comic quality that everyone saw for himself. The ambiguities were delicious; had the pilot, the moralist, busted minimums? Had his business meeting been so important to him—it was possible—or could he not accept the thought of being *unable to make it*? No one would ask him about it, because one could so easily anticipate the smile, the gently humorous disclaimer, "Really, you know, it wasn't bad at all!"

He is a skillful pilot; I believe he could handle whatever came along, but he depends, as we all do, on good luck, and he does take chances. But you have to take chances, and, I suppose, you have to balance the precariousness of your risks against the breadth of your experience and the completeness of your expertise. He is a kind of air-going Wallenda; you would not advise most people to walk a high wire, but you admire one who does it with impunity—admire him, in fact, more than you admire ordinary people. So you do not consider him a fool to risk his life for nothing; and when he finally falls, you feel that the whole world is the poorer for the loss of such an admirable fellow. Pilots aspire to that same kind of absurd heroism. When we fly a homemade single-engine plane across the Atlantic and the Pacific we are fashioning, by that elaborate Russian roulette, a frame for our portrait, an ennobling decoration for our self-esteem. To fly into a hillside during a rainstorm when one could have been sipping coffee at an airport several miles back may seem more stupid than ennobling, and indeed by any measure it is, except by the measure of the pilot who made the mistake (which became a mistake only because it ended badly); because if he was pigheaded, obstinate, vain, reckless, and shortsighted, he was also, in the same way as the Light Brigade, indomitable, fearless, and bold. It is that imaginary parallel action in which a flight home for dinner is interchangeable, through the mind's metaphors, with a mission in battle, and in which discretion melts into cowardice and recklessness into courage, that seduces novice pilots into incredible blunders, and that makes the advice of pilot moralists, easily given, so difficult of application.

I have made it sound, no doubt, as though all airplane accidents were produced by the will, the judgment, or the emotional compulsions of pilots. Obviously not all are; the National Transportation Safety Board collects data on accidents and tabulates circumstances and causes, which are then digested by a computer and emerge as long, foul-smelling lists of the permutations of frailty, human and mechanical.

In one tabulation for 1976, the pilot is a "broad cause/factor" in almost 84 percent of accidents. When the types of pilot contribution are tabulated, however, they are scarcely homogeneous. By a long margin the most common error attributed to pilots in fatal accidents is failure to obtain/maintain flying speed (caused 183 accidents), followed by continued VFR flight into adverse weather conditions (98), improper inflight decisions or planning (80), and spatial disorientation (80). These categories overlap, and a single fatal accident could be produced by all four: the pilot fails to get a good weather briefing, goes on into worsening weather until he plunges into a cloud, becomes disoriented, spirals out, emerges from the bottom of the cloud near the ground in a strange position, pulls up, stalls, spins, and gets killed. In this case, the pilot could certainly be faulted, several times over, on the level of judgment, volition, flying technique, or self-control. In some of the less destructive categories, however, such as failure to recover properly from a bounced landing or to maintain directional control on landing, the pilot simply made a physical mistake; he thought he was doing it right, he meant well, but he blew it.

Since flying is a skill that some people will acquire to perfection while others never really get the hang of, a certain number of accidents will always arise from errors of technique. Airplanes are not excessively tricky to handle, for the most part, and the combined effect of years of design refinement and of the licensing procedure has been to make the dangers of unskillful operation rather slight. Still, a few borderline situations exist in which skill is very useful. Landing on a short strip in a gusty wind, a crosswind, let's say, when there are ridges of snow piled up on either side of the runway, is frankly difficult, and being difficult it's dangerous. It may be more dangerous for one pilot than for another; some will always do it successfully, some should never attempt it at all, and some will believe they belong to the first category and find out that they are of the second.

Since incompetent plane-handling is rarely of much significance elsewhere than in taxiing, taking off, and landing, and blunders develop in a more or less controlled context, inept piloting produces few fatalities, though a good deal of property damage. People will apparently never stop hand-starting airplanes with the throttle wide open and a small rock wedged beneath one wheel for safety, and a certain number of parked airplanes each year end up looking as though they have been put through a food processor. Terrified friends are removed unhurt from the cockpit of the runaway plane, needing a stiff drink, and armed for life with an effective horror story.

Less amusingly, people are maimed or disemboweled by propellers, often not precisely by the negligence of pilots so much as by the same sort of assumptions about the intentions of others that we always make when driving. In one incident at my home field a while ago a newly licensed pilot took a friend of his up for a joy ride. The friend felt sick, and on their turning off the runway after the first landing asked to be dropped off while the pilot made a few more takeoffs and landings. Cautioned about the propeller, the passenger left the plane by the right side door, walked around the tail, said a few words to the pilot through the left window, and then, with a graceful and unexpected movement, swung beneath the wing strut into the whirling propeller and was instantly eviscerated. It is a rule constantly violated that when people disembark from an airplane no propeller should be turning. It is violated because we assume, with good reason, that people possess intelligence and that if they are aware of the propeller at one moment they will not suddenly, inexplicably forget about it at the next.

I find it a little hard to sympathize with the mentality that condemns as recklessness an operation of this kind, purely in the light of its gruesome conclusion. A more Olympian observer could say that operating airplanes in the first place is reckless in itself, and to do so for pleasure alone is madness; for a critic then to argue that certain subdivisions of this madness are more blameworthy than others is mere pedantry. A certain danger is inevitable; however many the layers of safeguards, people will contrive to penetrate them. The pilot whose friend was killed by the propeller will—if he ever flies again—undoubtedly turn off his engine before he lets a passenger open the door; and if he goes through the rest of his life without ever cutting another passenger to pieces, he will congratulate himself on the success of his safeguards. On the other hand, other pilots will disembark hundreds of passengers with propellers whirling on every side, and not hurt a soul. Time and chance happeneth to them all.

The danger of flying that I find most frightening, and which seems to me the most ironically merciless, is that of a mechanical failure having nothing at all to do with the pilot's performance. To some extent even mechanical failures can be laid at the pilot's doorstep; if he failed to detect the fuel leak that set the engine afire it was an inadequate preflight inspection, or if he put off checking the excessive magneto drop until the next stop, and lost an engine on the way, it was reckless operation. But there are also materials failures that give no telltale signs, and breakdowns of the electrical or vacuum systems that no preflight inspection could foresee. Valve assemblies, fuel and oil pumps and lines and fittings, are popular causes of death and damage. The lines and fittings may give some indication of incipient damage, and sometimes are accessible for inspection; but valves and pumps stare back at you in the same way whether they are healthy or sick. Crankshafts, rods, cylinders, pistons; you don't get a look at them from one year to the next.

Airplane structures and mechanisms are designed to the conflicting requirements of lightness and strength, efficiency and reliability. The basic light airplane is an extremely simple device, made for the most part of materials of a high quality and avoiding systems and mechanisms that require extreme delicacy of fit, care of operation, or regularity of maintenance. Airplane engines are large for their power output—two pounds and two cubic inches displacement per horsepower are typical values—and even at full power are not in distress. They are expected to run one or two thousand hours between major overhauls without serious problems. Properly run and maintained, they will do so; but many are not properly run and maintained, and don't. They are surrounded, furthermore, by interfacing equipment far inferior in quality to the engine itself. The push-pull controls operating throttle, prop, and mixture are wretched things, prone to break apart internally, creep, or come loose from the fragile mountings that support them. Engine compartments get dirty; dust mixed with oil grinds away at moving parts; light aluminum brackets and baffles crack. But all these things are rather costly and difficult to replace, and since their wear is often progressive they are left from one inspection to another. Money plays an inevitable role; if the mechanic says that a part ought to be replaced and will cost $225, but that it will most likely be all right for another hundred hours, the pilot who is eager to spend his money (and there are many) will go for immediate repair, and the one who is in a bind will opt for delay.

The economic pressure against impeccable maintenance exists at every level, from the hobbyist with a thirty-year-old Cessna 140 to the airline with a 747. Little parts that ought to cost next to nothing, like hoses that carry fuel, oil, or air, are made to specifications dreamed up by the military, which has money to burn, and are specially fabricated in small numbers for airplanes. Not that they are perfect by any means. In fact, the fancy liners and braids concocted to protect fuel lines against fire, solvents, chafing, impact, and heat sometimes turn out to do more harm than good, and the exotic fittings connecting hoses to appliances are difficult to install, prone to leak, and liable to plug the line in the very process of being attached to it. Industry practice is a hodge-podge of highly conservative traditional techniques that involve more labor than anyone can afford, and modern simplifications borrowed from automobile practice. Some of the improvements are valuable; some are inadequate, interface badly, are insufficiently protected against vibration (which is far worse in an airplane than in a car), or seem to embody the assumption that the airplane, like a car, is only going to last five years anyway.

Between the uneven quality of design and construction evident in light airplanes and the vast uncertainties of maintenance, a person must be very optimistic indeed to imagine that the air is free of the kinds of junk heaps that infest the highways. It is not free of them at all. I used to suppose that the buyer of a used airplane was protected by the required inspections and logs; but having owned my own airplane for a few years and having seen, day by day, what comes and goes in a maintenance hangar, I have entirely changed my ideas. Of course, that may be like judging the health of the human race by the traffic in a hospital corridor, but since the problems of airplanes are problems of design, construction, and maintenance, all of them human responsibilities, I think it not unreasonable to believe that when I see everyday evidence of carelessness and incompetence, those nemeses are surely abroad elsewhere than in the hangar alone.

Because airplanes may be flawed on a number of levels—condition, design, materials, manufacture—a good pilot has to learn to foresee problems, understand his airplane, and react to difficulties with good judgment. Experience is the best teacher; but it cannot replace a positive effort on the pilot's part to learn about his equipment. It's useless, I suppose, to expect the occasional pleasure flyer—the fellow whose accident rate is worse by a factor of ten than that of the professional—to become an expert in what for him can only be a sideline. He rents airplanes, he has to depend on the owner to provide him with something that will work and is safe. His chances are fairly good, and for all the unkind words that I have said about the state of manufacture and maintenance, the statistical reliability of airplanes is excellent. But the airplane owner who flies regularly and plans to go on flying for the rest of his life owes it to himself and his passengers to be thoroughly acquainted with his airplane. He ought to take the trouble to learn how all its systems work and what the symptoms of malfunction may mean. He should follow a mechanic through an inspection, or do one himself for practice. He should be able to distinguish the essential from the decorative, and to know what system can produce what symptom, and by what other system the symptom might be relieved.

In addition to education, he should have instrumentation. Personally, I can't have too much. I would like to know the temperature, pressure, and voltage of everything in the airplane; otherwise I'm flying through wild guesses. Light airplanes are usually lightly instrumented because most of the time the instruments just sit there saying the same thing year in and year out; you might as well just look up the numbers in the owner's manual. Trainers rarely have so much as a cylinder head temperature gauge. Simplicity is desirable in a trainer, of course; but it has, as I have said before, the unfortunate consequence of leaving the trainee in the dark about the complexities of the more sophisticated airplanes he is sure to fly in the future. The student is not generally forced to become acquainted with every system in his Cessna 150 or Piper Tomahawk, and airplanes in which something is going wrong are simply pulled off the line until they are fixed. There are few opportunities for the trainee to get an understanding of what can go wrong, how long things take to go wrong, what is serious and what is not. It's likely that, in addition to not knowing how to cope with problems, a student barely knows how to interpret the information on the simplest instrument panel. Not understanding how the ammeter is wired, he does not know whether it will reveal an alternator failure or a battery short circuit, or what the signs would be and how to react. He has never seen a cylinder head temperature gauge, and so when he gets into an airplane equipped with one he pays no attention to it; the same with an exhaust-gas temperature gauge (EGT). On the other hand, presented with a fuel pressure gauge that is labeled as a fuel flow gauge, he tries to set his mixture by it, ignoring the EGT gauge right beside it; and then he wonders why he cannot get the same fuel flows as the handbook lists, or why his cylinders last only 400 hours, or why his plugs foul.

Though every pilot who does not make a profession of knowing all there is to know about his airplane is liable to be in the dark about one system or procedure or another, it is the occasional pleasure flyer, the hobbyist, or the wealthy professional who buys a complicated airplane as a diversion, who is likely to know far less than he ought. The renter submits to an hour-long check flight to qualify to rent an airplane. If he seems able to fly capably and is not completely reckless, the renter will rent to him because he makes money by doing so; he would soon go broke if he subjected each of his prospective clients to a flight engineer's exam. But the pilot's knowledge of the airplane is slight. If something begins to go wrong, he will have no idea what to do to fix it. He will not know whether engine roughness is due to routinely fouling spark plugs or perhaps to a sticking valve; he is depending, to some extent, on luck to spare him any difficulties while he's flying the strange airplane.

Even some owners are strangers to their airplanes. A doctor or a lawyer gets a license and then contemplates ownership. The school at which he got his training encourages him to get an airplane and put it on leaseback—all the talk about tax writeoffs is right up his alley—and so he buys an airplane that will rent well, perhaps encouraged by the school to provide something that will fill a void in its lineup. A used single-engine retractable with full avionics. He does not know what to do with all these radios and instruments; he rarely turns them on. He flies away on a weekend afternoon with wife and friends to a resort; returns the following evening, having taken off later than he planned, and arrives home to find clouds covering the airport—a condition he never thought to consider. It is dark and he is trapped on top, ironically surrounded with IFR equipment that he does not know how to use. He had some instrument training while getting his private license, however, and a few more hours afterward when he was thinking about getting the rating. So he calls a tower and ends up with approach control making an approach; the controller knows from the things he says that he isn't qualified, but doesn't challenge him because now there is no alternative, and besides he thinks that to challenge the fellow might make him lose his nerve. The pilot is on his way to becoming a "pleasure flying" statistic.

Without making too much of a happenstance of naming, we might reflect that the terrible safety record of "pleasure flying" might suggest that flying ought not to be quite so much of a pleasure. Not, at any rate, for the pilot. When he begins to carry passengers, his family, his friends, new acquaintances, they reasonably expect him to provide them with the same safeguards, more or less, as are provided by commercial carriers. They expect him to be competent. To be competent in an airplane requires more than just a taste for kicks; it requires concentration, hard work, study, seriousness, and a thoroughly adult sense of responsibility. It precisely does not require the mentality of the boulevard drag racer; but that is exactly the mentality of many pleasure pilots. Pleasure pilots crack up for hundreds of reasons, but there is enough similarity among many of their accidents to show that one of the common problems is lack of self-discipline, combined with ignorance of flying technique, airplane systems, or of the wind and the weather. Lack, in short, of what can only be acquired by subjecting oneself to a certain amount of unpleasantness. But pleasure pilots didn't come to aviation for unpleasantness, hard work, discipline, or self-denial; they came for pleasure. With deplorable regularity, they get more than they bargained for. The economic pressures to produce more and more of the least knowledgeable, least responsible kind of pilot is great. As long as hungry manufacturers have wares to sell, and declare that "Anyone Can Fly" and that this is the year to "Discover Flying," and as long as the FAA takes an indulgent attitude toward instruction and licensing, the dismal accident record will remain just what it is.

# 14

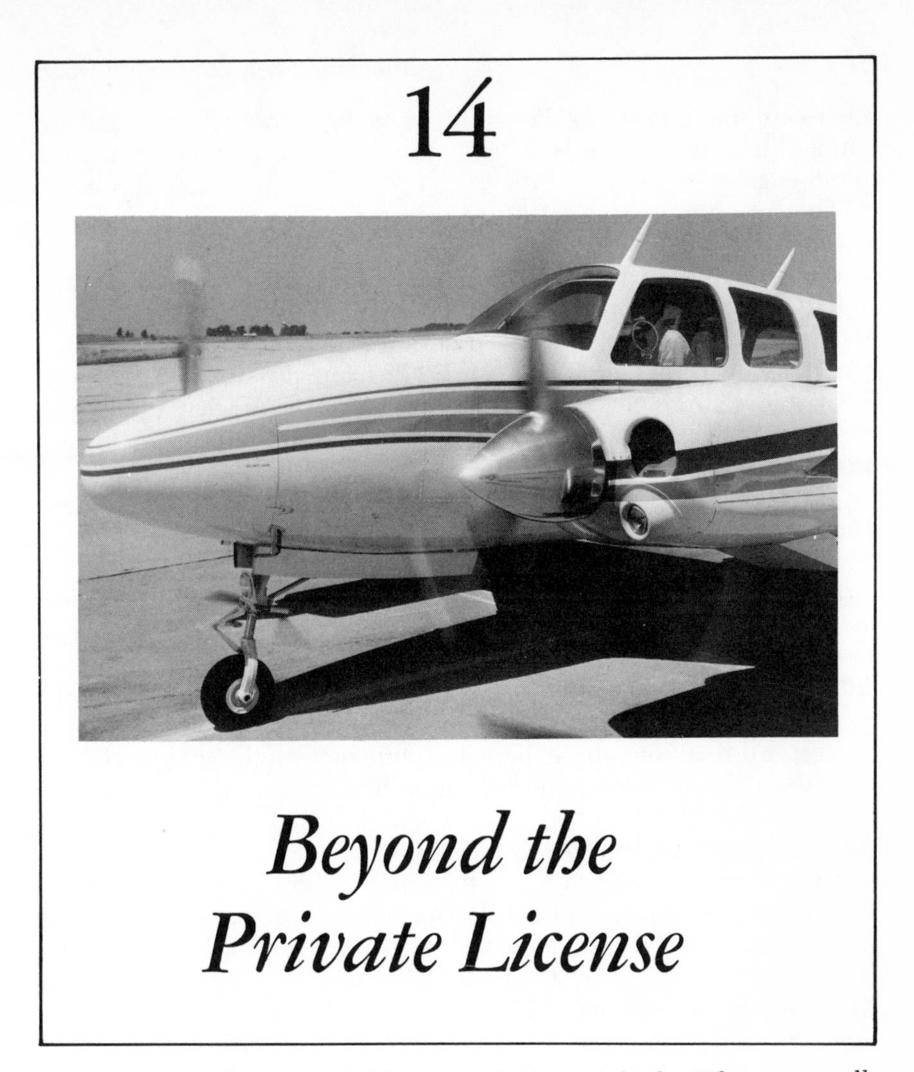

# *Beyond the Private License*

You can make of flying a hobby, a profession, or both. When you walk away from the check ride with a license in your pocket, you have crossed the first hurdle. You have permission to go ahead.

There is a rather complicated structure of licenses and additional ratings, covering both overall levels of competence (Student, Private, Commercial, ATP) and specialized areas (Instrument, Instructor), as well as classes of aircraft (single-engine, multi-engine, centerline thrust, glider, rotorcraft, balloon, landplane, seaplane) and individual types (Learjet, DC-8, and so on). Type ratings are required for "large aircraft" and for turbine-powered aircraft. Some pilots collect ratings; this appears rather adolescent, but a sympathetic writer once pointed out that collecting ratings was a way for pilots who had no other excuse to fly to justify their continuing to do so. Practically speaking, however, there are two ratings that one needs to be a "compleat pilot": the instrument and the multi-engine.

There is no minimum total time requirement for the multi. You can get your private license in a multi-engine airplane; and in that case, curiously enough, you have a private multi, but no private single, and you have to go back for further instruction and a separate check ride to get the single-engine rating. Now, you obviously don't really need a multi if you never own, rent, or borrow a twin. But so many airplanes are twins, even at a relatively low level of cost and performance, that a pilot who does a lot of flying, especially commercial flying, is almost certain to have to fly a twin at one time or another.

The reason why twins require a special rating is that they have certain peculiarities that make them quite a bit trickier to fly than singles—though only after one of the engines has quit.

In nearly all twins the engines are located on the wings, several feet away from the centerline of the airplane. Each engine is usually capable of keeping the fully loaded airplane aloft by itself, if the density altitude is sufficiently low; but, except in the case of very powerful airplanes like twin turboprops or jets, the climb performance on one engine is very meager. Furthermore, this marginal performance can be attained only in a narrow range of speeds, and only after the airplane has been "cleaned up." Because the thrust of one engine is off the centerline, it is a problem just to keep the airplane going straight ahead.

Suppose you are taking off in a twin from a short runway, and just as you lift off one engine quits. It doesn't stop turning, of course; it continues "windmilling," the propeller driving the engine because of the forward speed of the plane. The windmilling prop has a lot of drag—more than a stopped or feathered prop—and your landing gear and flaps are still down too. In this configuration, the airplane is incapable of climbing. You have to move fast. You're out of runway, and the terrain ahead doesn't admit of a forced landing. You raise the landing gear, milk up the flaps, and try to get to the single-engine best rate of climb speed, all the time clinging to your altitude. You identify the dead engine—the side on which you're stomping on the rudder pedal with all your might to hold heading is the side of the *good* engine—and you pull the prop control back to feather, which aligns the blades with the airstream, stopping the windmilling and greatly diminishing the drag. Finally you get your climb rate—which might be as much as one or two hundred feet a minute on a summer day.

This is a difficult procedure. The pilot must make a number of steps, he must make them rapidly and in the correct order. Certain mistakes—feathering the wrong engine, feathering while leaving the gear and flaps down, or letting the speed bleed off—could cost him the airplane, or his life. Indeed, deaths resulting from mistakes in single-engine procedures are frequent.

Because it has twice as many engines, a twin has on the face of it at least twice the chance of an engine failure that a single has. Then if you consider its more complicated systems and pre-takeoff and inflight checks, and the consequently greater likelihood of oversights and errors, there may be more than twice the chance for trouble. And even beyond that, the presence of a second engine might make pilots more readily overlook a funny noise or vibration, or a doubtful magneto check; or make it easier to delay needed maintenance, especially in light of the fact that while twins may cost no more to buy, used, than singles, they cost much more to maintain; so that the mere fact of an airplane's having two engines might make some pilots less cautious in its operation. All things considered, I would be surprised if twins did not experience engine trouble not just twice as often as singles, but more than twice as often; but there is no way rigorously to verify this, because no one collects statistics on engine trouble as such—only on certain types of dramatic failures, or failures that lead to accidents or deaths.

You would still think that twins would be safer, because even if their engines fail more frequently, when one does fail you can keep going; whereas in a single, when one engine fails you go down. The consequences of the same failure would seem less dire in the twin. But not so. It appears that the fatal accident rate is higher for twins than for singles. Students of these statistics offer the explanation that when in a single the engine fails the pilot gives his undivided attention to the ensuing forced landing, whereas in a twin he does not consider a forced landing, but instead turns his full attention to the complicated procedure of trying to continue on one engine—which, aside from the pitfalls in the procedure itself, under many conditions of loading and density altitude simply cannot be done. So the arrival at the ground, when it comes, takes the pilot by surprise. He has not given attention to arriving in a good place, at a good speed, with his shoulder belts tightened and his fuel and electrical systems shut off. Thus the second engine, under some circumstances, may turn out to serve less as a backup than as a booby trap.

Almost all twins have a single-engine minimum control speed that is higher than their stalling speed, and below which directional control cannot be maintained on one engine. The possibility of a loss of control must thus be added to the hazards of settling into the ground and of the ordinary stall-spin, which accounts for the death of a number of single-engine pilots each year. Some pilots take the position that until a certain speed, altitude, and state of cleanup have been reached, an engine failure in most twins—this would include all light twins except the Cessna

Skymaster—should be treated just as it would be in a single, and a controlled forced landing straight ahead should be the normal response. But it is one thing to say that and another to do it. Most pilots—probably including those who advocate the forced landing—would, if they thought they had a ghost of a chance of staying airborne, try to do so.

The Cessna Skymaster is unique among present-day production light twins in mounting its two engines on the centerline of the fuselage, one on the nose and one behind the passenger cabin. (The tail surfaces are carried on twin booms extending aft from the wings, clear of the rear propeller.) An experimental airplane called the Rutan Defiant (Rutan built it; "Defiant" is supposed to sell it) combines this arrangement with a canard layout and fixed landing gear to produce a light twin in which an engine failure puts no additional duties whatever on the pilot (in the Skymaster, climb performance still depends on the pilot's retracting the gear, raising the flaps, and feathering the dead engine). Another prototype, the Learfan, from the late William P. Lear of Lear Jet fame, gears two turbine engines together, as in many helicopters, to drive a single tail-mounted propeller. But with the single exception of the Skymaster, the industry continues to produce, more from force of habit than anything else, twins with engines installed off the centerline, and with all the attendant problems of asymmetric thrust. Presumably, were this unnecessary and dangerous arrangement to be abandoned, the multi-engine rating, at least as applied to light twins, would become a superfluous anachronism.

More basic I think for pilots in general than the multi is the instrument rating. When you fly VFR only, weather seems like a perfectly legitimate reason for canceling a flight or, depending on where you live, even for skipping all flying sometimes for weeks or months at a stretch. Weather can also seem like a sporting adversary against whom one normally takes certain risks. The risks do not seem foolhardy; they appear rather like part of the acceptable overall risk that flying entails. When you get the instrument rating, however, these perspectives change. Weather no longer seems worth much risk at all, and you routinely expect to make a flight, regardless of weather, with very few exceptions. Heavy fog, freezing rain, and solid thunderstorms are about the only weather conditions that stop you. Weather of one sort or another is almost ubiquitous; the best way to avoid trifling with it is to avoid temptation. Now that the air traffic control system is such as to permit IFR flights to terminals almost everywhere, and there are instrument approaches even to small and unimportant airfields, blind flying is as integral a part of flying as is navigation or the ability to take off and land. The instrument rating seems to me not so much an exotic addendum to the private license as its natural second half.

The importance of the instrument rating can be inferred from the rules relating to commercial licenses. The commercial is required for carriage of passengers for hire, for instruction, and so on. It used to be that 200 hours total time was required for the commercial, and that one could have a commercial license but no instrument rating. Those rules were changed a few years ago to require 250 hours total time and, what is more significant, to limit commercial pilots without instrument ratings to daytime flying and to cross-country flights of not more than 50 miles. Without the instrument rating, then, the commercial license is good for little more than day VFR instruction, sightseeing rides, demonstration flying, and certain kinds of helicopter work (helicopters are rarely flown IFR anyway).

From the way these rules are now written you can judge that night flight, or cross-country flight for a greater distance than one could, from 7,000 feet, see with the naked eye, was thought to be so hazardous, absent the instrument rating, that paying passengers should not be unwittingly exposed to it. (The families and friends of non-instrument-rated private pilots, contemplating these rules, might wonder why they are not considered worthy of the same protections.) As a matter of fact, the limitations on the commercial are extraordinarily conservative. Perhaps it was thought that the pressure to make and complete a marginal flight would be greater on a paid professional pilot than on an amateur, and so the risk to his passengers would be proportionately greater.

If a commercial pilot needs an instrument rating to fly at night or to fly farther than he can see, then every other pilot might conclude that he too needs one for his normal flying, which is likely to be quite a bit more ambitious than that. Obstacles of time and money prevent many people from getting the instrument rating, as does a paradoxical idea that instrument flying will expose them to more danger, not less. The rating is indeed demanding; to get it you must have 200 hours total time, 100 of them as pilot in command; and 40 hours of simulated or actual instrument time, of which 20 can be in a ground trainer or simulator. The other 20 must be in an airplane, normally flying under a hood rather than in actual instrument conditions. These are minimum requirements; I spent more than 60 hours of instrument training getting ready for my instrument check ride.

In addition to flying skills, the instrument rating requires knowledge of the air traffic control system, which is quite complicated; of numerous rules and technicalities; and of radio navigation. The last you pick up, to some extent, in your VFR flying, particularly if, knowing that you will eventually be wanting an instrument rating, you organize your VFR flights as though they were IFR flights, and use IFR charts in addition to Sectionals or WACs. The symbology of IFR charts is much more easily mastered a bit at a time, while using them in flight, than by trying to memorize the whole legend at one sitting. Using the charts also makes clear which are the really important symbols that you have to recognize immediately, and which are the odd ones that appear rarely and that you can, in a pinch, look up. When I took the instrument written test it was much simpler than it is now, and I barely passed it, having had no formal ground school and having relied, in my home study, on an antediluvian air force manual that, among other omissions, made no mention whatever of VOR. I went to the test prepared to navigate by four-course ranges, at about the time that the last four-course range was removed from service. Today I doubt that I would have gotten by with such slapdash preparation. These days students get large and modern systems of programmed learning, formerly called books; many take weekend cram courses to propel them, on pure momentum, through the exam on Monday. As with the private, the distribution of information in the instrument written does not much resemble that in real life; but no matter. The test is a thing in itself, and has to be undertaken on its own terms.

As is true of the private license too, the instrument rating is no more than official permission to go out and learn. It signifies that the holder is more or less able to take a clearance, follow an airway, fly an approach, and recite a regulation. It is no guarantee that he will do these things correctly every time, or that he will cope intelligently with emergencies, or that he will stay calm in the cockpit when faced with a sudden change in the weather or in a clearance, or even that he will always, or regularly, tune in the right frequency on the right radio and follow the right radial in the required direction. It tells little about his knowledge of weather conditions in different parts of the country; or of the customary shortcuts used by air traffic control; or for that matter of the peculiarities of alternators, vacuum pumps, gyros, and airspeed indicators.

In fact, the IFR flight test always involves certain local procedures. The student practices them hundreds of times. He becomes so familiar with the BOZZO Transition to a Runway 14 ILS, followed by a missed approach and a procedure turn to the Runway 32 NDB approach, that he executes them automatically, consulting the charts merely for show. Take him elsewhere, and he becomes again as a little babe.

Many pilots get commercial licenses without specific prospects of using them. I got one, after the instrument and before the multi, and I don't think I have ever carried anyone or anything for hire. It simply seemed to me like the thing to do, as, having become a cub scout, a young person might automatically go on to be a boy scout or an eagle scout or what have you. The prestige of the commercial license may occasionally be of some practical use; but the difference between the words "private" and "commercial," which to my ear sounds as great as that between diapers and trousers, is really an illusion.

However, if you want to pursue a career in aviation, you pretty well have to get a commercial license. The ultimate aviation career, at least in the sense that most career pilots longingly aspire to it, is no doubt that of the airline pilot. The supply of highly qualified aspirants greatly exceeds the demand, and the years of waiting to be accepted become a lifelong joke for the majority of would-be captains. They put in applications with all the airlines, and then wait. After a year they go in to update their files and show continuing interest; and this goes on year after year. From time to time a few get hired, fueling the hopes of the rest. While waiting, they instruct, fly charter, cropdust, get corporate jobs, or drift into something other than flying. After a certain time elapses, they know that their prospects are growing dim because of their age; since airlines operate on a seniority system with time in service the main determinant of who moves into a vacant seat when one appears, an old copilot would be a senile captain.

Instruction is the most common occupation of those who stand and wait—unfortunately so, because many instructors thus turn out to be people who have really no taste for teaching. But there are other kinds of jobs, particularly for the footloose. There are charter, sightseeing, air taxi, cargo, survey, photographic, and bush jobs all over the world. Alaska is crawling with pilots who came up from the lower forty-eight to find bush work. Not that a far greater number did not also come, search, find no work, and eventually go back home; but there are jobs. They are not jobs for which one makes applications and gets interviews; if you are there when a seat becomes available, if you can fly, if somebody else doesn't beat you through the door, you get it.

Planes are put to uses most people aren't aware of. They are used to hurry checks from bank to bank, in order to minimize the time your money spends not making the bank money. They carry air mail to places not served by the airlines. In the back country an airplane, however small and slow, that can land on water or snow or a river bank, can cover in ten minutes a stretch that might take surface transport ten hours; and so in undeveloped places all over the world people even take the plane to town to shop. Airplanes are used for pipeline patrol, mapping, firefighting, smuggling, sampling, traffic watch, police surveillance, hunting, counting game, spotting fish, towing gliders and carrying sport parachutists, towing banners, skywriting. They race, do air shows, compete in aerobatic contests. One can even use them for magazine writing. Aviation is a big field; many colleges now offer courses and degrees in many of its aspects, of which actually flying is only one. But it is the best one.

Professional flying may seem exotic, but it isn't; it is routine. Airline pilots fly the same routes month after month in the same equipment with the same crews, talking to the same controllers, facing the same weather.

They spend a lot of time in motels, which are the same even when they are not the same. But airline flyers also get a lot of time off, and the usual reason people give for wanting to be airline pilots is that the work consists mostly of well-paid vacation. It isn't the flying that attracts them at all; it's the *not* flying.

A friend of mine flew charter and air tour work in Hawaii. It was monotonous, and he thought it was unnecessarily dangerous to boot, because the planes were poorly maintained, and although the company was licensed only for day VFR operations the pilots were under powerful pressure to complete their flights come what may. He eventually quit in protest over the working conditions, even though he knew he had little prospect of finding another job flying

Another friend of mine was a Learjet charter pilot—a chauffeur for the very rich, for celebrities, for important people. The work, he said, consists mostly of waiting. And you can practically kiss your social life good-bye, because you're always on call and when you leave you never know exactly when you'll be back. A corporate pilot's life is much the same sort of thing: lots of waiting, always on call, the whims of the boss or the boss's wife or girl friend; always on one's best behavior for the baksheesh of a night on the town, tickets to a show in Vegas, a weekend at a ski cabin. Not exotic, but of all the kinds of work, many must be worse.

Not even test pilots, those knights of the air, have exciting lives. A few make famous saves or become astronauts, but for most it is a life of clerkish data-gathering, as commonplace, tedious, and routine as that of any instructor.

The part of flying that is romantic, I think, the part that makes all these people keep doing it, is not the part that is accessible to certain pilots—those flying supersonic jets, bush planes, rescue helicopters, or what have you—and not to others. It is the part that is accessible to all pilots: the chain of intermittent moments, the proverbial hours of boredom and the instants of terror or delight, which are imbued by their very monotony with a continuity and a wholeness that produces, eventually, the same love and yearning as one feels for a companion of many years. Only to be around airplanes, to fly them, is in itself a small but satisfactory romance. The romance is not in the planes, but in the pilots, like that romance of the road that absorbs truckers. It can be quite boring for outsiders, this uncontrollable interest in airplanes, weather, geography, the sky, air crashes, airports; they are puzzled that, were it even the middle of the Miss Nude America judging, the pilot would keep glancing upward, by an automatic and unconscious nervous reaction, when the drone of an airplane engine was heard overhead. Nor does the pilot himself know what he hopes to see in the passing airplane. He sees it without seeing it, as people see the time without seeing it who glance at their watches and have to glance again if you ask them, a second later, what time it is. Or as people glance at their reflection in a window; and indeed, as in the passing window, I think that what the pilot sees in the passing airplane is himself. For him all longings for escape, for mystery, for excitement and passion, for change, for youth or immortality, for disappearance, for power or for salvation, are bound up, however vainly, in that little dot that recedes obliquely in an azure sky.

One of the liabilities of books and articles about flying, when they concern themselves, as this one does, with getting along safely in the real world of airplane operation, is that they read like cautionary tales. They make the world seem like a place where one threads one's way from pitfall to ambush, and whence only saints and heroes emerge unscathed. In reviewing these pages I see how one could conclude that to fly for a year or two without at least once skidding off the runway, running out of gas, getting lost, straying into a thunderstorm, making a forced landing, crashing, getting killed or at least undergoing a few periods of sheer terror, must be a very rare thing indeed.

In fact, nothing of the sort is true. The reason for the emphasis on all the things that can go wrong is that in airplanes, the consequences of error can be so serious. You cannot, as pilots always say, pull over to the side of the road, fix a tire or hitch a ride, and so the time to avoid trouble is before the trouble occurs. Hence all the warnings about all the kinds of trouble. But in fact most pilots never have any trouble at all. Most fly thousands of hours without so much as a murmur of uneasiness from their engines; most find their destinations without incident, and land smoothly. They get to bed on time and sleep well. Frightened passengers flying for the first time find that there is nothing to fear, and enjoy what they thought they would loathe. To find a pilot who has had an engine failure or a forced landing, or has done even minor damage to an airplane, is rare.

The memories that years of flying leave are, on the contrary, almost always pleasant ones. There are certain assets that make a life more pleasant to live, like money or good looks; mobility is one of them. The essential thing that flying brings into your life is not fear or danger or uncertainty; it is mobility. It is that one unquestionable benefit of progress, the one thing that modernity, more than any other, implies and provides. It is the implication of the wings of angels and the omnipotence of gods; and much more than a boat or a car, an airplane gives it to you.

So do not be discouraged by the weight of responsibility, or by the turns around a point, the practiced forced landings, the radio navigation, the restricted areas and forbidden zones, the treachery of weather, or the mystery of night. The emphasis on danger and mischance is for instructional purposes. It does not reflect the true nature of the flyer's world. Don't take flying as a struggle, when it has so much else to offer. Go out, use your head, and enjoy it.

# INDEX

# INDEX